Of Marriage
and the Market

Of Marriage
and the Market:

women's subordination
in international perspective

edited by Kate Young, Carol Wolkowitz
and Roslyn McCullagh

Of Marriage and the Market: women's subordination in
international perspective was first published by CSE
Books, 25 Horsell Road, London N5 in October 1981.
Copyright © CSE Books
Cover design by Chloe Nevett

British Library Cataloguing in Publication Data
Of Marriage and the Market
1. Women—Social conditions
I. Young, Kate   II. Wolkowitz, Carol
III. McCullagh, Roslyn
305.4′ 2   HQ1154
ISBN 0 906336 24 4
ISBN 0 906336 25 2 Pbk

Photoset in Bembo by Red Lion Setters, London WC1.
Printed by Whitstable Litho, Whitstable, Kent.

Contents

Introduction

The articles in this collection are all written by women who have been active in the women's movement in their own country or taken part in the debates raised by the feminist challenge to the orthodox interpretations of women's position in society. Most of the writers too have lived for some time or undertaken research in a third world country.

For those of us who have lived in the third world, we found that our experience of inequality in our own country gave us a particular way of focussing on the inequalities we observed in the countries in which we were working. But not only were we concerned with the apparent subordinate position of women, many of us also attempted to understand the wider changes which were transforming these countries. Most of us came to be influenced by one particular theory of social change – Marxism – yet found the economistic categories of traditional Marxism inadequate to explain many of the forms of relationships, including gender relations, that we saw. However, we were in a paradoxical situation in that the feminist debates which most interested us tended to be rather domestic in focus and were not concerned either with the question of imperialism and its effects on women in third world countries, or women of third world origin in our own countries. Yet on the whole the literature dealing with imperialism and development issues ignored questions of women's subordination. Of the literature specifically concerned with 'women and development', much was deeply unsatisfactory from a feminist perspective. In particular we disagreed with the way these discussions tended to isolate women as a separate category. In our view the theoretical object of analysis can not be women, but rather the relations between men and women in society.

It was in this context that some of the writers in this volume came together with others to form the Subordination of Women Workshop (SOW). Our aim was to develop better analytical and conceptual tools for the development of a theory of social relations which would encompass not only the so-called economic relations of society but also what have been called the relations of everyday life. In our discussion we found that we developed a language which does not make use of many of the standard terms current in discussions of women's position in society, such as exploitation, oppression or patriarchy. This arose from our feeling that we had to find a term which conveyed the general character of male female relations while reserving such terms as oppression for historically specific forms that these relations may take. In part this stemmed from our common point of departure that relations between men and women are social relations; they are not immutable and fixed. Thus the form that social relations of gender take in any given historical period of a socio-economic formation are specific and have to be constructed analytically; they cannot be read off from a specification of other relations within a society. Yet despite the historical specificity of social relations of gender, we were concerned to understand how it is that within differing socio-economic formations, whether pre-capitalist, feudal, neo-colonial, capitalist or socialist, so many common elements are present when the relations between men and women, particularly within the marriage bond, are examined: men's greater access to social resources, whether they be food, political positions, or land; their greater physical mobility; their lesser responsibilities in terms of self-maintenance or of care for the young and the old; their privileged position in terms of command of labour, particularly women's labour; their less confined sexuality. What we wanted to investigate was the realm from which these asymmetical relations sprang, and the articulation of this area of social life with the one which has been so much more the object of inquiry and theorising – the economy. This tension between specificity and universality made us anxious to avoid explanations which analysed the various forms of social relations between men and women only in terms of their function for capital, or for the reproduction of capitalist relations of production. We preferred to use concepts such as subordination and the social relations of gender, and then to specify the nature of such relations in a given context. In this way we hope to indicate, albeit partially, what a theory of gender in society would have to include.

A number of articles in this volume come directly from our discussions in the SOW workshop, the others from the Conference that was organised at the Institute of Development Studies, Sussex, and at which over 600 women from all parts of the world had week long discussions on common interests. The focus of the Conference was the effect on women of the changes taking place in third world countries as their economies are gradually being transformed along the lines of either capitalist or socialist forms of production and distribution. At the Conference, as in the Workshop, a number of divergent views were expressed and theoretical positions argued for. Although we cannot represent them all in one volume, we have tried to make a selection which adequately represents the diverse emphases in the work of both SOW and women elsewhere working towards a feminist theory of development. A further volume is being prepared which will focus more specifically on the effects of economic change on women in third world countries. For this volume we chose articles which have a common concern with a number of themes which are critical in feminist analysis generally.

One of these themes is the relationship of the household to women's subordination. While the household is neither a natural unit nor a universal category, the domestic sphere, its separation from the public or social world, and relations between men and women within different households, are fundamental to gender subordination. In the main, family based households (whether nuclear or extended family) are hierarchical structures characterised by male dominance. Women are made vulnerable by the isolation of domestic life, and are largely dependent on the men who represent them 'outside'. Women generally, and wives in particular, often do not have direct access to the market; their access is mediated, either directly, by men, or indirectly through their acceptance of male ideologies of appropriate female roles. Women have less access than men to external sources of income, and are thus often dependent on household income. However, women frequently have less command than men over household resources and consumption goods, despite the fact in theory these are commonly shared. Even where women work outside the household they rarely have the same degree of control as men over their individual wage and how it is spent.

Intra-household relations can not however be understood without reference to the wider society of which they are a part, and to the sexual division of labour in that society. The sexual division of labour – minimally defined as the system of allocating particular tasks to men and others to women – has been a recurrent theme in feminist analysis. One of the issues that has concerned us most is to understand why it is that women are allocated those tasks (broadly defined as domestic labour and reproductive work) which are neither given value nor commensurated by the market. This is especially important when we consider that it is precisely these privatised, financially unrewarded tasks, that form the basis on which society rests.

This brings us to another theme discussed in some of the articles – class. In orthodox class analysis, the reproduction of class relations has been examined only at an abstract level; upper class women for example have usually been viewed merely as members of the privileged dominant class. What is also crucial is an understanding of how class relations are reproduced through time. Thus the role of women as reproducers of the next generation, and the control of women's procreative capacity, must also be analysed if we are to understand how class privilege is perpetuated. This question of biological reproduction is itself part of a more general concern with women's sexuality, and how it is constructed in relation to that of men such that men's sexuality sets the parameters within which women's can be expressed.

Many of those writing about women's unequal position in society have argued that if women had full access to the market – in the form of control over sale of produce, sufficient jobs, equal pay, provision of nurseries for all children and so on – women's subordinate position in society would end. The articles here reject such a view, arguing that by concentrating solely on the process of production it ignores other fundamental causes of gender subordination. For the subordination of women continues when women enter the public sphere of wage labour, and also continues in societies where there has been a socialist transformation of the relations of production and distribution. Indeed an investigation of the position of women in socialist countries highlights the inadequacy of economistic analyses of gender relations.

Finally, we want to emphasise that the point of specifying these themes and of writing all the articles here is not one of academic interest, but of political struggle. By attempting to identify the diverse elements and mechanisms of women's continuing subordination, our aim is to contribute to women's struggle against the many forms of our subordination.

We have a number of people to thank for helping to get these articles into a publishable state. First all those who commented on various drafts of the manuscript, and especially Robin Murray, whose enthusiasm for the volume was a great encouragement. Second we have to thank Fiona Pearson; without her hard work – and good humour – the manuscript would never have reached a readable state.

Kate Young
Carol Wolkowitz
Roslyn McCullagh

July 1981

Gender and Economics

The Sexual Division of Labour and the Subordination of Women

Maureen Mackintosh

All societies exhibit a sexual division of labour. That is, there are some tasks which are allocated predominantly or exclusively to women, others to men, while some may be done by both men and women. As societies undergo economic change, the nature of work changes, and so does its distribution between men and women. And at any point in time, of course, the division of tasks varies from country to country. But the existence of some sexual division of labour, some sex-typing of activities, is a very persistent fact of human society.

Feminists have long been interested in this persistent fact, arguing that to understand the sexual division of labour is crucial to any attempt to understand, and to change, the social position of women as a whole. In taking up these arguments in this article I have two aims. First, I survey the reasons why the sexual division of labour is an important problem for feminist analysis, and the theoretical difficulties raised by attempts to explain the creation of such sexual divisions. And second, I seek to use this discussion to address the general problem of the relation between the economic position of women – that is, the type of work women do and the relations within which they do it – and the broader subordination of women in society.

While this article introduces a number of themes which are taken up again in other articles in the book, it concentrates on economic aspects of women's subordination. Many social and cultural aspects of subordination, discussed in detail in other articles in the book, are not addressed here.

SUBORDINATION AND SEXUAL DIVISION

Two questions of definition need to be discussed at the outset. The first is the distinction between 'gender' and 'sex'. Feminist writers (see for example Oakley, 1972; Rubin, 1975) have come to distinguish sharply between biological sex, and socially constructed categories of gender. Although I continue to use the established phrase 'the sexual division of labour', what I mean by it more strictly is the division of labour along lines of gender. Thus the subsequent discussion uses the concepts of 'gender' and 'gender relations' in the discussion of the activities and relations of men and women, and does not assume that any of the divisions studied can be deduced from differences between the biological sexes (see also, on this point, Elson and Pearson, this volume).

The second concept requiring definition is that of 'subordination'. I am using the concept of female subordination – the subordination of women to men – as the focus of my analysis because this centres attention on what one might call the feminist problematic: the relations between men and women within the social process as a whole and the way those relations work to the detriment of women (see Whitehead, 1979 for an extended discussion of this). If we take the subordination of women to be our central problem, we can then analyse the relation of this gender subordination to other afflictions of women, such as economic exploitation, without conflating the conceptual and political issues.

Feminists, then, are interested in the sexual division of labour in society because it appears to express, embody, and furthermore to perpetuate, female subordination. This can be easily illustrated. In areas where both women and men work for wages, women workers tend to be segregated into certain industrial sectors, and into certain occupations within those sectors. Within these jobs, women are typically lower paid, defined as less skilled, low in the hierarchy of authority and have relatively poor conditions of work. This situation is quite well documented now for developed industrial countries (see Phillips and Taylor, 1980, and the papers in Amsden, 1980), and there is also substantial evidence for the Third World (Elson and Pearson, this volume; Lim, 1978; Blake and Moonstan, 1981; Grossman, 1979; Heyzer, 1981; Stoler, forthcoming; Banerjee, forthcoming). Moreover, it is striking how rapidly, as new factories and plantations are established, new categories of 'women's work' become established, with relatively disadvantageous wages and conditions (see for example Mackintosh, forthcoming; Pearson, forthcoming). In this way the sexual division of labour is created and recreated as the wage labour market develops, and one form of women's subordination is perpetuated.

The existence of a sexual division of labour is not of course limited to the sphere of wage work. In non-wage work, whether in farming, in urban self-employment in trading or manufacturing, or in 'domestic' tasks such as cooking or child care, a sexual division of labour is also a continuing fact, and frequently works to the relative detriment of women. Women work as unpaid labour in household-based activities – agricultural and non-agricultural – for an often meagre share of the benefits. In poor agricultural areas, the development of cash cropping and new farming methods, and the shifting of food processing outside the home, have brought changes in the sexual division of labour, creating financially profitable activities for men, and segregating women in the less productive activities (Rogers, 1980; Bukh, 1979; Palmer, 1977 and 1978; Roberts, 1979 and forthcoming; Boserup, 1970). And finally, in very many societies, the division of labour by gender is very marked in what I have called above 'domestic' tasks. Where women undertake all the domestic work, this work may be socially under-valued, and sharply restrict women's ability to participate in cash earning activities. In very many areas of the world, the sexual division of labour in the home forces women to work for longer hours than men, to achieve at the end of the day a lower standard of living.

Gender subordination is thus embedded in the sexual division of labour. As shown, the sexual division of labour, reorganised and often strengthened as the cash economy spreads, tends to act to the detriment of women. Feminist analysis of such sexual divisions therefore starts from the premise that they are not 'natural', that they do not merely embody complementary roles for men and women. Rather, we can turn such a proposition on its head: only in a society where men and women constitute unequal genders is there any reason why gender should be an important organising principle of the social division of labour, with the exception of the physical process of childbearing. For nothing in the fact that women bear children implies that they exclusively should care for them through their childhood; still less does it imply that women should also feed and care for adults, nurse the sick, undertake certain agricultural tasks or work in electronics factories. A society where men and women were equal would be one where the arbitrary fact of sexual difference did not mark out the possibilities and limitations of economic activity for the individual.

The evidence thus strongly suggests a link between the sexual division of labour and the subordination of women. But how then can the creation and perpetuation of the sexual division of labour itself be explained? I survey below some of the types of theoretical explanation which have been offered, and the problems they present. The discussion is intended not as an even-handed summary of differing points of view, but rather as a distinctly partisan examination of some of the theoretical difficulties involved, concentrating on the difficulty of integrating economic analysis and gender into a theory of the development of categories of women's work.

THE ADVANTAGES OF WOMEN'S WORK FOR CAPITAL

An understanding of the sexual division of labour in any society requires that we examine, not only the jobs that men and women do, but also the relations under which they do them. So much is already clear from the discussion in the previous section. Thus the implications of the sexual division of labour for women depend on whether they work as wage workers, as unpaid household members, as self employed traders; in other words, they depend on the social relations of production under which the work is performed. This concept of the social relations of production, and its importance to an understanding of the division of labour in society, is one of the most useful insights which Marxist economic theory has brought to an understanding of sexual division.

This insight is employed in one area of the literature on sexual division of labour, where the approach has been to ask, what are the benefits of women's work to capital? Writers using this approach, based in Marxist economic analysis, have examined the various categories of 'women's work' – wage work, for example, or small scale farming or domestic work – and have asked how, in different ways, each category of such work is of benefit to the owners of capital (that is, to those who own and run private sector enterprise in mixed economies). The implicit assumption behind such an approach is that if one can show that capital, the dominant economic power in non-socialist economies, benefits from the sexual division of labour and from the economic subordination of women which it implies, then one will have at least a partial explanation for the existence of such subordination and for its perpetuation once established.

The method of argument in this approach is to try to show that, because of the existence of the sexual division of labour, capital is able to extract greater profits from its workforce than would otherwise be the case. Within the sphere of wage work, for example, women have long formed a cheap labour force, paid less relative to their productivity than men, and the effect of this has been to increase profits both within developed industrial capitalist countries and in the Third World (see Sally Alexander's introduction to Herzog, 1980, and Elson and Peason, this volume). It has also been suggested that capital benefits from using women as a 'reserve army' of labour: a flexible supply of workers who can be absorbed in a phase of expansion, and thrown out – not merely out of work but out of the labour force, back into dependency within the home – when a crisis sets in (see Bruegel, 1979, for an examination of this hypothesis in the context of recent British experience). Women form one of the cheapest and most vulnerable parts of the wage labour force, and are thus open to a high level of exploitation. Furthermore the material divisions which emerge in the work force between men and women – difference in pay, competition for jobs in situations of unemployment – lessen the strength of workers as a whole, allowing capital to divide and rule and thus to increase profits at the expense of wages.

A similar line of argument has been applied to women's work done outside the wage labour force, such as unpaid work within the household. Within Europe and North America, a recent debate about the analysis of domestic labour, or housework, focussed on the advantages of such work for capital. Housework is work done within the home, producing goods for immediate consumption within the household (cooked meals, clean clothes, child care). How then, it was asked, is the process of capital accumulation assisted by this mass of unpaid labour? (See Himmelweit and Mohun, 1977, for a summary of the debate and bibliography). The unpaid labour within the home, almost all done by women, raises the standard of living of the working class above that provided by wage alone, and provides the services of care and socialisation of children, that is, of the future labour force. These are services which could only otherwise be provided, less effectively and at high cost to capital, by the state.

In addition, still on the subject of housework, there is an unresolved debate concerning the effects of women's housework on the average level of wages paid by capital (see Beechey, 1977, for a contribution to this debate). It has variously been argued that the performance of housework lowers wages below what they would otherwise be, by providing goods which would otherwise have to be bought with the wage, and that its performance by women excluded from the labour market may tend to raise the wage of those in work (in particular, the wages of men), by allowing them to fight for a 'family wage' to cover dependents' consumption (for the last argument, see Humphries, 1977; for a critique see Barrett and McIntosh, 1980). This is a continuing debate and one which cannot be resolved at the level of theory alone. There are many conflicting influences on the general level of wages in any geographical area or historical period, and the relation between housework and wage levels may well be a question for economic history as much as general theory.

All these analyses seek to show that women's work, as cheap wage workers or as housewives, is of benefit to capital. Critics of this approach to the sexual division of labour have generally argued, not that it is incorrect, but that it is insufficient as an explanation. For it does not seem to explain why it is *women* who perform these tasks. The problem becomes clear when we move outside the developed capitalist countries. Thus Bennholdt-Thomson (this volume) takes the line of argument that housework lowers the value of labour power, and stretches it to its logical conclusion. That is, since it is the unpaid nature of housework which is crucial, one may use exactly the same framework of analysis for other productive activities such as subsistence argricultural production which are performed by both men and women, and contribute to the standard of living of the capitalist labour force (Meillassoux, 1981, makes an analytically similar argument). Therefore simply to analyse the benefits of this type of work for capital is insufficient to explain why women predominate in particular areas of such work.

THE LIMITS OF ECONOMICS AND THE LIMITS OF MARXIST THEORY

In order to explain the sexual division of labour therefore we have to move beyond an explanation solely in terms of the benefits of women's work to capital. This need for additional explanation is reinforced by the observation that some form of sexual division of labour predated the spread of capitalism in virtually all countries. Historically, as wage work has spread, capital has seized upon pre-existing division between men and women, and has incorporated that division within its own workforce to its own advantage.

That capital should seize upon existing division in this way is the result of the form of organisation of capitalist production. Production is organised on a hierarchical and exploitative basis, by a management constantly attempting to increase its level of control of the production process in the face of various forms of worker resistance (see for example Brighton Labour Process Group, 1977). Any existing divisions, such as those based on gender or race, tend therefore to be exploited and worsened to increase management control, and become embedded in the internal hierarchies of the production process. The spread of the wage economy thereby brings new forms of the sexual division of labour, and new forms of subordination of women embodied in that sexual division of labour (see Elson and Pearson, this volume, for examples of this process).

The theoretical problem then arises: if women's subordination within society predates capitalism, then surely we cannot hope to explain it solely in terms of the inherent logic of the capitalist system? Or to put it more generally, if women's subordination has existed across different modes of production, then surely one cannot hope to explain it by the demands of any particular set of production relations?

This takes us to the heart of the debate about the limits of economic explanation – or more generally the limits of Marxist theory – in the analysis of women's subordination. The problem just outlined has led many feminists to argue that even the sexual division of labour (an apparently economic phenomenon) cannot be explained solely in terms of the demands of the production system. Rather they have argued (see in particular Hartmann, 1979) that our central problem of analysis is, or should be, the relation of women to *men*, not to capital or other economic forces; accordingly it is proposed we have to go beyond the bounds of Marxist analysis, since the object of study of Marxist theory is production or production relations, a different object of analysis from that of feminists.

Their alternative proposal is that we seek to understand the sexual division of labour in society as the intersection of two sets of social forces: capitalism and patriarchy. It should be said that the argument along these lines has so far only been developed for capitalism, not for other sets of production relations in societies incompletely dominated by capital. Patriarchy is used in this argument in its most general sense of the social dominance of the male. This general usage has been criticised (Beechey, 1979; Edholm et al, 1977); critics have suggested that we should keep 'patriarchy' for situations where society is organised under identifiable patriarchs,[1] (e.g. for lineage societies, or for peasant households dominated by the oldest male), and not weaken it to include more general and socially diffused systems of male dominance. Defenders argue that if we wish to understand male dominance in society we have to analyse the social processes of the creation of two unequal genders, and that the family remains under capitalism the central site of that process: hence the appropriateness of the term.

The question then immediately arises, if we do want to divide up our objects of analysis into capitalism and patriarchy, what kind of analysis of patriarchy are we looking for? Is the analysis of the creation and recreation of a society divided into unequal genders an analysis entirely outside economics, in the realm of ideas or ideology? Is the analysis of sexuality, which such an analysis necessarily involves, an analysis of social processes which are outside the realm of production relations?

Many feminists, myself included, have a strong desire to answer no to both of these questions. First, on the question of ideology, the influence of Marxist theory has led us to seek to root our understanding of ideology in material processes, and what the Marxist tradition has generally understood by material processes are those in the realm of economic relations. Ideologies, we tend to believe, do not persist if they are not supported by and embedded in material processes. However, the attempt to understand ideologies of gender differentiation suggests that we may have to widen our concepts of the 'material' beyond economic processes to include the area of sexuality. The relations of sexuality, several feminist critics of an earlier draft of this paper pointed out, are surely as material as production relations.

Second, however, even if we widen the concept of material in this way, this still leaves open the problem of the relation between sexuality and economic processes. Most[2] feminist writers do not seek to conflate production and sexuality in theoretical terms, but the close links between the organisation of production and the operation of sexual relations have been traced by feminists in the areas, for example, of prostitution, inheritance and economic relations within marriage (see Millett, 1975; Phongpaichit, 1980; and the papers by Stolcke and Whitehead, in this volume). Rubin (1975) has made a plea for the development of a 'political economy of sex' which would precisely trace the links between sexuality, marriage and kinship on the one hand, and economic relations and accumulation on the other.

The search for a material understanding of women's subordination has therefore led some feminists to study in more detail one particular area of the sexual division of labour: that area of work, so frequently the exclusive preserve of women, which consists of the care of children and the provision of a range of domestic services for adults. This work has often been referred to in the literature as 'reproductive' work (see for example Beneria, 1979). The reason for using the term reproductive is that this work has seemed to be particularly closely related to the areas of sexuality and the reproduction of human life, which in turn are important to an understanding of patriarchy. A clearer understanding of these domestic tasks, and the social relations under which they are done in different societies, has therefore seemed to provide a link between the operation of the economic and the non-economic factors in the maintenance of women's subordination.

THE ECONOMICS OF REPRODUCTION

Reproduction has been a very vexed concept in feminist theory. It has been used with a variety of different definitions, and the theoretical debate in this area is still very much open. I am only discussing a small area of that debate (for discussion of the conceptual issues, see Edholm et al., 1977; and Harris and Young, 1981), concentrating on the relation between productive activity (and its associated sexual division of labour) and reproduction.

For my purpose here I need to distinguish several meanings of reproduction. The first has been called the reproduction of labour (Edholm et al., 1977) and involves the production of people: not merely the bearing of children (which might be called biological reproduction) but also their care and socialisation, and the maintenance of adult individuals through their lives, processes which create individuals to fit more or less into the social structure of society and so ensure the continuation of that society in the next generation. It should perhaps be said that there is nothing inevitably successful about this or any other process of reproduction: it is a contradiction-ridden process, often threatened with failure in certain societies.

Included within the concept of reproduction of labour is a narrower concept, also found in the recent feminist literature: that of human reproduction (McDonough and Harrison, 1978; Bryceson, 1980; Mackintosh, 1977). The relations of human reproduction are generally taken to centre on the relations of marriage and kinship in a society, or, put more broadly, those relations which circumscribe and determine the operation of fertility and sexuality, and construct the context for the bearing, care and socialisation of children.

A further meaning of reproduction is mentioned merely to distinguish it from the above, but I shall not be further concerned with it in this article. This is the concept of social reproduction: the process by which all the main production relations in the society are constantly recreated and perpetuated. Thus, for example in developed capitalism, social reproduction involves not only the production and maintenance of the wage labour force, but also the reproduction of capital itself, through the processes of production and investment under the control of a restricted class within the society. Needless to say, this kind of reproduction under capitalism is also contradiction-ridden and unstable.

I am chiefly concerned here then with the reproduction of labour and the narrower concept of human reproduction. What is immediately clear is that the process of reproduction of labour contains within it a great many productive tasks. There is in other words no way in which we can divide up social activity into distinct spheres of production and reproduction. The two concepts are not of the same order, and this fact alone has caused a good deal of confusion. The reproduction of labour includes many of the productive activities undertaken in society, although not all of them. Under developed capitalism for example, it includes the production (under conditions of wage labour) of the goods and services consumed by the working class; it includes the provision of state services such as health and education, and it also includes domestic work.

This list of productive activities which reproduce labour includes a large part of the productive activity of society. However, what has concerned feminists is that certain of these activities, in particular societies, appear to be more closely tied into the relations of human reproduction than do others. What I mean by this can best be explained first by the example of developed industrial capitalism. In such societies, the marriage-based household is an institution constructed by definition on the basis of gender. Economic relations within such households are highly structured by gender (see Whitehead, this volume), and despite some moves towards the sharing of housework the allocation of the domestic labour (especially child care) to women is extraordinarily persistent and still defended by many non-feminist commentators as natural and correct. In these societies then, housework and childcare are the activities most directly influenced by the relations of marriage, or the relations of human reproduction as defined above. They are *therefore* the activities where the sexual division of labour is most rigid, and where any change in the sexual division of labour is often perceived as a serious threat to established forms of gender identity (that is, established understandings of masculinity and femininity).

I have also observed (Mackintosh, 1979) this greater rigidity in the sexual division of labour in child care and in such areas as cooking, cleaning, caring for the sick and old, in an agrarian West African society still dominated by non-wage labour. The allocation of these tasks largely to women constituted a sexual division of labour which showed itself much more rigid than the agricultural sexual division of labour, in a period of great pressure for change in work patterns, and great pressure on women's working time. The question then is, why is the sexual division of labour so rigid in these areas of production?

Any answer can only be tentative for the moment, more a specification of areas for further study. We know that child care and what I have called 'domestic' tasks are not always in all societies allocated to women (see Rogers, 1980, for a summary of the evidence), but they are predominantly female tasks. We also know that these tasks in many societies become tightly tied to the concepts of gender identity, although other tasks may also become involved in gender-definitions in this way. One might expect to find that those tasks where the sexual division of labour is most rigid, are also those for which that gender allocation of tasks is most crucial to the perpetuation of existing forms of the relations of marriage, procreation and filiation. That is, gender-typing is most rigid in areas crucial to the social relations which I have called the relations of human reproduction, and which generally incorporate male dominance and control of women's sexuality.

Thus in developed capitalism the household has become a kind of mediating institution, mediating that is two sets of social relations: those of marriage and filiation, which act to constitute the household and determine the context of much of child care, and the wider economic relations of the society. Women's performance of domestic work, especially the care of children within the home, both expresses their dependence and subordination within marriage (since men actively benefit from this work) and also weakens their position within the wage labour market, contributing to their low wages and poor conditions as wage workers. The constraints put by domestic responsibilities on women's participation in wage work is shown by the rapid rise in part-time work for married women in Post-war Britain (Hurstfield, 1978), and has also been discussed in the feminist literature (e.g. Herzog, 1980; Beechey and Perkins forthcoming).

Women's domestic work therefore is the economic expression of the fundamental inequality of the marriage contract. The implication of this argument is that the subordination of women through an unequal division of labour in the wage sphere, described in the first section of this article, is ultimately derivative of subordination within the marriage-based household. I am not implying by this that one depends solely upon the other: on the contrary, once established each area of economic subordination has considerable independent momentum and acts to reinforce the other. The implication of this is that in the long run inequality in the wage sphere can only be overcome – and indeed could be relatively easily overturned – were the relations of reproduction, and the form of the household which they create, first to be transformed.

I have cast this argument so far in this section largely in terms of the sexual division of labour in and outside the home in developed industrial capitalism. But similar kinds of questions can also be asked, I suggest, about the implications for women of the spread of capitalism elsewhere, whether this occurs through increasing wage labour, or through the reorganisation of small-scale production for the market. One can ask there too, what are the areas of production where there is most resistance to a reorganisation of the sexual division of labour? How is this resistance tied into the organisation of marriage and household forms, and male dominance of those institutions? If in crucial areas such as child care the sexual division of labour is being reorganised, is it to the detriment of women's position within the marriage contract (whether formal or informal)? An analysis – which clearly has to be historically and geographically specific – of which areas of an existing sexual division of labour are most resistant to change, and why, is clearly useful to any attempt to abolish the division of work by gender and the subordination of women that it implies.

THE SEXUAL DIVISION OF LABOUR: A POLITICAL ISSUE

This has brought us then to the question of women's struggle against the sexual division of labour. The implication of this discussion is that whatever the theoretical disagreements the sexual division of labour is an important political issue for women. The form taken by the sexual division of labour is perpetually being transformed and recreated as economic and social change occur. Thus for example the opening of new factories and plantations in the Third World bring new forms of division of labour by gender, and therefore new forms of the hierarchy between men and women.

Once firmly established, these new forms of sexual division of labour, and the subordination of women which they embody, are hard to challenge. Once, for example, young Asian women in textile or electronics factories have become a super-exploitable workforce for capital, once particular jobs have been cast as 'women's work', then the sexual division of labour within wage work takes on an autonomy of its own. Once men and women workers have been created as two relatively non-competing groups within the labour force, with men relatively privileged in terms of wages and work conditions, then there exists a material division between men and women (however much as workers they also have in common), which can be exploited by management, and which reinforces women's social and economic subordination in the new economic sphere. Thus gender hierarchy and the subordination of women, however much they may be based within the household or marriage relations, nevertheless become an embedded feature of the wider economic structure.

Furthermore, once established, different areas of the sexual division of labour tend to reinforce one another. In some societies inadequate wages trap women within marriage-based households. The need to support and care for children weakens women's bargaining position in the labour market throughout the world. Men acquire a vested interest in women's services within the home, and more generally in their own relatively favourable position in the economy. In many countries the state will operate to support an unequal sexual division of labour once it is established: for example, by legislating against industrial action to improve pay and conditions, by turning a blind eye when women are paid below minimum legislated wages, or by reinforcing through legislation women's unequal position within the household. Thus social service provision in Britain treats women as the dependants of men, so reducing their ability to survive and support children without male support (McIntosh, 1978). Elsewhere, legislation on marriage and divorce, rules for the allocation of public housing, indeed a wide range of social legislation, may operate to weaken women's economic and social position (Land, 1977). Agricultural development policy too, implemented by government, may operate to the detriment of women's position in production (Rogers, 1980; Roberts, forthcoming). Thus, as the sexual division of labour is transformed and recreated by the spread of the cash economy, any struggle against new forms of sexual division tends to involve not only a struggle against employers but also against state policy (LEWRG, 1980).

The emergence of new forms of the sexual division of labour, then, should always be a matter of concern to feminists. New divisions of labour by gender embody new forms of subordination of women, and once established acquire a momentum of their own. Any strategy aiming to change the sexual division of labour has to take into account the benefits of that division to men, as well as those to the dominant economic class in society. To leave either benefit out of one's calculations is to underestimate seriously the scale of the problem.

To return to the general theoretical issues raised in this article, it is true to say, I think, that the analysis of the sexual division of labour proposed here raises important issues for a feminist understanding of class in any society. Women workers' perception of the class of which they are a part, is of a class containing deep material division between men and women. These material divisions are then reflected in the forms of organisation of different groups of workers. Women are so frequently marginalised and ignored by formal union organisation (from Britain, see Coote and Kellner, 1981, to West Africa, Mackintosh, forthcoming, to Indonesia, Stoler, forthcoming) resulting in their often resorting to sporadic 'wildcat' protests (Heyzer, forthcoming; Cardosa-Khoo and Khoo, forthcoming). Feminists are frequently accused by male socialists, both in Britain and elsewhere, of undertaking divisive political activity, dividing the working class by creating conflict on gender lines. The implication of the analysis above is that the working class is already materially divided, women's subordination being embedded in a sexual division of labour relatively favourable to men. Feminists have therefore replied that, far from being divisive, to struggle against those divisions is necessary if the divisions are to be overcome.

NOTES

This paper owes a great deal to discussion with all the members of the Subordination of Women Workshop, and the participants in the Conference on the Continuing Subordination of Women in the Development Process, Sussex 1978. Particular thanks for comments on earlier drafts to Carmen Diana Deere, Maxine Molyneux, Olivia Harris, Kate Young, Ros McCullagh, Ruth Pearson and Gaby Charing.

1   This point was made by a conference participant, Awa Thiongane.
2   Some feminist writers would however, argue that relations of
    sexuality can for women be treated exactly as if they were produc-
    tion relations. Claudia Werlhof made an argument to this effect at
    the conference.

Subsistence Production and Extended Reproduction

Veronika Bennholdt-Thomsen

A basic contradiction within the capitalist mode of production is the separation of subsistence production from social production. This article investigates how this separation relates to the accumulation of capital and how it is reproduced with capital. My central argument is that the separation is fundamentally necessary for the accumulation process. Within the present capitalist world economy, housewives and peasants (men and women) are the main subsistence producers; in different concrete forms both reproduce labour power for capital without compensation. It will be argued that these two groups are integrated into the capitalist mode of production through their marginalisation, i.e. they form the consolidated mass of the industrial reserve army of labour, and as such they are continuously reproduced as part of the process of extended reproduction of capital. Housewives and peasants embody a basic form of capitalist relations of production. Although this form is subordinate to the valorisation process, it is distinctive, and has gone unrecognised theoretically.

CAPITAL ACCUMULATION AND THE PRODUCTION OF LIFE

The capitalist mode of production is composed of two areas of reproduction: extended reproduction or accumulation and subsistence reproduction. Extended reproduction includes the valorisation process as analysed by Marx in the second volume of *Capital* (Marx, 1978, Ch.21). The reproduction of life and of the working capacity of individuals is the necessary precondition for extended reproduction. Marx does not, however, discuss this aspect of reproduction in any detail. And up to the present, it has been (incorrectly in my view) conceived in political economy as being given by nature. Capital does not directly exchange with labour as part of nature; rather nature is appropriated by means of work, in both production and the reproduction of human life. Precisely because the valorisation of labour power by capital is based upon previous expenditure of labour, subsistence production must be included in the analysis of political economy. In order to do this the reproduction of human life has to be examined. I shall call this aspect of general social production *subsistence production*, since it is here that human life and vital capacity to work are continuously produced and reproduced. Subsistence production includes work related to pregnancy, childbirth, nursing and education of children, as well as that required in the production and transformation of food, clothing, housing, and the physical and psychological demands associated with sexuality (see Evers, 1980; Werlhof, 1980a). In short, subsistence production is largely women's work (wives, housewives and mothers) in the metropolitan countries. However, it is also necessary to include the subsistence production of peasants (men and women) in the so-called Third World because by means of such production, nature is directly appropriated for consumption (see Werlhof, 1980b).

The relation of production central to extended reproduction is the exchange between wage work and capital; the relation of production central to subsistence production is the family. Under capitalism, subsistence production is subordinated to valorisation. It is important to stress that the production and reproduction of individuals' capacity to work simultaneously result in the availability of labour for capital. When we consider that the domestic production of housewives is generally dependent on the wage, the fact of their subordination to capital and consequently to the capitalist valorisation of their labour becomes evident. This is, however, less obvious for peasant production in underdeveloped countries. Recently a start has been made to develop such an analysis but it is still incomplete (see Singlemann, 1978). I shall at this point outline the subordination of small peasants' subsistence production to the conditions of extended reproduction, and then attempt to show both the similarity between the position of the housewife and the small peasant as subsistence producers confronted by the

accumulation process, and the nexus between the two types of reproduction.

The subordination of peasant production to capital takes three main
forms:

1. wage labour: some members of the family work as agricultural labourers for the whole or part of the year,
2. the market: peasants sell some of their produce on the capitalist
   market,
3. credit: capital succeeds in controlling the process of peasant production by means of credit agreements, thereby ensuring the appropriation of a surplus product for a specific capital.[2]

That part of production which is directly consumed by the peasant
serves to reproduce labour which is available to capital. For example, a
peasant who periodically works for wages spends a considerable part of
necessary labour-time on self-provisioning, thereby increasing the
amount of surplus-labour appropriated by the employer. This becomes
obvious in the case of temporary wage labourers in agriculture or low-
paid workers in the so-called world-market factories, particularly
women, who cannot cover their minimal necessities for existence with
their wage and have to support themselves by additional means or be
supported by relatives engaged in subsistence production (Meillassoux,
1981; Fröbel et al., 1980). A similar process occurs when peasant
households produce for both subsistence needs and the market. In this
case, however, it is not labour but products which are sold.

There are of course a number of differences in the social and class situation of housewives, above all white metropolitan ones, and poor
peasants in the Third World. Nevertheless, we feel that it is useful,
especially from the point of view of the reformulation of the marxist
theory of value, to emphasize the similarities on a general level before
entering into a discussion of the differences on a more concrete level. A
whole range of housewife types exist: the white metropolitan, bourgeois or proletarian; the coloured, generally subproletarian in the
metropolis; the upper class wife in the periphery (who is generally much
better off than the bourgeois metropolitan housewife because she has
servants and therefore cannot really be called a housewife); the housewife of a permanent factory worker; the housewife in the slums, who is
often an all-round subsistence producer getting a very small contribution from her under- or unemployed companion; and finally the poor
peasant's wife.

Despite these differences there are three sound arguments for considering peasants and housewives to be similar in their position as subsistence producers:

1. We are talking about one form of the social division of labour within the capitalist mode of production – that between immediate subsistence and industrial commodity production. This division of labour can appear along sex lines – in fact, the sexual division of labour is a part of the social division of labour – but it need not necessarily be so.

2. The housewife is one special form of labourer that has emerged with capitalism, and is now the generalised form responsible for subsistence production within the First World. From the point of view of the daily performance of the subsistence production process the metropolitan housewife has more in common with a Third World peasant than with the wife of a bourgeois in a Third World country who has servants.

3. The sexual division of labour within peasant production in the present Third World does not (yet) conform to the pattern of women in the house, men in the fields. Rather women do all kinds of work (Boserup, 1970). When we speak of peasants, we therefore refer to women as well as to men. Nevertheless, it is true that a process in which peasant housewives are being created can be observed with the spread of credit programmes. This and similar processes (see Bennholdt-Thomsen, 1980) can best be understood in terms of an analysis which starts by conceptualising subsistence production as a whole within the present capitalist world economy (Wallerstein, 1974).

In the first place, an aspect common to peasants and housewives is their production for consumption under conditions of generalised commodity production. The production of exchange values prevails in extended reproduction, whereas the production of use-values prevails in subsistence reproduction (see Otto-Walter, 1979). Here, there is direct appropriation of work for consumption (services and products), without the interference of exchange of commodities. However, it would be wrong to consider the production of use-values as being outside the capitalist mode of production, even though at first sight it may not seem to be integrated into generalised exchange relations. It would also be wrong to consider it to be another mode of production articulated with the capitalist mode, since it is an integral part of capitalism. Capital cannot operate without subsistence production, for extended reproduction is based upon subsistence reproduction; products from the latter area are essential to the former. Under capitalist conditions, use-value always has its counterpart in exchange-value; they are the two faces of the same coin. However, exchange-value of subsistence products is not always immediately apparent. Similarly the appropriation of labour power by capital is not immediately apparent, when such appropriation occurs under exchange relations which do not adopt the wage form. In this case, the amount of labour which is realised as surplus is neither directly controlled nor fixed by a concrete capital in the production process itself (unlike the wage form, divided as it is into necessary labour-time and surplus labour), but only afterwards in circulation.

The use-values of peasant producers and craftsmen which are sold as products are subsumed by the capitalist valorisation process and are transformed into exchange-values through prices. In this way, labour power reproduced outside commodity production is brought into the sphere of commodity production. This phenomenon is the same as that of the peasant who is simultaneously a wage worker. Only the mechanisms of exchange with capital are different; here the commodity is not a product, but labour power itself. With respect to housewife-production, it is possible to regard it as private and concrete work (Himmelweit and Mohun, 1977). But we must also recognise that it becomes social and abstract afterwards. Consequently it is not correct to say that this work is not commodity production – it is! – but a certain time lag is built in. The housewife, like the peasant, produces use-values – this is the goal of her production process – but these use-values become exchange-values the moment when the labour-power, produced and reproduced within the household, is sold.

Another important aspect of this disguised relationship between use-value and exchange-value is the producers' attitudes towards the products. Subsistence producers measure their product in terms of use-values; they do not calculate the exchange-value in advance. The conversion of these use-values into exchange-value is outside their control and is unfavourable to them. The housewife does not think (consciously at any rate) of her labour process as producing the commodity 'labour power'. As far as she is concerned, she is rearing human beings and working for the well-being of her children and husband. In effect, what she is creating becomes a commodity. The same applies to peasants. Even when they cultivate cash-crops, a use-value-oriented way of treating the crops prevails, and it is exactly this attitude which makes this form of agricultural production so profitable (Martinez-Alier, 1967; Eckstein et al., 1978; Bennholdt-Thomsen, 1980).

In general, the handicraft production process is bound to be excessively exploited. It is closely related to subsistence production but is indeed often extended to enter commodity production. It is characterised by the same fundamental aspect of all subsistence production within the capitalist mode of production: the producers themselves are in charge of the work of reproducing their own labour and that of their family. Capital does not assume any responsibility for it. It is unpaid work, which, in turn, is the exact definition of surplus-labour. What on the part of capital appears as the cost of labour power, on the immediate producer's part appears as a cost also. However, capital's outlay represents payment for provisions only and not payment for the work of reproduction. This can also be demonstrated for petty commodity producers. Precisely because they are *not* part of a precapitalist mode of production with productive forces, relations of production, distribution and exchange of its own, they are increasingly forced to sell a part of their product in order to get money to buy basic provisions. This money is entirely spent on acquiring heating oil, medicines, roof tiles, etc., but not on daily food. Equally, peasants who are also wage workers pay for some necessary purchases with their wage but they have also to produce their own supplies of food.

The work of the housewife is also not paid. The husband's wage or salary is only spent in buying goods for the family's daily consumption. If the wife's work were to be paid from the wage, the level of the normal wage would be grossly insufficient.

What ideological mechanisms legitimise such exploitation? Common to the three described forms (commercial peasant, housewife, wage-earning peasant) is an absence of any consideration of this expenditure of labour power in terms of purchase and sale. It is not covered by legislation nor is there even an economic concept for this relation. It is lack of legal contracts, the informal method of subordination to capital, the valorisation process hidden behind anonymous market mechanisms, and the mediation of the familial organisation, which make the exploitation of all this work invisible. The presumption of familial affection and the love of husband and wife obscure this economic relation; hence it is a question of ideology. The husband has another person work for him, without remunerating this work, and this is justified by love. The wife depends on the husband because she has no 'professional' qualifications, because she gets a lower salary if she sells her labour power, because she does not own any property, etc., and because of the needs of childcare. These same ideologies apply to the use of family labour in peasant production. As for the heads of peasant units, it is the illusion of independence within production itself which makes them accept personal responsibility for their own survival as something normal. But in fact it is the fraction of capital which has subjected peasant producers to its interests of valorisation, that is responsible for their extremely low standard of living.

THE RELATION BETWEEN SUBSISTENCE PRODUCTION AND EXTENDED REPRODUCTION FROM AN HISTORICAL POINT OF VIEW

The separation of subsistence production and social reproduction in general, and the specific relation between extended reproduction and subsistence production in the capitalist mode of production, have to be understood in the context of the historical process of the development of capitalism. In all modes of production prior to capitalism, subsistence production was also social production, and vice versa. Separation developed with the emergence of classes – which was rooted in the first form of division of labour, namely that between sexes – when a dominant class began to expropriate from others labour and/or part of their subsistence products. Nevertheless, even in the mode of simple commodity production, all production continues to be use-centred, i.e. directly subsistence or consumption-oriented, and exchange, being one of equivalents, is not yet mystified. Only with the emergence of generalised commodity exchange and socially determined wage work does subsistence production become relegated to a sphere which is considered to be either not properly social or even outside or apart from social work.

This process of separation is accompanied by transformations in social structure, namely the continuously decreasing size of the social unit, which manages subsistence production, eventually ending up as the patriarchial nuclear family. The housewife and the patriarchal nuclear family appear with capitalism. A similar process occurs (although somewhat later) in the peasant production systems described above; it appears with mature internationalised capitalism and is mostly confined to Third World countries.

Capital confronts human beings as a strange force that determines their life, although, in reality, their life feeds capital. The autonomy of accumulation, is the face of the production and reproduction of life, is only an appearance, and men and women have to shake off this golden disguise in order to assume the determination of their own lives.

However, to date the critique of political economy has not offered any analytical tools which would help us shake off this disguise. How is it possible that the basis of accumulation itself, the production and reproduction of the human capacity for labour, has been excluded from the analysis of capitalism? Here we have to point to the ideology of male-chauvinist Marxism which accepts the appearance of the separation of so-called social production from subsistence production as something real, thereby accepting the basis for alienation. I call this way of thinking the fetishism of capital accumulation. It includes a belief in the absolute progress of the capitalist mode of production, the development of productive forces by capital, and the denial that artisanal work, production for direct consumption, or exploitation under non-wage forms, may be intrinsic elements of the capitalist mode of production. The way to avoid concrete analysis of subsistence production is to exclude it from the capitalist mode of production as the devil, and to call these forms pre-capitalist or non-capitalist.

The lack of understanding which renders subsistence reproduction something like a black box in present marxist analysis, can be partly traced back to Marx's own thought. He assumed that with the development of capitalism, all work would adopt the wage form. It is therefore not surprising that Rosa Luxemburg in her reformulation of Marx's reproduction schemes focused precisely on this point – the total neglect of subsistence production in Marx's theory of extended reproduction. Since value-theory seen as *the* theory to explain and measure exploitation under capitalism is an outcome or integral part of a model of extended reproduction which excludes subsistence, it cannot be used to reveal the capitalist exploitation of subsistence work. Value theory itself starts from an ideological assumption, namely that the separation of subsistence production from social production is something real. By our criticism we do not mean to deny the utility of value-theory for the analysis of non-wage labour, but rather to emphasize the need to broaden it. This means it must be applied in an orthodox but not sterile way.

We owe to Rosa Luxemburg the first steps in such an approach, in that she maintained: 'For its existence and future development capitalism needs non-capitalist forms of production as its surroundings' (Luxemburg, 1951, p.289). She was however unable to develop her insight to its ultimate consequence. Despite certain inconsistencies, Luxemburg's propositions lead us nearer to reality than the conceptualizations of Althusser, Balibar and their followers, (Althusser and Balibar, 1970), who theorise precapitalist modes of production when referring to

Veronika Bennholdt-Thomsen 23

relations of production which not only are maintained by but have emerged with capitalist development. Luxemburg, on the other hand, was careful to refer to *non*-capitalist *forms* of production. Notwithstanding her clear-sightedness concerning historical reality with its many forms of production, in contrast to the restricted analysis derived from pure logical models, she still upheld Marx's belief in the tendency within capitalism to the generalisation of wage work. As a result her conclusion that the capitalist mode of production, having eliminated all non-capitalist forms, would be unable to reproduce itself and would thus perish because of its own contradictions, is entirely logical.

Luxemburg has been severely criticized for her self-destruction thesis, but the real blame should be laid on Marx. Instead of recognizing this, critics sought to defend Marx against Luxemburg, and thereby ignored her valid contribution to Marxism, as a true anti-imperialist with real anti-capitalist bias. It was nonetheless Rosa Luxemburg who, in a certain sense, started a discussion which is only today being taken up by Marxist feminists and anti-imperialists.

The reason why Marx and Luxemburg both adhered to the view that wage work would become generalised within capitalism can be found in the historical contexts in which they lived (see Córdova, 1977, for further discussion). In their time imperialist penetration in the colonial countries had not yet dominated all social relations in the form of generalised exchange of commodities. It still could be said that the domination of exchange-value over social relations had its basis in a form of organisation in which labour faced capital directly in the form of a commodity – labour power. Since Luxemburg's time, however, commodity production has imposed itself universally. There is no country today where wage work has not become the determinant social relation, even in those cases where it does not prevail quantitatively (i.e. where there are more peasant producers than wage workers). At the same time we cannot close our eyes to the evidence that the transformation of all work into wage work is not taking place. Worldwide there are more unpaid subsistence producers than wage workers. Hence we come to the conclusion (to paraphrase Luxemburg) that capital itself reproduces its own non-capitalist surroundings, in the imperialist as well as in the dependent countries.

SUBSISTENCE PRODUCTION AND MARGINAL SUBSUMPTION

Those who start from the premise of the real subsumption of all work to capital must logically expect the progressive dissolution of peasant production and, although this has not been explicitly formulated, the dissolution of housewife production. But in fact, quite the opposite has happened. In Third World countries small peasant production is reinforced or reintroduced by bourgeois agrarian reforms or is ultimately even sponsored by the World Bank itself (Bennholdt -Thomsen, 1980). And in the metropolitan countries after the proletarianisation of women, the housewife reappears. Accordingly, the generalisation of wage work (extended reproduction) and of small peasant and housewife production (subsistence production) is a result of capitalist development in its late phase. How do these relations of subsistence production emerge? What are the mechanisms which maintain and reinforce them in capitalist society?

Extended reproduction determines subsistence production: the reproduction of subsistence production inside the capitalist formation is given by the 'general law of capitalist accumulation', that is the progressive production of a relative surplus population or industrial reserve army of labour (Marx, 1976, Ch. 25). All modes of production have their own law of population; in other words, the social conditions under which human life is produced and reproduced are different in different historical epochs. Originally relations of production and reproduction were the same, but as class society developed, they differed more and more, finally becoming opposed in a contradictory unity. Under conditions of generalised commodity production, the law of population is derived from the needs of the valorisation of capital. The production relation that determines society – the capital-labour relation – also determines the law of population. As a result, production and reproduction of life also depend on the contradiction between necessary labour and surplus-labour. Capital will pay for necessary labour as long as it can appropriate surplus-labour, but it constantly endeavours to reduce necessary labour-time in favour of surplus-labour. We call a part of the labour rendered to capital necessary because it is necessary for the workers to reproduce themselves. When a part of the wage-working population is surplus to capital's requirements because its surplus-labour is not required for the average needs of valorisation, it becomes unable to appropriate its necessary nourishment by means of wage work. This process concretely takes place through the constant revolution of technology, and the consequent development of a superfluous population – or the industrial reserve army.

Today we can clearly observe how capitalism renders one part of the working population relatively superfluous. The introduction of new techniques in for example the metal and printing industry is threatening the jobs of a large number of workers in the Federal Republic of Germany. It is not yet clear whether workers will become directly superfluous or forced to accept less skilled jobs. On the other hand, in under-developed countries, a vast army of potential workers for industrial valorisation has existed for years. In these countries industrialisation took place at a highly developed technical level and required little labour. As the development of productive forces under capitalism involves a decrease in employment of living labour in favour of dead labour (embodied in machinery), the possibility of absorbing the freed labour-power in these countries steadily declines. Industrialisation and generalisation of commodity production and the expansion of the world market destroyed precapitalist modes of production, freeing labour power for capital. At the same time not all this freed labour power is needed by capital for wage work. This liberation of labour can thus become structural unemployment.

The result of all these mechanisms is the increasing consolidation of an industrial reserve army. Since this is an extreme manifestation of a relative surplus-population, extreme because its permanent absorption by capital remains unlikely in the near future (Hobsbawm, 1969), we need to find a specific concept for this part of the population. We have chosen to call it the *marginal mass* (see also Bennholdt-Thomsen, 1976). The members of this marginal mass work under any conditions; their aim is not to achieve a higher standard of living, they only struggle to survive. They are the urban poor who collect garbage, are shoeshine-boys, house-maids and prostitutes; in the rural areas they are small peasants who obtain land by any means in order to survive, the para-chutists who invade land, the mass of migrant day-labourers, the primi-tive artisans – all those who sell their products and labour for less than minimum subsistence. Somehow these people survive (although many of them are condemned to an early death), by working and producing just to reproduce themselves and their families.

In spite of being structurally superfluous, they are not superfluous in absolute but in relative terms, which, under capitalist conditions, means that they provide an available reserve of labour-power by virtue of their very existence. In analysing this industrial reserve army, emphasis has focused on its function in lowering the general level of wages. This is true, but a reserve army has other functions too. Here again one can note in existing analyses an almost hypnotic preoccupation with the employed, male, industrial worker; little or no attention has been paid to the livelihood of the industrial reserve army. The important point is that the marginal mass is in charge of its own reproduction and, being an available reserve, it makes its labour-power (directly and indirectly through the product) cheaper for capital. It is this particular point we want to emphasize in our analysis. When a section of the population is responsible for its necessary subsistence work, the appropriation of surplus-labour for capital increases enormously. Furthermore, the mere fact of being subsumed as a whole by capital and predestined through their sheer existence to be used as available labour-power, makes any work rendered by the marginal mass exploitable.

The marginal mass is not outside the capitalist system but in fact very much within it. Therefore, we chose to call its position in relation to capital *marginal subsumption*, borrowing the expression from the related situation of real subsumption (Marx, 1976, Appendix). Marginal subsumption is not another term for the industrial reserve army, but indicates that these workers and their work take diverse forms, and that their work is valorised by capital, although they themselves are responsible for their own subsistence. This means that only a minimal part of the necessary work for their reproduction appears as a cost for capital. (See also Bennholdt-Thomsen, 1977).

The most diverse forms of subsumption to capital arise from marginal subsumption, and a typology of these production relations should be elaborated, based on empirical research. However, marginal subsumption can serve as a generic term to indicate the specific socio-economic position of this vast majority of producers within the capitalist mode of production, their specific relation to capital, and the mechanisms by which their social position is reproduced.

There is nothing peculiar nor new in the fact that a large area of subsistence production exists within the capitalist mode of production, nor is the position of these subsistence producers as reserve in relation to capital either new or peculiar. Women have formed a potential industrial reserve army, whose working power is absorbed or rejected according to accumulation cycles and epochs, since the capitalist mode of production came into existence. Nevertheless, this fact has been treated as a black box within Marxist thought. Now the huge numbers and nature of the industrial reserve army in underdeveloped countries have awakened our attention to these facts and have helped to throw light on the essential features of subsistence production and the way it is connected to accumulation within the capitalist mode of production in general.

Veronika Bennholdt-Thomsen 27

In analysing the so-called underdeveloped countries, we also become aware that in the so-called developed countries a marginal mass exists as well. Metaphors like – 'women, the slaves of our society' or 'women, the colonised of our society' – have real meaning from this perspective. Women are bound to form a structural part of the industrial reserve army – the housewife emerges with capitalism – and their subordination to capital should therefore be seen as one important type of marginal subsumption.

TOWARD A NEW AND INTEGRATED THEORY

Our exploration of Marxist theory indicates three basic points of weakness which in our view must be resolved for understanding of the world capitalist system to be enhanced: firstly, value theory must be reconsidered so that subsistence production is included in it; secondly, a new reproduction scheme must be worked out which includes subsistence reproduction as well as extended reproduction; finally, the class situation of women, housewives, and poor peasants as the marginal mass must be specified and their common aspects and differences analysed.

To summarise the preceding arguments, we think it is possible to establish the framework within which the analysis should be carried out: the laws of accumulation themselves reproduce capitalist reproduction relations which do not adopt the wage form. It is the general law of accumulation, the *progressive* production of an industrial reserve army, that reproduces these non-wage forms which are directly linked to subsistence production.

NOTES

1. The author is a West German scholar working on Latin America. The thesis proposed in the article has been formulated within the framework of the Latin American debate on dependent capitalism and especially on marginalisation and the Western European debate on modes of production and housework. Ideas in the article were developed during discussions at a series of conferences on 'Underdevelopment and Subsistence Reproduction in the Middle East and Arab Countries, South and Southeast Asia, Black Africa and Latin America', organised by the Working Group on the

Sociology of Development at the University of Bielefeld, of which the author forms part and to whom she feels very indebted.

2. The importance and variation of these forms differ in the different regions of the Third World. The empirical background of the present analysis is the situation in rural Latin America, especially Mexico. For results of research on the historical development of these forms in different regions of the world see Research Group on Households and Production Processes at the Fernand Braudel Center (1978).

Women's Labours

The Naturalisation of Social Inequality and Women's Subordination

Verena Stolcke

Polemics over the roots of women's subordination in class society have frequently been marked by a strong economistic bias. Feminists – both radical and liberal – and Marxist social scientists have generally centred their attention on the economic constraints of marriage and the family as the basic impediments for women's emancipation. Consequently, little attention has been paid to the ideological construction of reproduction in class society or its effects on the definition of sexual roles (cf. Rowbotham, 1974, p.69; Meillassoux, 1981). In addition, no distinction has generally been drawn between the role of bourgeois family structures and ideology and that of the working class family in the reproduction of social class relations.

Though from different angles, both Marxist and feminist scholars converge in attributing women's subordination, at least in class society, to the burden of maternity and the ensuing sexual division of labour which prevent women from participating on equal terms with men in so-called productive labour. Women are seen as subordinate because the functions executed by them are subordinate. For Marxists this is so because domestic labour is privatised and therefore unproductive. For many feminists women's subordinate status is due to the apparently universal constraints on their activities exerted by their responsibility for procreation, which prevents them from participating in social production and the public sphere, i.e. those activities from which men appear to derive their social and political pre-eminence. In my view, neither of these explanations is adequate. The Marxist position on the one hand, by focusing primarily on production, has failed to consider the essential connection between the interdependence of relations of production and reproduction and the perpetuation of social inequality. On the other hand, the feminist position has bypassed the question of cross-culturally diverse definitions of sex roles and the specific organisation of social reproduction and its social meaning in different historical contexts.

As a logical conclusion of this politico-productivist bias, many Marxists and feminists advocate women's incorporation into productive labour and the elimination of the sexual division of labour as the only path to women's emancipation. By attributing women's subordination to the inferiority apparently inherent in domestic labour however, one ends up taking one of the effects of women's subordination in class society as its cause. Moreover, one fails to ask the fundamental questions of why woman is ideally confined to the home or why domestic labour, as opposed to so-called productive labour, is viewed as inferior. My aim is not to demonstrate that domestic labour in capitalist society is productive after all, but to discover the social roots of its ideological valuation. This is in part a question of perspective. A similar issue has been raised by Himmelweit and Mohun with regard to domestic labour:

'domestic labour was invisible to Marx because he considered labour-power from the perspective of capital . . . But if the proletariat is seen from its own perspective, that of the production and sale of labour-power, that is, if labour-power is seen from the point of view of its own production, of its value aspect rather than its use-value aspect, then not only does domestic labour become a visible category but also Marx's tendency to analyse the family and the problem of equality between the sexes from a specifically male perspective can both be understood and corrected' (Himmelweit and Mohun, 1977, p.22).

I want to suggest that this correction can contribute to a better understanding of the working class family, but not of that of the bourgeoisie.

By adopting a productionist perspective, students of women's subordination have often been blinded to the specific nature of women's subordination, which lies precisely in the socially necessary role which the family plays, not initially in the reproduction of cheap labour power but in the social reproduction of class relations. Born of the nineteenth century notion of progress, which regards as socially valuable only those activities related to material production, the work and achievement ethos characteristic of and central to bourgeois society largely obscures the specificity of women's subordination. According to this ethos, it is men who work; it is only work which produces; and it is thus only men who actively participate in the progress of society, and accordingly deserve respect and power. As Naredo has argued,

> 'this phallocratic position celebrates production as the only source of wealth, and treats women just as it treats nature, i.e. as passive and dominated objects which offer themselves without any counterpart to the predatory desires of the father work, . . . depriving them of any transcendental meaning they possess' (Naredo, 1979, pp. 63-6).

Engels' interpretation of the origins and role of monogamous marriage in class society and its effects on the condition of women looms large in most recent Marxist analyses of the roots of women's subordination. His interpretation lends itself to two quite different emphases, although the implications of only one dimension – the economic structure of society – have generally been pursued.[1] Engels initially attributes woman's subordination to her degradation to 'a mere instrument for the production of children' for her husband in the interests of rightful transmission of private property (Engels, 1972, p. 121). To guarantee the paternity of children, the absolute sexual fidelity of women had to be enforced; thus monogamous marriage arose, granting men ample sexual freedom but subjecting women to absolute control by their husbands. The nuclear family is the end product of these transformations. As regards woman's economic role, this transformation meant that

> 'household management lost its public character. It no longer concerned society. It became a *private service*; the wife became the head servant, excluded from all participation in social production' (ibid., p. 137).

I will come back later to the biologist bias in this argument. For the present argument it is relevant to notice how Engels shifts his ground from an initial concern with reproduction to the sphere of production, and in this process inverts the determination:

> 'The legal inequality of the two partners [presumably in family law, which defines mutual rights and obligations between spouses] bequeathed to us from earlier social conditions, *is not the cause but the effect of the economic oppression of the woman* (ibid., pp. 136-7, my italics).

Now, man's preeminence and woman's subordination are seen as the product of their relative position with regard to 'social production':

'In the great majority of cases today . . . the husband is obliged to earn a living and support his family, and that in itself gives him a position of supremacy without any need for titles and special legal privileges.'

The conclusion that

'the first condition for the liberation of the wife is to bring the whole female sex back into public industry' follows logically (ibid., pp. 137-8).

This shift in Engels' argument is not arbitrary. It derives from the economistic bias in Marx and Engels' notion that bourgeois society abolished 'all feudal, patriarchal, idyllic relations' – even within the family and between the spouses – and instituted the cash nexus as the only social relation (Marx and Engels, 1958). They insisted, that is, that bourgeois society necessarily eliminates, even within the family, the most intimate sphere of social life, all elements of what one might call extra-economic coercion. Under capitalism, the relation between spouses is supposedly determined exclusively by their respective economic roles, in terms analogous to those that define the social relations of production: 'within the family he is the bourgeois; and the wife represents the proletariat' (Engels, op. cit., p. 137).

Lenin also maintained time and time again that

'as long as women are engaged in housework their position is still a restricted one. In order to achieve the complete emancipation of women and to make them really equal with men, we must have social economy and the participation of women in general productive labour. Then women will occupy the same position as men . . . You all know that even with the fullest equality, women are still in an actual position of inferiority because all housework is thrust upon them. Most of this housework is highly unproductive, most arduous, and it is performed by women' (Lenin, 1972).

Women's contribution to the recovery from the ravages of the war in the Soviet Union was no doubt essential and may in part explain Lenin's emphasis on the need to incorporate women into productive labour. Freeing women from domestic isolation and economic dependence is of course desirable, but the question remains, to what extent does Lenin's solution attack the roots of women's subordination?

Lenin and others saw clearly that some of the parallel requirements for women's emancipation were the granting of full political and legal rights and the socialisation of domestic labour (Trotsky, 1970, p. 61; Lenin, op.cit.). The need to free women from the controls over their sexuality in marriage was however less clear; in fact Lenin was highly critical of the emphasis women workers gave to the questions of sex and marriage (ibid). Thus, the Soviet government, rather than abolishing marriage as an institution regulating the relation between the sexes, modified the laws on marriage and introduced easy divorce. Lenin also rejected the specificity of the women's question and the need for separate organisations for women.[2] The relatively greater sexual freedom in some Western countries in recent times has shown that a sexual revolution does not necessarily entail a social revolution. But equally, without a radical transformation of those institutions – marriage and the family – which perpetuate social and sexual inequality, any social revolution will be incomplete.[3]

In order to revise these biased views of the family and women's subordination, the crucial issue is to understand the ways in which the institutions of marriage and the family lend support to, and serve to perpetuate, social inequality and relations of power, and the particular way in which the subordination of women is one of the prerequisites for the maintenance of social relations of domination. I would argue that while class oppression and the social division of labour have their origins in unequal access to the means of production, it is social reproduction, i.e. the perpetuation of class relations and domination – mediated directly by the institutions of marriage, the family and inheritance – which requires (and thus determines) both women's primary assignment to domestic labour and the undervaluation of this function.

In class society, in other words, the sexual division of labour – women's domestication – is ultimately the product of man's control over women's reproductive capacity in the interests of perpetuating unequal access to the means of production. Because historically women's sexuality and reproductive capacity have been conflated, this involves the control over women's sexuality by men as husbands, fathers and brothers.

It is of course misleading to speak in general terms of *the* family or *the* role of women in class society, for the institutions of marriage and the family may be only formally identical for the bourgeoisie and the working class; their social meanings are distinct and they must be dealt with in distinct terms. Moreover, the social control of women through marriage differs by class and has different implications for economic roles in different classes.

Nonetheless, just as capital cannot be conceived without labour, any explanation of the persistence of the working class family must take into account the interrelation between the bourgeois and the working class family. A consideration of the working class family purely in terms of its economic functions for capital, e.g. the contribution of unpaid domestic labour to the reproduction of labour power, is insufficient to explain its persistence. It is only with reference to bourgeois ideology that we may understand how marriage, the family, and inheritance serve, within the working class, both to reproduce workers and to maintain existing workers. Since it is the dominant class which sets the rules of the social game, a first step towards understanding the institutions of marriage and the family must be an explanation of the persistence of these institutions among the bourgeoise. Due to lack of space, my discussion will be confined to this question.[4]

INHERITANCE AND HEREDITY: THE PERSISTENCE OF THE
BOURGEOIS FAMILY

Neither monogamous marriage nor the family is particular to capitalist society, nor did they originate with it. In other hierarchical social formations, e.g. caste or feudal societies, both monogamous marriage and the family are central institutions. Marriage always concerns the allocation of a number of distinguishable classes of rights to the spouses in their respective attributes, e.g. their sexuality, labour and property (Leach, 1961). Rules of inheritance always concern the transmission of specific rights between generations (cf. Goody et al., 1976). It is through marriage patterns and rules of inheritance that a person's social condition is partially or totally defined. This is most obvious in social formations like caste or lineage societies, whose members' position is determined by birth.

Within bourgeois society the persistence of the family based on relations of personal dependence and the subordination of women is a paradox. As Hobsbawm recently argued,

'the crucial point is that the structure of the bourgeois family flatly contradicted that of bourgeois society. Within it freedom, opportunity, the cash nexus and the pursuit of individual profit did not rule.' (Hobsbawm, 1975, p.239).

An analysis purely in economic terms is insufficient to resolve this paradox.

That social position is determined by ascription is seemingly out of place in societies (most typically bourgeois society) in which the condition of the individual is supposed to be the result of his/her own personal achievements. John Stuart Mill well perceived the contradiction between the liberal ethos and women's subordination.

'At present, in the more improved countries, the disabilities of women are the only case, save one (royalty), in which laws and institutions take persons at their birth, and ordain that they shall never in all their lives be allowed to compete for certain things ... The social subordination of women thus stands out as an isolated fact in modern social institutions; a solitary breach of what has become their fundamental law [competition and individual achievement]; a single relic of an old world of thought and practice exploded in everything else but retained in the one thing of most universal interest (Mill, 1977, pp.236-7).

Is it at all tenable to consider the subordination of women a relic in bourgeois society? Indeed it is striking that it is precisely in Victorian England, at the height of competitive capitalism, that we find the bourgeois family in its most repressive form.

The emergence in the most advanced Western countries of biological theories to legitimate social inequalities in the nineteenth century is a crucial fact which helps us understand the apparent contradiction between a family structure based on the subordination of women and children, and the bourgeois ethos of equality of opportunity for all. For the development of class society, which is based on – and generates – profound social inequalities, has been accompanied by the spread of the myth of equal opportunity, which serves to obscure the potential conflict inherent in class relations. There is thus a permanent tension between a hierarchical reality and a seemingly egalitarian ethos. It is the definition of woman's role primarily in biological terms – woman's function in life is motherhood because nature made her so – which serves to bridge this contradiction. But at the same time, this ethos of equality of opportunity also provides the conditions for women to struggle to overcome their subordination.

By the nineteenth century, the profound effect of the consolidation of class society, the increasing misery of the masses and growing working class militancy on the dominant ideologies, were evident. In the seventeenth century, liberals had accepted the market freedoms of emerging capitalist society, but had been oblivious to their class concomitants. But by the early nineteenth century liberals increasingly had to include capitalist relations and thus class divisions in their models of society. The effects of the system's excesses were however to be attenuated by the granting of universal franchise as the basis of representative government, which, in turn, was seen as neutral, standing above sectional interests (Macpherson, 1977). Also, as Hobsbawm has pointed out, the bourgeoisie could no longer justify social inequalities purely in terms of an ethic of abstinence and effort, that is in terms of personal achievement, not least because these attributes did not seem to explain any longer the success of the bourgeoisie itself:

> 'Hence the growing importance of the alternative theories of *biological* class superiority, which pervade so much of the nineteenth century bourgeois Weltanschauung. Superiority was the result of natural selection, genetically transmitted. The bourgeois was, if not a different species, then at least the member of a superior race, a higher stage of human evolution, distinct from the lower orders which remained in the historical or cultural equivalent of childhood or at most adolescence' (Hobsbawm, 1975, pp.247-8).

This came very close to being a racist theory of social inequality. Some have interpreted this as essentially a product of colonial expansion to legitimate the apparently civilizing mission of the colonial powers. I would suggest however that the pervasiveness of biological theories of social inequality was as much an ideological mechanism to explain away the growing social inequalities in the home countries as a legitimation of colonial expansion.

For instance in Germany – which was not a colonial power – in the second half of the nineteenth century, élites responded to the polarisation of society with various types of racist theories, all of which attributed social inequalities not to a functional division of labour, but to radical, inherent, differences between human beings. The emphasis was placed on heredity much more than on environment (Struve, 1973). In England and the United States, toward the end of the century, widespread racism found its expression in the dominance in academic circles of eugenics, the root of which was a pervasive fear about the likely consequences of differential class fertility, based on the view that social class expressed at least in part men's genetic endowment (Searle, 1978; Gordon, 1977). Élite supremacy could only be protected either by guaranteeing that its rate of reproduction could compete with that of the lower orders, or by preventing the latter from overtaking the former in their birth rate.

All of these theories coincided in rejecting, in varying degrees, environmental factors as explanations for social inequalities; all were predicated upon the hereditary transmission of relevant characteristics. But interest in eugenics was not restricted solely to academic circles. Rather it expressed, in the form of an apparently scientific theory, a much more widespread racial sentiment. The fact that by the 1930s the political impact of the theory was slight in Britain, France and the United States, while in Germany eugenics furnished the scientific legitimation for the virulent racism of the Nazi regime, is probably related to the different degrees of consolidation of the bourgeoisie in these countries. In the former countries too, the repudiation of eugenics was in part a reaction precisely against the rise of Nazism. Yet, even today, biologism has not vanished as a diffuse social sentiment.[5]

What are the implications of this biologism for an understanding of women's subordination and the role of marriage and the family in class society? An expression of this biologism, which is no more than the attempt to define as natural what are social facts, is the tendency to collapse *inheritance* and *heredity*, i.e. to confuse social attributes with biologically transmitted traits. This is revealed in Western thought by the propensity to attribute the special social prerogatives accorded to relatives to the existence of *blood*, i.e. biological, ties. Blood is thicker than water, as the saying goes, yet anthropologists have shown that different kinship systems imply different notions of descent, and common blood and substance, and different patterns of sociability which have little to do with biology (Sahlins, 1976). The phrasing of social relations in biological terms is in effect an ideological mechanism to turn social facts into natural and therefore immutable facts.

Equally symptomatic is the ambiguous definition given to the term *to inherit*, meaning not only 'to receive property, rank, title by legal descent or succession', but also 'to derive (quality, character) from one's progenitor' (Concise Oxford Dictionary). Character traits, like material things, are inherited. Since the rules of heredity are unchangeable, they furnish the most persuasive explanation and justification for social inequalities. In a society which purports to assure freedom and equality of opportunity to all its members, the apparently anachronic value attached to heredity in Western society, as 'the tendency of like to beget like' (Concise Oxford Dictionary), is the ideal way of explaining the fact that some are more equal than others.

Again the widespread ambivalence about adoption, particularly among the propertied classes, reveals the same tendency. While by law, adopted children generally enjoy rights identical to those born to a couple, such children are nevertheless often regarded with considerable unease. At times, adoption is rejected because of the supposed hereditary blemishes the child might carry.[6]

Nineteenth-century socialists assailed the institution of inheritance as one of the bases of social inequality; some bourgeois thinkers (consistent with the ethos of equal opportunities) also regarded inheritance as incompatible with bourgeois society. Durkheim, for instance, argued for the necessary disappearance of the right of inheritance; for this 'injustice, which strikes us as increasingly intolerable, is becoming increasingly irreconcilable with the conditions for existence of our present-day societies' (in Lukes, 1973, p.184). What Durkheim was in fact expressing was the apparent incompatibility of inheritance and the achievement ethos. For him, it was the social division of labour that ordered modern society. But in his explanation of the place assigned to the members of society within the social division of labour, biologism again makes its appearance. Instead of the position of each individual within society being determined by birth,

'the only cause determining the manner in which work is divided, then, is the diversity of capacity ... labour is divided spontaneously [and generates solidarity rather than conflict], only if society is constituted in such a way that *social inequalities exactly express natural inequalities*' (Durkheim, 1964, pp.376-8, my italics).

Again it is by appealing to natural differences in capacity that an attempt is made to reconcile equality of opportunity and the social division of labour. But natural differences can only come to mean social inequality in an unequal society (Dobzhansky, 1973; Chomsky, 1978).

If social inequalities are thought of as natural differences, genetically transmitted, and if inheritance follows the dictates of heredity, then monogamous marriage, i.e. the exclusive right of the husband over his wife's sexuality, becomes a critical social mechanism to ensure that reproduction occurs between socially, and thus supposedly genetically, equal partners. As Leach put it some time ago:

'in a very fundamental way, we all of us distinguish those who are of our kind from those who are not of our kind by asking ourselves the question: Do we intermarry with them?' (Leach, 1967, p.19).

In class society the same kind means the same class. One way of maintaining class supremacy is class endogamous marriage and the control of women's sexuality in it.

This collapsing of social and genetic attributes and its consequences for a woman's right to decide about her sexuality, emerge very clearly in the renewed debate over abortion on demand in countries with zero population growth rates such as France. Although it is clear that this decline cannot in any way be attributed to the introduction of the French abortion law of 1974, Michel Debré has recently argued

'abortion on demand is the suicide of a people' (Debré, 1979, p.50).

The underlying issue is, in fact, the alleged depopulation of France, which, as the opponents of abortion on demand argue, will eventually produce a situation in which the active population will be largely composed of the children of immigrants (ibid., p.46). The falling birth rate is no longer seen as a menace to class domination in one country, but as a threat to the preeminence of the first world. Women's refusal of their patriotic duty to produce more babies for the Nation will lead to

'producers without a market, pensions which the State will no longer be able to pay, a social legislation put totally in question, *a dangerous isolation of ageing Europeans in an over-populated world in which the Third World plays the card of natality...*' (ibid., p.50, my italics).

Contraception and abortion on demand have led to

'the substitution of the instinct of procreation by the will to procreate' (ibid.).

Women's freedom to decide over their sexuality is thus seen as a menace to the First World's political cum racial supremacy. In Debré's call of alarm it should be noted that the nineteenth-century French revolutionary notion of the Nation as a political community constituted of all those who profess its principles, is contradictorily replaced by the much older notion of a Nation as a community of all those born to it, i.e. who are of the same genetic stock.

It is within the terms of these biologistic ideologies that Engels' argument that monogamy has as its prime aim to prevent any doubt about the *true* paternity of offspring – in order to safeguard the rightful transmission of property – also makes sense. For, as the old Latin saying has it, *pater semper incertus*. For purposes of inheritance it should in principle make no difference whether paternity is biological or social, as long as it is defined as such.[7] Engels' explanation of the rise of the patriarchal family as a consequence of increasing wealth which

> 'made the man's position in the family more important than the woman's, and . . . *created an impulse to exploit this strengthened position in order to overthrow, in favour of his children, the traditional order of inheritance*' (Engels, 1972, p.119, my italics)

is just one more example of the pervasive tendency to 'naturalise' social facts. Engels presupposed some kind of paternal instinct which would lead men, once they had something to transmit, to want to bestow this on their *own* children. But it is in fact the deeply ingrained belief, contained in bourgeois ideology, that social identity is equal to genetic indentity, which requires the control of woman's sexuality. As Bachofen pointed out, maternity is a natural fact whereas paternity is always social. Paternity requires social mechanisms to make it visible, whereas maternity is incontestable; only its negation would require such mechanisms (Bachofen, 1967). The aim pursued by imposing sexual fidelity on women is to prevent bastardy. But it is social cum biological bastardy that is seen as the true threat to class dominance.

In order to draw out the implications of my argument for the subordination of women, I shall refer to the role of marriage and the family in two explicitly racist societies, nineteenth-century Cuba and Nazi Germany (cf. Martinez-Alier, 1974; Mason, 1976; Rupp, 1977; Koonz, 1977). Their explicitly racist character reveals more clearly some fundamental and general features of the problem which may be less obvious in modern class society.

Nineteenth-century Cuba was a slave society. An individual's social condition was not exclusively determined by ascription, i.e. birth or racial origin. Economic attributes could to some extent offset racial status, but interracial marriage was outlawed. Although the norm was for marriage between racial and social equals – as the Cuban proverb had it, *cada uno con su cada uno* (like with like) – the very existence of the law indicates that it was not always observed. The incidence of interracial marriages contributed to heightening the concern of the white dominant class with racial purity. In fact, apart from wealth, the marks of superior status were whiteness and racially unmixed origin. The perpetuation of class supremacy depended not only on the transmission of property according to the prevalent rules of inheritance but equally on the preservation of racial purity through control over heredity.

This was achieved, very much as in Victorian Britain, through severe control by upper-class men of the sexuality of the women of their class, and women's consequent domestic seclusion. A woman's purpose in life was ideally to bear legitimate, i.e. racially pure, children to her husband. It was through women that family attributes were seen to be transmitted from generation to generation. The role of men consisted in being the providers and guardians of the women of the family. They fulfilled the supporting function of seeing to the socially satisfactory transfer of social attributes and administering the family's patrimony. This notion of women as the repositories of family attributes is quite explicit in nineteenth-century laws regarding the so-called crimes against honesty and adultery, which dealt extremely severely with women but very leniently with men:

> 'a sensible and just differentiation because apart from the consequences of any infidelity between spouses in weakening social bonds, in attacking good manners, in introducing war and discord into the home, *the woman can bring bastards to the marriage*' (Martinez -Alier, 1974, p.117).

The case of Nazi Germany is different in several ways. In nineteenth-century Cuba, women of the propertied class were absolutely confined to the home. Germany in the late twenties had seen a rapid increase in the employment of women wage-earners and white-collar workers, the latter recruited predominantly from among the lower middle and middle class. With the economic crisis at the end of the decade this trend was abruptly interrupted. Also, birth rates and family size were steadily declining by the early thirties. These two factors found expression in the violent reassertion by the Right of the traditional image of woman as mother. This ideological position was translated into policy when Hitler, after seizing power, ordered employed women to return to their homes and to rear large families. By 1937 however, and as Germany prepared for war, this policy was reversed, and women were once more incorporated into industry to participate actively in the war effort.

Still, the growing involvement of women in production did not seem to have a marked effect in altering society's image of a woman as basically subordinate. Women were excluded from all positions that implied any measure of participation in decision-making, and were relegated to the mere execution of the urgent tasks at hand. This is clearly connected with the Nazi regime's persistent emphasis on motherhood and the home as an expression of its aggressive racist ideological underpinnings. As Mason has noted:

> 'all racialist movements which take the biological, pseudo-scientific elements in their ideology seriously, are bound to attach particular importance to women's procreative role . . . The purity of blood, the numerical power, the vigour of the race were ideological goals of such priority that all women's activities other than breeding were relegated in party rhetoric to secondary significance' (Mason, 1976, pp.87-8).

An apparent paradox was the fact that the most extreme expression of Nazi racism, the so-called breeding camps, in which specially selected unmarried girls should give birth to racially pure children, involved turning a blind eye to sexual taboos and marriage (Koonz, 1977). In this case the state determined the adequate choice of partners in procreation and thus controlled women's sexuality. German women, in fact, enjoyed no greater freedom to follow their own inclinations – for instance, by making love to a Jew – than white women had in nineteenth-century Cuba to marry a coloured person.

All this provides evidence that when social hierarchies and supremacy are explicitly or implicitly explained in terms of natural attributes (race, biologically transmitted capacities) rather than as products of environmental factors (for instance the unequal access to the means of production), *heredity* becomes a fundamental concern. This has immediate consequences for women: the perpetuation of social preeminence depends on effective control over procreation in the form of control over women's sexuality. In discussing the implications of artificial insemination for the right of inheritance, a rabbi recently argued that

> 'the semen of any man not the husband, even if there has been no sexual intercourse, produces adultery' (Folha de Sao Paulo, 1978).

The central issue is clearly not sexual but social purity. As the definition of the verb 'to adulterate' reveals, adultery is the act of 'falsifying by admixture of baser ingredients' which produces a stained or counterfeit product (Concise Oxford Dictionary). In this respect, the difference between overtly racist societies and class society is only one of degree.

Finally, what is the connection between the role of monogamous marriage in perpetuating class privileges on the one hand, and the bourgeois ideal of woman's confinement to the home and the low value attached to domestic labour on the other? If women's primary function in life is to produce genetically legitimate heirs, she must be effectively controlled by the men of her family. This control is achieved by confining her as far as possible to an exclusively female sphere, from which all men but those of her own family are excluded – the home – which is also the sphere in which those activities related to motherhood are carried out. The men of her family – her father, brothers and husband – appear as her natural guardians and providers. But at the ideological level, the domestic confinement of women required by the production of legitimate heirs also requires that women accept motherhood as their primary mission in life, and dependence on and domination by men. Motherhood is presented as *the* source of gratification for women, and it is impressed on women that this is their *natural* function, that they are innately incapable of anything beyond this and the tasks related to it. Thus women are characterised as a different species from men, weak and dependent on men and their protection. Moreover, since bearing and rearing children are women's *natural* vocation, they do not require any special skills. They are not *work*, and thus deserve no compensation beyond the so-called joy of satisfying women's innermost instincts of bearing children and seeing their offspring prosper. This does not mean that motherhood is not recognised by society as a valuable function. In fact, it is considered so valuable it needs to be protected and controlled. And what better way to justify and exercise this control effectively than by instilling in those to be controlled their dependence and need for protection by men, i.e. by demonstrating their inferiority. It is in this way that men's domination is legitimated. And it is this 'inferiorisation' that then contaminates all other activities of women. It should be stressed, however, that at issue is not motherhood as such, but the consequences this has for the position of women in class society.[8]

The institutions that are at the root of women's subordination in class society are thus the prevailing arrangements of social reproduction, i.e. marriage and the family. It is through these institutions that the propertied classes reproduce themselves. No modern industrial society has in fact abolished these institutions, despite the lip service which is paid to liberty and equality of opportunity. The growing professionalisation of bourgeois women has not menaced the family or existing property relations. Women continue to be socially defined primarily as mothers. Their incorporation into production is largely determined by the fluctuating needs of the labour market and not seen as their inherent right. Even where greater professional opportunities have given women greater economic independence, this is generally achieved at considerable cost: either the double burden of domestic and extra-domestic work, or foregoing motherhood. Moreover, despite women's greater sexual freedom through the greater availability of means of birth control, class endogamy continues to prevail, and appropriate social reproduction is assured. While the spread of contraceptives has made it possible to separate procreation and sexuality and grants women greater sexual freedom, it also makes it possible for class society to absorb this freedom by providing the means to prevent pre- or extra-marital, and possibly socially inadequate, sexual relations producing undesirable consequences, i.e. 'adulterated' offspring. Finally, even if the greater professionalisation of women of the propertied class generates new tensions within conjugal relations, and liberates women from economic dependence on their husbands, the institution of divorce, by providing relief for cases of conjugal crisis, functions precisely to safeguard marriage as the basis of the family. It is indicative that the majority of divorced people tend to remarry (Shorter, 1977).

CONCLUSION

It may be argued that attempting to explain women's subordination in terms of the role of women's procreative capacity in social reproduction reduces the problem to the physiological differences between the sexes, i.e. adopting a form of biological reductionism. In fact I disagree with the position of radical feminists who attribute women's subordinate status to the greater share women have historically taken in perpetuating the species, and who propose such extreme and to my mind frightening solutions as test-tube babies as the way to end inequality between men and women (see Firestone, 1979).

Obviously, if intrinsic differences are taken to explain social inequalities, then logically equality can only be achieved through identity. But the proposition that only by abolishing biological differences can sex hierarchies be eliminated is much like proposing that racism will only end once all people are of the same phenotype. Racism is not the product of ethnic differences as such, but rather, where racism exists, phenotype – real or imaginary – is used to mark the underlying sociopolitical inequalities. Similarly it is not physiological differences as such which explain sexual hierarchies, but rather their social usage and the social meaning which is attributed to them. The radical feminist position bypasses the crucial issue of the way different societies make use of biological difference to perpetuate themselves. Sexual hierarchies presuppose social inequalities, and both are only legitimised by attributing them to natural facts.

As regards the sexual division of labour, different spheres of activity and segregated sexual roles do not necessarily entail subordination or hierarchy (Leacock, 1978). The issue is rather whether segregated roles fulfil complementary functions to the benefit of the collectivity or whether they are an instrument to perpetuate social inequality. If women's subordination is attributed to women's exclusion from production, then equality between men and women will depend on women's incorporation into production. But this reasoning is based on the idea that only by making accessible to women the defining attributes of men within class society, i.e. their non-involvement in procreation and involvement in so-called productive labour, only by converting women into men, will equality be achieved. Even those who argue for the incorporation of women into production on strategic grounds, i.e. as the only way for women to achieve consciousness of their exploitation and to organise, tend to see struggle in exclusively male terms. To propose that women have first to become like men in order to become free is almost like suggesting that class exploitation might be ended by making it possible for workers to become capitalists.

The subordination of women is not resolved by depriving women of their procreative capacity or by converting women into workers. As Emma Goldman insisted a long time ago, independence, emancipation and equality will continue to be illusory if the narrowness and the lack of freedom in the home is exchanged for the narrowness and lack of freedom of the factory, sweatshop, department store or office (Goldman, 1970, p.14). What is required is the elimination of hereditary class privilege and forms of domination for whose persistence the subordination of women is as fundamental as the exploitation of labour.

NOTES

I want to thank specially Martha Ackelsberg, Olivia Harris and Pepe Roberts for their careful reading and many useful suggestions for this paper.

1. See, for instance, the 'domestic labour debate'.
2. The role played by the family in perpetuating social privilege persists in a number of socialist societies. As Bahro, a left dissident in

the German Democratic Republic has recently pointed out, the bureaucracy sees to it that the children of party cadres lose no privileges. Because their parents work in the state apparatus they are considered to 'pertain to the working class' and are thus entitled to attendant benefits (Bahro, 1979, pp.245ff.). Equally the reluctance to consider the abolition of marriage remains: when Havemann, another German dissident, suggested that future society would probably entail the abolition of marriage, he was attacked for propagating polygamy (Havemann, 1967, p.189).

3. For similar developments in post-revolutionary Cuba, see Verena Martinez-Alier (1974).

4. The implications of bourgeois ideology for the role of the working class family and the condition of working class women has been further discussed in Verena Stolcke (1980).

5. See G.R. Searle (1978).

For an excellent discussion of the politics of eugenics and their implications for the conditions of women in the United States see Gordon (1977). The recent popularity of socio-biology particularly in American social sciences is a further example of the tendency to naturalise social processes. This is not the place to discuss at length this new approach to evolution. Suffice it to say that it is based on an application of the Darwinian notion of fitness as the ability of the individual to pass on his genes through his own reproduction. The central ideas, formulated in what is called inclusive fitness or kin-selection theory, are that mating strategies in human society, such as incest, endogamy, exogamy, types of marriage, can be explained through genetic imperatives, such as the tendency of the individual to maximise his genetic stock. This has produced such bizarre propositions as that

'Human females, as good mammals who produce few, costly, and therefore, precious, offspring, *are* choosy about picking mates who will contribute maximally to their offspring's fitness, whereas males, whose production of offspring is virtually unlimited, are much less picky. Hence, the widespread occurrence in human societies of polygyny, hypergamy, and double standards of sexual morality' for 'the most direct way of ensuring the survival of one's genes is, of course, to procreate and to see to the survival of one's offspring' (Barash and van den Berghe, 1977, p.813).

E.O. Wilson – the pope of sociobiology – has set out its

central tenets (Wilson, 1975). A radical refutation is contained in Sahlins (1976). As Sahlins has pointed out, underlying Wilson's interpretation of the natural progress of genetic transmission as a struggle for resources is again the idea to conceive 'inheritance, which initially referred to the continuity of goods over generations of people . . . to denote at a later date the continuity of the generational "stock" itself'. (p.105). One of the most recent products of this 'biologist' reaction is Symons (1980).

6.   As Goody has recently shown, in hierarchical ordered societies such as China, India, Greece and Rome, an adopted heir was often selected from within the descent group (Goody, 1976). This would seem to be related to the fact that in hierarchical societies socio-economic status is ascriptively defined. By choosing someone from within the descent group, the social and economic integrity of the group is not challenged. In modern European societies adopted children are usually non-kin. It is surely precisely this which causes anxiety.

7.   Thus, the Napoleonic Code ruled that any child born to a couple was to be legally considered the offspring of the husband. This constituted a way to resolve the contradictions between the emphasis given to paternity in ideology and law and the actual difficulties at times to enforce sexual fidelity of women.

8.   Marilyn French (1978), dramatises this well – men as protectors but also as jailers and predators.

Households as Natural Units

Olivia Harris

The sense that women are natural beings while men are able to transcend nature and become fully cultural, is deeply embedded in European
thought (De Beauvoir, 1972). The values attached to nature are not all
negative, but whether viewed as a haven or a threat it is a force that is
subject to control. The ideological basis of women's identification with
a 'natural' sphere has been increasingly recognised and subject to
critique; assumptions about nature and the natural are powerful metaphors that endow what are often quite transient states of affairs with an
air of finality and eternity. Feminists have long been concerned to
undermine the image of femininity as a natural quality; in particular the
associations between physiological specialisation and a set of universal
attributes that supposedly derive directly from them have been questioned, and shown to be culturally and historically specific – a means of
guaranteeing the hierarchical organisation of gender relations. Nature
as a concept is in fact a product of particular cultures, and ideas about
what is natural, and the values assigned to it, vary correspondingly
(MacCormack & Strathern, 1980; Hall, 1979).

Naturalistic assumptions about femininity derive particularly from
physiological characteristics and also from the organisation of family
relations. It seems to me that similar naturalistic assumptions underlie
also the way we think about the domestic domain, although here the
assumptions are in general more concealed and less coherent. It has been
generally accepted from Engels on that the key to women's subordination is to be found in their identification with the domestic sphere.

Some have argued that domestic labour is a hidden form of exploitation; others that women's responsibility for the personal, emotional lives of household members structures their lives in such a way as to exclude their participation in social and political life; others have pointed to marriage as the key social relation by which women's subordination is secured; yet others have argued that women's status in the public domain can be positive only when there is little separation or differentiation between domestic and public spheres. Through a whole spectrum of arguments it is agreed that the domestic sphere is the site where gender subordination is produced and re-enacted.

In feminist discussions it is normal to talk of 'the' family, 'the' household, 'the' sexual division of labour, in a way that seems to impute some universal significance to these terms. Other writers are quite explicit about claims to generality. For G.P. Murdock, an anthropologist, the nuclear family is a universal form of organisation (1949, p.2); P. Laslett, a historian, has claimed that nuclear households did not arise with the development of capitalism but are typical of European societies for a far longer time-period (1972). A model of the sexual division of labour, as a division whereby women remain in the domestic sphere while men go out of it usually to do what is termed productive work, is deeply embedded in the literature. Both Marx (1976) and Engels (1972) take this to be the natural division of labour, and the same assumption resurfaces frequently even in contemporary feminist writing.

On the other hand, it is well-known that the division of tasks between women and men varies significantly from one culture to another (e.g. Oakley, 1972; Friedl, 1975) and from one historical period to another (e.g. M. Roberts, 1978). Anthropological research makes clear the enormous variety in kinship systems and residential arrangements (Goody, 1972); a spate of historical research on family and household particularly in Europe makes it possible to move away from some supposedly universal institution to perceive variation and its causes, and to reintegrate the variety of forms into a broader social and historical context (recent syntheses include Flandrin, 1979; Anderson, 1980; Donzelot, 1980; see also Chaytor, 1980).

Why then, given all we know about the variation in domestic arrangements is it so common to find the domestic domain treated as a universal, or at least very widespread institution? Even those who recognise that the co-resident nuclear family is a historically specific idea will in the next breath talk of 'the' family, 'the' household in a way that surreptitiously reintroduces an assumption of universalism.[1] Working as an anthropologist I have often noticed myself perform this same slippage and have wondered why it comes so easily. One explanation is that the image of the household as a separate, private sphere is so powerful in contemporary capitalist organisation that we extend it to cover other radically different structures, using our own categories of thought to interpret different realities. There is clearly some truth in this, but we need to understand more about how that image comes to be so powerful.

One assumption which reinforces the image of the domestic domain as distinctive and universally recognisable is that household units coincide with families. Many writers have pointed out the problems of treating these concepts as synonymous and argued for their rigorous separation (e.g. Goody, 1972; Creighton, 1980); others have documented the points at which in Western Europe the term 'family' ceases to refer to all those living under a single roof and is restricted to genealogical relatives (e.g. Flandrin, 1979). It is clear that the terms family and household are used interchangeably in many contexts, but they also refer to different sets of meanings. Feminist writers have pointed out that this confusion of terms is no mere accident; the prevailing familial ideology of capitalist society insists that members of a nuclear family should live together, and that people not related in this way should not live together (Rapp et al., 1979). McIntosh (1979) further points out that even in a country, like Britain, where this ideology is deeply rooted and reproduced in social legislation, a surprisingly large percentage of households do not conform to the ideal nuclear family type (see also Stivens, this volume).

The assumptions made today about the natural – and proper – organisation of family life can be shown to have arisen in particular historical circumstances (Hall, 1979; Donzelot, 1980). The definitions of motherhood, childhood, fatherhood, the representation of the home as a 'haven in a heartless world', have been forged out of veritable ideological and legal campaigns, and are subject to constant renegotiation as needs and circumstances change (see Rapp et al., 1979). However, the fact is that in most parts of the world recruitment to domestic groups does take place ideally through relations of kinship and marriage. Marriage may provide for the recruitment of new members to already existing units, or it may form the basis for the creation of a new unit, but it also provides a means by which families are reproduced from one generation to the next. Thus what is initially a contractual relation becomes absorbed into the language of genealogical (that is physiological) relations through the bearing of children. It is also common for household members who are not genealogically related to core members to be treated as kin, either through the formal process of adoption or simply by ascribing a kin status (for example, living-in servants are often treated as children of the house, albeit of a lower status; unmarried adults may be assigned the status of uncle or aunt, regardless of their real relationship to household members). Thus, while we know that kin relations have different meanings, different values in distinct situations, the fact that relations between members of a single domestic unit are thought of so often in terms of kin relations has important consequences. Kin relations, derived as they are from the biologically-founded ties of parent-child and siblings born of the same parents, are imbued in most cultures with ideas of natural behaviour, natural morality.

While the supposed coincidence of family and household presents the domestic unit as a domain in which relationships are based on natural law, I think there are other important dimensions in the assignation of natural status to the domestic domain. The English term household denotes an institution whose primary feature is co-residence; it is overwhelmingly assumed that people who live within a single space, however that is socially defined, share in the tasks of day-to-day servicing of human beings, including consumption, and organise the reproduction of the next generation. Co-residence implies a special intimacy, a fusing of physiological functions and a real distinction from other types of social relations which can be portrayed as more amenable to analysis. It is undoubtedly the case that whether or not it coincides with the family of procreation, household organisation is fundamental to ideologies of womanhood, and that households are in material terms the context for much of women's lives.

THE DOMESTIC MODE OF PRODUCTION?

In recent years several influential theories have been put forward of what is variously called a domestic or family mode of production. Fundamental to such theories is the assumption that as organisational forms the household or family transcend both historical and social boundaries, that they contain some inner logic separable from the context in which they are embedded. In the work of Christine Delphy the proposal of a family mode of production stems directly from her concern with how to interpret the subordination of women (1977).

However some economic anthropologists have also developed theories of a domestic mode of production in an attempt to understand the logic of economic systems not dominated by commodity exchange and the law of value. The most elaborate formulation is to be found in the work of the anthropologist Marshall Sahlins (1974), and it has been developed in a rather different direction by another anthropologist – Claude Meillasoux (1981). Its intellectual roots are however far older. Sahlins in particular draws on the work of the Russian economist A.V. Chayanov, who in opposition to the prevailing Leninist orthodoxy of his time argued that the peasant economy was not based on the same calculations as a capitalist enterprise but rather was oriented to the consumption needs of the household. Since the aim of this family-based enterprise was continued subsistence, it would exploit its own labour until the needs of all its members were satisfied, and no more (Chayanov, 1966).

Influential in recent years, Chayanov's theory has also been subject to much criticism (e.g. Harrison, 1977; Ennew, Hirst & Tribe, 1977). One aspect common to many theories of the household, is to treat this form of enterprise as an isolated unit whose functioning can be analysed without reference either to wider social or economic structures, or to the nature of relationships within the unit. It is premised on assumptions which are the more significant for rarely being rendered explicit. In particular, the supposed or ideal self-sufficiency of the individual household suggests a fundamental separation between this unit and the rest of society. This has various consequences: either society is construed as a series of identical units, held together in some ill-defined way (this would appear to be what Marx had in mind when he described the French peasantry of 1851 as a 'sack of potatoes' (1968); it also underlies the models of Sahlins and Meillasoux); or society is seen as being in some sense outside or in opposition to the household. This seems to underlie the distinction between domestic and public spheres and the theories that have been built on it (see below); it is also the basis for the supposed anti-social tendency of the household, that is, that the interests of individual households are in opposition to the interests of more inclusive social groups (e.g. Sahlins, 1974; Ortner, 1974; Bourdieu, 1977).

Chayanov's theory in fact depends on something which is scarcely mentioned – the market. In the situation he discusses, that of the South Russian peasantry at the turn of the century, there was a market for both land, labour and produce, which set the parameters for the economic behaviour of the peasantry. This means that households have an *appearance* of autonomy since relations with other households are mediated through the abstract form of money. It is because the relations between peasant households were vitally affected by commodity exchange that the household as an individual unit appeared so distinct, and based on a unique structure of non-commodity relations.

The consequences of this supposed autonomy of the individual household, which in fact derives from dependence on the market, can be seen especially clearly in the work of Marshall Sahlins. His domestic mode of production, which is apparently held to characterise all primitive and peasant economies, is premissed on two main assertions. First that while households are never entirely independent, autonomy and self-sufficiency are ideals which affect economic behaviour – the 'centrifugality' thesis. Households will tend to self-sufficiency unless other countervailing forces prevent this centrifugality (such as, for Sahlins, political power). Secondly, and more important for his overall argument, Sahlins asserts that there is a difference in the form of circulation, or distribution of goods and of labour, that takes place *within* as opposed to *between* households. For him, intra-household economic relations are characterised by pooling and what he calls generosity, while those between different households are termed exchange, i.e. a two-way, balanced transaction. There is thus in Sahlins' view a clear-cut discontinuity between inter- and intra-household relations.[2]

This distinction in forms of circulation provides the justification for treating the household as an economically isolable and independent unit. If economic relations between household members were really so different from those with non-members, then that would give weight to the view of households as self-contained enterprises. However this distinction in forms of exchange relies heavily though covertly on the categories of commodity exchange, which make possible the abstraction of objects exchanged from those who exchange them. It is in fact only in conditions of generalised commodity circulation that we can make a radical distinction between pooling, and the two-way transactions of the market-place. In such conditions though the individual household may well be isolated it is anything but independent, since it relies for its reproduction on the circuits of commodity exchange. On the other hand, in situations where commodity exchange does not prevail, for example in many peasant societies, the individual household is not more autonomous, but less. The conditions for individual production are reproduced in such agrarian societies through historically-specific relations that limit and structure the disposition of land and labour

(Friedmann, 1980). There are many empirical illustrations of the centrality of commodity exchange in transforming how households are reproduced, both historical (e.g. in Medick, 1976; Middleton, 1979) and contemporary (e.g. Rogers, 1980).

With the development of generalised commodity exchange, there is a case for treating domestic units as economically distinct and related only through exchange; that is, for asserting a discontinuity between intra- and inter-household relations. This distinction is co-extensive with that between exchange-values and use-values in Marxist analysis. One of the defining characteristics of domestic labour under capitalism is that it produces use-values not exchange-values.[3] Where commodity relations prevail, the circulation of use-values as use-values is effectively curtailed. Conversely where commodity exchange is absent, use-values are produced and consumed within an integrated circuit; this latter economic form is significantly termed in classical Marxism the 'natural economy'. For both Marx and Engels the natural economy, and the natural (sexual) division of labour, are characterised precisely by the absence of exchange relations.[4] In their terms, then, the domestic formation is a natural one, and this would presumably include households within advanced capitalism.

Starting from assumptions about the discontinuity in forms of exchange within and between households under capitalism, it is easy to read backwards to other, non-capitalist economic systems and see the same discontinuity. This appears to be the basis of Sahlins' domestic mode of production. In even less explicit ways, it is also presumably a fundamental criterion by which the domestic domain can be assigned a transhistorical identity (Meillassoux for example sees the household of advanced capitalism as a direct continuity of West African lineage communities, which have merely been deprived of their productive functions, 1981). An important consequence of the unacknowledged significance of commodity circulation in defining the boundaries of domestic units is that whatever economic activity is carried on within the household is given the same status. At worst it is characterised as 'natural', at best described as an absence – the absence of exchange relations, as though a polarised distinction between consumption and exchange could encompass the multitude of ways in which objects and labour circulate other than as commodities. Thus while most writers fall short of Meillassoux's universalism and are careful to maintain a distinction between households which are units of production and those which are not, the distinction lacks theoretical vigour if at the same time households are conceived as an abstracted, individual ideal type, separated from wider social relations.[5]

THE HOUSEHOLD HEAD

Ill-articulated assumptions about different forms of circulation are it seems to me fundamental in the ways that households are represented. If relations between households are characterised as exchange, distribution within households, where it is mentioned at all, is usually conceived as pooling, as for example in Sahlin's work. From his other writings (e.g. 1974, Ch. 5) it is clear that pooling involves first centralisation and then reallocation. This process presupposes a centre from which redistribution is effected, though Sahlins himself never makes this explicit. In the case of Marx the structure is clearer though still vague since for him the agent who allocates both labour and the product of labour is what he calls the patriarch (e.g. 1976, p.171). The same term is used by Chayanov (1966; see also Harrison, 1977).

These writers are representative of many others in their unquestioned assumption that households are organised by and around a household head. They offer no suggestion of the multifarious forms of allocation within households. Often the unspoken assumption is that distribution is based on the criteria of sex and age. While Marx for example recognises that the reproduction of human beings includes a 'historical and moral element' (1976, p.275), many writers assume that consumption levels, defined according to sex and age, are constant in all circumstances (i.e. again given in nature). It is clear however that economic relations within a household do not always take the form of a centralisation of resources followed by their distribution by the household head. In agrarian societies men and women may own different sorts of property and control independently what is produced from it; or economic transactions between wife and husband can take the form of commodity exchange, as is found in parts of East and West Africa (see Edholm, Harris & Young, 1977; Roberts, forthcoming; Caplan, forthcoming). Children too cannot be assumed to be under the direct, exclusive control of a household head. There are many examples of womens' control of the labour of their children, a control which is jealously guarded (e.g. White, 1976).

Where all or most of household income takes the form of money it might be assumed that money, being more abstract and depersonalised than concrete products, would more likely be pooled and distributed by a single authority. However recent studies of family income in Britain show that the origin of money is often taken into account in how it is spent, and that there is considerable variation in how different portions of household income are allocated (see Hunt, 1978; Grey, 1979; Whitehead, this volume). We cannot therefore take for granted that household heads exercise exclusive control over distribution. Neither do concepts such as pooling, sharing and generosity enhance our understanding of the forms of circulation within a domestic group, imbued as they are with normative and value-laden connotations. This does not of course mean that the concept of household head is an illusory one. In many cases it obviously does involve real control; but the nature and extent of this control need to be investigated and specified, rather than assuming an undifferentiated autocracy, or even an undifferentiated communality, within domestic units. As many studies have shown, shifts from household production for subsistence to household-based petty-commodity production, to an economy based on the sale of labour-power, affect radically the structure of households, power relations within them, and the resulting changes in the power to command the fruits of one's own labour (e.g. Tilly & Scott, 1978). Medick too investigates in detail the different forms of authority of household heads in early modern Europe, and sheds interesting light on the effects of these differences for household organisation by comparing peasant households with what he calls the 'proto-industrial family' (1976).

While such work has made a valuable contribution in showing the effects of different economic conditions, it would be mistaken to assume thereby that each economic system produces its own specific household form. It is highly misleading to talk without further qualification of the peasant household, the feudal or the capitalist household. Deere (1978) and Middleton (1979) show for feudal regimes how changes in the form of rent affect the structure of producer households. Similarly an enormous literature on variation in household form and size leaves little doubt that many other determinations must be taken into account – ecology, technology, precise inheritance rules, class position, and demography.[6] While an appreciation of the complex ways in which household membership is determined is obviously relevant to an understanding of relations both within the domestic domain and between members of different domestic groups, it should be emphasised that a concern with formal structures and rules does not necessarily enhance the analysis of economic relationships.

On the other hand, the authority wielded by a household head should not be conceived solely through economic funtions of production and distribution. Meillassoux (1981) for example places great emphasis on reproduction as the determining structure of what he calls the domestic community.[7] While the nature of the control exercised is in his theory quite specific, unlike the vague assumptions of many other writers, it is interesting that for him too the criterion by which the domestic unit is defined is via the identification of an authority-figure.

In the work of Christine Delphy we find what must surely be the apotheosis of concentrated focus on the household head (1977). Delphy is fully aware of the pitfalls of discussing household organisation outside its historical and economic context. However, after enumerating carefully the many different ways in which work performed in the domestic setting is inserted into wider economic structures, she then goes on to treat these differences as insignificant for understanding women's oppression. Whatever the class position of the households in which their lives are constructed through birth or marriage, all women for Delphy have in common the unpaid domestic services they are obliged to perform for the household head. Her analysis thus turns on the power relationship between husbands and wives: whatever demands husbands make, wives are bound to serve their interests, ('Whatever the nature of women's tasks, their relations of production are the same', 1977, p.31).

In drawing attention to the power relation between women and men rather than trying to squeeze sexual divisions into the pre-existing categories of political economy, Delphy's analysis is important. But it is one thing to locate the subordination (or exploitation in Delphy's terms) of women in the domestic domain, and quite another to treat this as sufficient explanation. The absolute identification of the household with its head and the interests of its head is taken as given. She thus asks neither whether this power is uniform in different conditions, whether economic control always coincides with jural authority, nor whence the power is derived. Her analysis too is of *individual* households, *individual* women and their husbands[8].

While change and variation in household form, and their effects on the nature of authority within the domestic unit have been documented, this is rarely combined with an investigation of the *sources* of that authority. It is curious for example that in Meillassoux's work, while the authority figure is central to the definition of a domestic community, the source of his authority is treated as unproblematic. Women are entirely omitted from his discussion of the domestic economy since for him they are by definition entirely subject to the elder. However it is clear from numerous critiques of his work and that of other writers who have used his material, that the source of the individual elder's authority derives from the collective monopoly, by elders as a social category, over the circulation of prestige goods and the disposition of women in marriage. To understand how the position of the household head is defined and reproduced takes us beyond the confines of the domestic unit itself. The authority located in a household head is not intrinsic to relations between household members, but must be sought in wider social structures. The sovereign body may be limited to a group of elders as in the West African societies discussed by Meillassoux, or it may be the community of adult males who collectively take and enforce certain decisions affecting those who do not have formal access to the structures of power.

If we turn from decentralised agrarian societies to those effectively dominated by an organised state, many aspects of male power over other household members can be seen to derive from the nature of the state (see Reiter, 1977; Ortner, 1978; Sacks, 1979). In most state formations, household heads are made responsible for paying taxes and other dues to the state, and are answerable in law for other household members. It is usually a male household head who negotiates contracts, makes sharecropping arrangements, leases land or other property, and thereby exercises control over the lives of his wife, children and dependent kin. The very *activity* of census-taking, fundamental to state organisation, normally organises and defines households precisely around the identification of a single person who is answerable for other members of the domestic unit. In the historical study of household forms this same criterion has generally been adopted in the identification of individual units (e.g. Laslett, 1972). Flandrin cites a definition of 'famille' from the Dictionnaire de l'Academie of 1694 as 'toutes les personnes qui vivent dans une même maison, sous un meme chef' (1979, p.5).

The organisation of domestic units around household heads derives enormous impetus from the bureaucratic requirements of state organisation, and also from the partial devolution of power to adult males by different state systems. However the allocation of authority is made more effective by being identified with the *family* head. It is surely no accident that Delphy whose emphasis on power relations within domestic units is so explicit calls her theory the *family* mode of production (as opposed to Sahlins' more economically-based domestic mode of production). Laslett himself draws our attention to the development in seventeenth century England of a philosophy concerning the natural rights and authority of the patriarch (1949; see also Tribe, 1978). The family or rather the position of the father within the family, was thus taken as the natural source of authority which could then be applied to political authorities such as the monarch.

The unproblematic way in which in so many different contexts households are identified with their putative heads is, then, to be explained by the assumptions of patriarchal philosophy, combined with an assumption of discontinuity in forms of circulation within and between domestic units. What distinguishes patriarchal philosophy is the supposition that the authority of the father is or should be total. As a philosophy it makes little discrimination between different domains in which authority may be exercised, for example political versus economic; the identification of the household head with the father reinforces the identification of the household as a natural domain unified by the exercise of authority. In France under the *ancien regime* a contractual relationship between the state and the head of the family gave him the right to have his children imprisoned, and was preserved even in the Napoleonic Code (Donzelot, 1980). In England even the authority a man had over his wife was conceived on the model of the father, as was that over servants (Hamilton, 1978).

An instructive contrast can be made concerning who, in the absence of a father, takes on the role of household head. In most parts of Europe historically a widow has replaced her dead husband, thus asserting that criteria of age and the status of parenthood are prior to those of sex. In Japan however, a boy however young would traditionally be preferred to an adult woman (Laslett, 1972, p.55). Again, it is important to understand under what conditions female-headed households form a significant proportion of the total. The evidence argues that this is the case mainly among poor and marginal social groups which are anyhow excluded from the structures of power. Female-headed households appear to be common in situations of migration, urban poverty, and chronic insecurity; nonetheless ideological elements also intervene. Some cultures appear to accept the existence of female-headed households more easily than others. In Turkey for example it is virtually impossible for a woman however bereft and unstable her situation, to live in a domestic unit without a titular male head (Kandiyoti, forthcoming).

In formal terms, then, it is general to identify domestic units with a male head, and the identification is guaranteed by endowing this figure with the ideology of paternal authority. Both the source, the content and the effectivity of that authority must be investigated if we are not to fall here too into naturalistic assumptions that eternalise the concept of the household. Even in cultures where patriarchal ideology has been extremely fully developed, the household head only enjoys unwavering power in certain conditions. In pre-revolutionary China for example, it was only among the gentry that the authority of the patriarch was fully realised. Among poor peasants, the ideal was subscribed to, but practice did not match the ideal (Wolf, 1974). In the legal system of contemporary Britain the authority of the male family head is not absolute even as an ideal. Married women still do not enjoy full civil citizenship, and in many contexts must be represented by their husbands, but they did gain political citizenship fifty years ago (Stacey & Price, 1980). Thus whatever the ideology, the authority exercised by a male household head is rarely absolute. The conditions in which a complete conjunction of powers is located in the household head should be treated as the exception rather than the rule.

THE PROBLEM OF THE DOMESTIC

While I have criticised the tendency of many writers to treat the household as a universal category, there are certain functions of the domestic unit which appear to be constant whatever the mode of production. These functions are frequently identified as 'reproduction'. The substantial confusions in the use of this term have been discussed elsewhere (Edholm, Harris & Young, 1977; Harris & Young, 1981), but in the context of discussion of the household what is generally meant is domestic labour.[9] Regardless of what productive activities are carried out, households are always the site of reproduction in this sense. (This is clearly what underlies Meillassoux's assumption of the universality of the domestic unit).

It is generally assumed, and indeed widely the case, that the way people live together is structured around the immediately physical needs of the human organism – food, sleep, cleanliness, clothing. Since these needs derive directly from physiology, it has been easy to separate off the servicing of the human organism in this way as a distinct kind of labour. Indeed the identification of this type of activity with the household as an organisational space is in a way circular, since the word domestic derives directly from the Latin word for house (*domus*). Insofar as people who inhabit a single physical space do not collaborate in these functions, they are thought to constitute at least partially separate households.

From this perspective too we find a close identification of the domestic unit with a set of activities construed as natural, in this case through their association with the human body. I suspect that it is also because of the base in physiology that such domestic activities have been virtually ignored by Marxists. As Mackintosh points out, writers such as Meillassoux and Sahlins who are explicitly concerned with the domestic economy, never so much as mention this type of work (1979; pp.176-7). Since the human body is ideologically presented as a natural given, outside of history (see Brown & Adams, 1979), it is easy to slide into treating domestic labour as a natural activity, also outside the scope of historical analysis.

It is apparent that the same approach has characterised assumptions about biological reproduction. The patently physiological process of procreation, birth and lactation have facilitated an entirely naturalistic approach to the place of these processes in social reproduction as a whole. Female fertility, and even infant mortality, are often treated, if they are mentioned at all, as invariant factors, or at best are thought to respond in some unspecified way to changes in the economy (Harris & Young, 1981).

The ideological presuppositions that must be uncovered in order to reconstruct an analysis of domestic work on a firmer basis are extremely powerful ones. Their strength is further reinforced by the fact that it is overwhelmingly women, who naturally produce children, that also perform domestic tasks. This association of the fact of childbirth with housework is taken for granted by many writers (e.g. Rosaldo, 1974; Bujra, 1978). However while it would be folly to deny the association, it is equally mistaken to accept it as a satisfactory account. The assumption that all women perform domestic labour precludes an analysis of the forms of cooperation and division of labour that are found in this category of work (Mackintosh, 1979). It is also clear that the nature of the domestic labour process changes radically with change in technology and size of household, as well as different forms of cooperation. Also human needs, while founded in undeniable physiological requirements, are also subject to cultural and social definition.

Again, even though domestic labour *is* overwhelmingly women's work, the degree to which it is oppressive and the ways in which it is burdensome differ greatly and must be taken into account. Quite apart from enormous variation in what work is entailed in the servicing of the human organism, the same tasks have quite different implications according to whether they are a basis for sociability and cooperation among women, or alternatively performed in virtual isolation with near-total dependence on the male household head.

One of the effects of analysing households as individual and autonomous units has been to miss the importance of the various forms of cooperation and collectivity in domestic work between households. While much of this type of work may well not involve a technical division of labour (that is, a complex division of skills), there are many variants of a social division of labour, for example where some women mind children and cook, leaving other women free to engage in wage labour. Whatever form cooperation takes, the degree of isolation on the one hand, collectivity on the other, will have important effects on women's position within their own households, as Rosaldo (1974) and Caplan & Bujra's volume (1978) among others have argued.

Whether or not it is assigned the status of reproductive work, domestic labour is overwhelmingly treated as distinct from productive labour. Under capitalism, as we have noted, the separation of domestic labour from socialised production coincides with the distinction between the production of use-values and the production of exchange-values in the form of commodities. The definition of use-values by Marx is closely associated with the idea of direct consumption (although not exclusively – for example the corn paid by a medieval peasant as rent and tithe is also seen as use-value). [10] As a result the denomination of economic structures within which commodities do not normally circulate as natural, in contrast to the *social* relations engendered by commodity production and exchange, is further confirmed. The concept of consumption, modelled on the ingestion of food and drink, is deeply imbued with naturalistic assumptions, either derived directly from physiology, or in more sophisticated versions from differences between consumers based on sex and age, again treated as having universal applicability. [11]

The domestic as a category is then defined in relation to a set of other concepts which mutually reinforce each other as natural, universal and not amenable to social analysis. These unspoken associations are important in that they continually reproduce the domestic as a separate, readily-identifiable domain. The very circularity by which the domestic is defined confirms the apparent transparency of this category – physiological needs, consumption, use-values inhabit a space whose identity emerged principally in contrast with another space defined by social rather than natural relations, exchange rather than consumption.

Various feminist writers have used a dichotomy between domestic and public spheres as a basis for trying to move beyond universalist assumptions about the household, and distinguish situations in which women have power in the social order from those in which they are subordinate to particular categories of men who represent them in public life (e.g. many of the articles in Rosaldo & Lamphere, 1974). This is a fruitful approach, since the degree to which different social systems define households as units is closely related to the degree of autonomy or dependence of households members. However as an explanation the distinction contains an implicit tautology.

We have already noted the circularity by which the category domestic is defined. This is often extended to the way that women are identified with the domestic sphere, men with the public or social. Thus the sexual division of labour is often identified with a division whereby women remain in the home and men work outside the domestic sphere; the woman is identified with the house, the house with the woman. In another rendering, men do production, while women's primary responsibility is the 'sphere of reproduction', i.e. housework. The problem with such identifications is that they serve directly to confirm the dualism already present in the sexual division. Clearly there is an empirical foundation to this dualism but to approach it in this way is, at best, to give only a descriptive account of the way that women's activities are typically confined to the 'domestic sphere' (see Maher, 1974). Too often, however such identifications move beyond the descriptive to the tautological; what women do is treated *by definition* as belonging to the domestic sphere, simply because women do it. One effect of this is to render invisible whatever activities women engage in that manifestly cannot be treated as domestic, for example wage labour. Anyone who has considered the problem of sexual divisions in capitalist society knows how easily women's waged work becomes invisible.

Since women and domestic units are so often mutually defining, any argument that women will be liberated by moving out of the domestic sphere must be viewed with caution. In many cases it may amount to no more than arguing that women will be liberated once they cease to be women.[12] While domestic units are defined frequently in economic terms, the public sphere, in contrast to which the domestic has meaning, is not merely the domain of socialised production and exchange, but also the sphere within which structures of power are defined to the exclusion of women. Where this is the case, it makes little difference whether or not women participate economically in what is called the public or social sphere. There is, then, often a slippage from definitions of the domestic in economic terms, to assumptions about power. However residential units do not always coincide directly with economic units, and still less do these necessarily correspond to politico-legal units, nor does women's involvement in social production necessarily correlate closely with high politico-legal status in the public domain.[13] To base the division between the domestic and the public on economic activities cannot explain the unequal social value attached to these activities and gives too little attention to the diverse sources of male power. To look at the sexual division of labour, or a division between production and reproduction, is to omit the ways that males guarantee collectively in many different types of groups, the power that each may wield in his own household.

CONCLUSION

My argument has been that the domestic as a category contains all sorts of assumptions about the natural status of the activities and relationships contained within it. Because of these assumptions, rarely made explicit, we go on talking of the household as a universal institution, outside and separate from the long march of history, even though there is an abundance of evidence of variation in the content and organisation of domestic institutions. Having said this, I would not wish to conclude that we should abandon the category altogether, but that we should use it with a fuller understanding of its ideological context. As feminists have long known, nature is an ideological means by which hierarchy and subordination are justified; to uncover the naturalistic notions embedded in the category of the domestic is, hopefully, to demystify it and thence enhance our understanding.

While my discussion has been chiefly concerned with what is written *about* households, my argument is not that confusions in the term domestic are simply due to the myopia of historians, feminist writers, or social scientists. Nor do I think that they result from an unthinking application to all situations of the way the domestic sphere is continually reproduced under capitalism as a separate and privatised domain. On the contrary it is evident that a domestic domain is easily identifiable in a multitude of different contexts. If we ask why this is so, one answer will inevitably be couched in terms of physiological needs and the organisation of consumption for subsistence. However it is equally clear that functionalist explanation of this sort is not conclusive. The constitution of a *sui generis* domain separate from the public or social world is also the means by which women are effectively controlled. The more households are organisationally separate, the more women are confined and isolated within the domestic space, the more total is their dependence on those men who represent them and speak for them in the world at large.

This means of subordinating women through the gender-typing of many activities and constraining those defined as female to a strictly circumscribed domain is found in many cultures and in widely-differing production systems. The ascription of natural status to this domain is certainly not restricted to western capitalist society, but again is found also in other contexts – a form in which the subordination of women is ideologically reproduced and their 'domestication' secured (in Rogers' apt term, 1980). But equally it is important to recognise that this is an ideology – that is, womens' subordination or domestication is never complete or guaranteed. Under capitalism the domestic domain is subject to continued intervention both directly through state agencies, legislation, welfare provision, and indirectly through the mass media, the structuring of wages, and through technological change that constantly alters the nature of work carried on within the home. In spite of this 'policing' of the household, only a limited number of units in fact conform to the ideal, as has already been noted. In other social and historical contexts too, whatever the power of domestic ideology, only a small number of units in practice approximate to it. Women can only be fully domesticated where men are wealthy and powerful enough to dispense with their abilities and labour and confine them to instruments of reproducing male stock, as Stolcke argues (this volume). It is surely because the project of fully subjecting women to the control of men is so contradictory that an ideological definition of the domestic in terms of a natural finality has remained so powerful and persuasive.

NOTES

1. Donzelot (1980) is a clear illustration of this contradictory tendency, as noted by Barrett (1980, p.199).
2. In another influential article written some years earlier Sahlins advances a theory of exchange based more on the idea of

continuum, in which degrees of kinship distance are correlated with the degree of balance in reciprocation (1974, Ch. 5).

3. This distinction has been made by many of those who contributed to the 'domestic labour debate', for example Gardiner, Himmelweit and Mackintosh (1975).

4. A point emphasised by Brown (1978). She adds that the natural in this context is not simply the opposite of the social. However it is certainly significant that Marx in the early chapters of Capital I refers frequently to the 'social' character of the labour by which commodities are produced (e.g. 1976, pp.163-187). By implication at least, use-values that are not also commodities in some sense are less social. This use of the natural is clear in Luxemburg's characterisation of non-commodity economies as 'natural' (1951).

5. While capitalism as a mode of production is characterised by the 'socialisation' of production, it is important to recognise that an enormous proportion of economic activity in advanced capitalist countries in fact takes place outside the market (e.g. Burns, 1975).

6. Many historians of the family work in terms of typical family forms for different historical epochs, e.g. Shorter (1977) and more recently Poster (1978), Tilly & Scott (1978). Anderson (1979) criticises this practice.

7. For critiques of Meillassoux see Mackintosh (1977), O'Laughlin (1977), Molyneux (1977), Edholm, Harris & Young (1977).

8. Even though in more recent writings she recognises the need to go beyond the individual marriage relationship and look at the ways this is both structured by social forces, and in turn affects the conditions of life of the unmarried (e.g. Delphy 1980). Molyneux (1979b) gives a useful summary and critique of Delphy. Engels, too, it should be noted, analyses gender relations in terms of a single, generic household (1972; see Brown 1978, p.45).

9. Bujra (1978) for example distinguishes production from 'purely domestic activities' and terms the latter the 'sphere of reproduction' (pp.30-32).

10. Marx (1976, p.131). In the same paragraph he states 'He who satisfies his own need with the product of his own labour admittedly creates use-values but not commodities.'

11. Delphy (1979) and Maher (this volume) give critiques of this assumption.

12. Some of Denich's writings fall into this circularity (e.g. 1977).
13. As Engels (1972), Sanday (1974), Sacks (1974) among others have argued.

Work, Consumption and Authority within the Household:

A Moroccan Case

Vanessa Maher

For many social scientists and institutes of national statistics, work and consumption patterns within the household are regarded as unproblematic, the assumption being that they are physiologically determined.[1] Here I wish to explore the organisation of work and consumption of men and women within the household among Berber-speaking people of the Middle Atlas, and argue that they are determined by social and political factors rather than physiological ones, and that the consumption and work of men, women and children are affected in different ways by changes in the overall economic environment. Many of these changes are mediated by the money economy to which men, women and children have access in different degrees.[2]

I shall discuss data from study of a cluster of Berber-speaking hamlets which are attached for commercial and administrative purposes to a small (11,000) Arabic-speaking town. The town's population consists to a large extent of people born outside the province: administrators and teachers from the northern cities, traders South of Marrakech and two batallions of soldiers from various parts of Morocco. Of more local origin are the artisans and technicians, small-time shopkeepers, hospital and post-office employees. Townsmen tend to marry women from the hamlets, and more women than men living in the town are of local descent.

About two-thirds of the hamlet population are engaged in agriculture, either on their own fields or as sharecroppers. Most plots are cultivated in association with implements, animals, land and labour being contributed by two, three or even four different people. Townsmen may be drawn in to supply funds for seed and fertilizer. Holdings are small, and the majority of peasants are able to provide for only about a third or a quarter of their needs from the land.[3] Even so, they regard their agricultural endeavours as the most important part of getting a living, although they are forced to find wage-work to enable them to live on the land. Thus the agricultural produce, comprising wheat, maize, lucerne, hay (rarely milk and eggs), pulses, root-vegetables, and in fortunate cases, fruit and nuts, is supplemented by sporadic wage-labour on the part of the household head or his adult sons. They may work as masons, road-builders (as part of the government's U.S. financed programme called 'Promotion National') or in some more regular capacity as miners or mechanics. The backcloth to this scene is a national unemployment rate of 20% which reaches 45% in the countryside (Ministère du Plan, 1964, p. 102). The emphasis which Moroccans give to the land is reasonable enough since it is their main source of economic and social security.

In the hamlets there are also several large landlords (i.e. who own more than ten hectares including orchards) who occupy administrative posts, hold shares in the lead-mines 35 kilometres away and are regarded as local notables. Their income from the land is trivial compared with that obtained from other sources, but the fact that they continue to live and own land in the hamlets entitles them to be regarded as members of the community. As notables, this commits them to certain kinds of behaviour towards the hamlet community (patronage, hospitality, mediation with the government bureaucracy). Notables who try to evade their community obligations are heavily censored.

In the rural areas and in the hamlets women are responsible for a large part of the agricultural work in addition to their domestic activities. About half of the hamlet women are also involved in spinning wool and weaving carpets or *djellabas* (robe-like garments). Only those whose husbands have no access to land work for wages. In the town, a few of the poorer women and girls sew in small sweatshops for a woman overseer; others knit, sew or embroider for clients on a strictly casual and private basis; others weave carpets at home for the cooperative of the

Union Nationale des Femmes Marocaines – all these work places being exclusively female. Finally a few educated women work as teachers, lawyers and nurses. Ideally women should restrict themselves to domestic matters, the 'public sphere' of market transactions and political relations being the concern of men. Women in the town are more strictly secluded, and if they do leave the house wear a *djellaba* and veil. It is the children who run errands around the town for their mothers, sisters and aunts.

In summary then, both town and countryside are economically and socially stratified. Many households have precarious sources of income, which not only restricts the access of all household members to consumption goods of all kinds, but is experienced differentially by men, women and children. For those families who cannot make ends meet the importance of credit cannot be overemphasised, with hamlet and town patrons and shop-keepers making good the permanent cash deficit which runs on from year to year.

THE SEXUAL DIVISION OF LABOUR IN THE HAMLETS

The division of labour between adult men and women rests on the fact that women's work concerns contacts with a known social world, while men have to deal with a negotiable and therefore unknown social world. The world of women need not necessarily be restricted to that of the family alone for women of different households may help one another with domestic tasks. Although it is considered shameful for women to work for wages, the return on credit and patronage often takes the form of poor women performing domestic services for the households of patrons and creditors, often within a framework of fictive kinship and common regional origin. So although they should restrict themselves to domestic matters, these can be the domestic matters of others.

A good example is the long and tedious job of removing stones from the wheat before it goes to be milled. This task is carried out by groups of kin, neighbours and clients in varied but predictable combinations. Men's work on the other hand, involves a managerial and representational function. In agriculture they concern themselves mainly with cereals, especially wheat which is the crop most often bought and sold and so serves as a link with the external and monetary world. All the operations in which men are involved have the quality of negotiating the conditions in which the family will get a living. Given the associational nature of Moroccan agriculture, a household head must find the land, hire the sharecropper, set up credit arrangements with shopkeepers in the town, which in turn involve him in obligations to buy consumer goods from his creditors or serve them in other ways. Then he must see to the equitable sharing of the crops among the associates and if necessary, to the sale of his quota to pay his debts. Perhaps the nicest illustration of the political and representational element in men's work is the irrigation system. The hamlets are built on ridges at intervals of about half a mile. Neighbouring hamlets control different parts of the valley which separate them so that they are bound to collaborate in the irrigation of their fields. The irrigation system with which I was best acquainted involved four different hamlets which used the water in turn for four day periods. The clearing of the irrigation ditches and the distribution of the water among the hamlets involved field owners in collaborative but potentially conflictual relations. In fact they were always complaining about the others' greed for water. Within the hamlet the distribution of the water was supervised by the *amghar-n-waman* ('elder of the water') – before this office was eliminated by the state administration – who was elected annually by the household heads.

All the agricultural operations for which men are responsible may involve commercial transactions or negotiations with outsiders at some stage. They consist of ploughing (with a wooden plough drawn by mules), manuring (manure is bought for cash from other households), the application of phosphates, sowing and harvesting. The seed is broadcast by the field owner who uses his own secret Islamic formulae to make it grow. The harvesting of the grain is carried out by teams of young southerners who travel north with their sickle; they are paid four *drahem* and 2 meals for an eight hour day. The field owner generally works with them, and his wife or female relatives prepare their meals. Threshing is carried out by driving a string of mules round and round in a circle over the grain. The threshing grounds are owned by the older families of the hamlet, and it is generally an adult male of the family which owns the ground who takes charge of the mules. He may thresh for families without mules or threshing grounds in return for the straw which is shared among the mule owners for fodder. The winnowing is usually carried out by the young unmarried women (i.e. not sexually active) although the presence of women in other circumstances is considered dangerous for the crop. Here we see again that where the operation does not require negotiating or collaborating with strangers, women can carry it out.

Women's work in the hamlets is composed of four main sets of activities: the care of animals; the cultivation of subsistence crops; the processing and cooking of agricultural products; the cleaning and care of the house and the care of its occupants including children, the aged and the sick. Many women add spinning and weaving to this list.

The care of animals involves cutting hay and lucerne for several months in the year, transporting enormous bundles of maizestalks after the harvest, milking the animals (rarely more than a couple of goats and a 'share' in a cow), and in some cases taking them to pasture. Most women keep hens as well. Women and children are especially concerned with the cultivation and harvesting of those crops which are thought of as 'for home use', that is, maize, root-crops and pulses, but they also weed the wheat.

Under the heading 'processing of agricultural products' we should include winnowing of grain, cleaning grain and pulses of stones, making of butter and sour milk. Further, there is the endless fetching of water from the streams, the gathering and transporting and chopping of firewood for cooking and heating. Bread in large round loaves is made daily, sometimes twice daily since it is the staple food. Most rural cooking is simple, but cooking in the town and for feasts is very time – and labour-consuming. A *cous-cous* may take three or four hours to prepare. Under cleaning and care of the house the annual tramp to the chalk-pits for loads of white-wash to disinfect the internal walls of the tamped mud houses has to be included. Then there is the washing of dishes, of clothes at the stream, the sweeping, dusting, tidying and beating of carpets which every housewife knows. Finally, women must take care of and educate children, feeding, cleaning and playing with the younger ones, whom they carry on their backs to the fields and around the house, and transmitting notions of correct social behaviour to the older ones, and to the girls all the domestic skills which they will need to call on.

In Morocco, women learn to do things because certain tasks are delegated to them as they grow up, and the women who are above them in the domestic hierarchy (see Maher, 1974, pp.122-123) supervise them in the performance of these tasks. It is this constant attendance of girls on older women and the involvement in their tasks which characterises women's lives. From about age four onwards, they look after younger siblings, fetch and carry, clean and run errands. The tasks themselves are arranged in a hierarchy of importance and attributed to women and girls according to their authority within the household. An elder sister would not dream of leaving to a younger sibling those tasks which are her own prerogative. A girl always experiences herself in a vertical relation of obedience and command. Girls of all ages from three to fifteen tend to play games together near the houses in case they may be needed to help. Boys tend to be freed from domestic tasks and spend their time in groups of peers who play marbles or trap birds, or play hide and seek among the houses until late at night. Relationships among boys are horizontal, allowing for personal assertion and competition among age mates.

Women's activities are continuous and repetitive and perhaps this explains why adolescent girls are already skilled especially in the domestic sphere. In contrast, it seems that the relationship between a man and competence in his work is a fragile one which may be consolidated only in maturity. Moroccans observe that a peasant needs a long and arduous training. It is possible that the difficulty of imparting agricultural knowledge is due, in part, to the physical distance which separates father and son for long periods of the latter's life, and, in part, to the fact that male tasks require concentrated bursts of activity in certain seasons of the year, and in between come long periods of idleness, A year has to pass before the repetition of each operation, making learning a long-drawn out process. This uncertainty about competence in work may contribute to men's authoritarian and distant presentation of self and their willingness to consider work irrelevant to their social role. To stroll up and down to the town, to chatter in the cafes and the markets, to sleep during the day, to spend hours gossiping outside the hamlet walls or at prayer in the mosque – these are all considered fitting manifestations of male roles.

For women, however, work is subsumed in their social role to an extreme degree. This is indicated by the fact that I found it almost impossible to collect accounts of daily activities without witnessing them myself. If I asked a woman what she had done during the day, she would look at me with a puzzled expression, and I would have to ask about specific activities causing considerable hilarity. Since these were inseparable from her social role, perhaps the only feasible reply to my question would have been 'I have been being a woman all day'. In sum, it is more difficult to separate work from women's roles than from men's, and one of the reasons is that women's work cannot be exchanged for money by the women themselves. Although they produce the bulk of agricultural crops (with the exception of wheat), spin wool and weave carpets and grassmats, only exceptionally do women go to market. Their marketing is done for them by men.

WOMEN AND MONEY

In so far as women do not have access to money, they are confined to that sphere of social relations in which not only work but also consumption are determined by ascribed and qualitatively differentiated social roles. Certain kinds of activities, e.g. the care of the sick which forms part of the definition of the female role, cannot be thought of apart from the statuses which predicate their performance. The value of the activity is determined by the status of the person who performs it. An example of this is the way clients price the embroidery which women carry out for them on a private basis. The higher the status of the girl's family, the higher the price she can demand for her work; the quality of the work is not the main criterion for setting a price, and poorer women are often indignant at the sum they are offered.

Money transactions tend to transform social roles by removing the activities attached to them from the sphere of rights and duties and giving them a quantitative aspect: so much work for so much pay. Where there is an ethic of work, conspicuous consumption comes to signify social worth. But I am not suggesting that consumption indicating social worth is what differentiates the monetary from the non-monetary sphere, for in both there is competitive consumption. The idea is rather that it is the work done which confers consumption rights in the monetary sphere, while in the non-monetary sphere it is your political status which does so. Where consumption is part of a social role it is attached to moral duties towards the collectivity, such as patronage or hospitality. Where consumption is mediated by money it appears to be a matter of individual choice, because the mechanisms which regulate it are more impersonal. They include such factors as price, determined by political and economic decisions which originate outside the community, or the 'hidden persuasion' of the mass media which promote certain life styles.

Women's relation to the monetary sphere is nearly always mediated by men. They cannot sell their own labour but it is a resource which men use in their negotiations with the outside world, as the following example shows. Poor peasants often buy standard grocery items on credit (sugar, tea or meat). They may or may not eventually pay for the goods. If the debt is not paid, the shopkeeper retains a claim on the services of the debtor. This claim is often realized in the form of domestic labour supplied by women of the debtor's family to the creditor's household. Another way in which domestic service is offered for credit is by inviting the creditor and all his family to a prodigious meal, prepared and served by the debtor's wife and daughters. The creditor, by accepting, assures his host that he will continue to be well disposed towards him and to give him what he needs. Thus within the non-monetary sphere of social relations, there is an exchange of goods for which no money equivalent can be obtained for services of a type for which no money equivalent should be offered. Both goods and services of this kind form an essential part of the total economic system and their exchange keeps women and money separate, and allows the head of the household to decide where women allocate their labour and what they consume.[4]

Women do not even control the income which derives from their agricultural work, since their products are sold on the market by the family head and it is he who is responsible for new purchases, though his wife may have a consultative role. As a rule women do not go to the *suq*, the big weekly market, where the family provisions are bought and the family products sold, that is, where relatively large sums of money may change hands. Other research showing that about eleven per cent of married women go to market regularly and about thirteen per cent in the absence of their husbands (Belghiti, 1971, p.360), almost exactly coincides with my findings. Most of the mothers who marketed were either widows or wives of miners or other workers who were away all day. However for a woman to buy or sell is considered 'shameful in God's sight'. Many of the women who go to market do so in an executive capacity and cannot buy at their own discretion, for the family head is considered chief trustee.

Many women resent this situation and most resort to petty intrigue to palliate it. All women have 'housekeeping money' but one woman told me that she would hide stocks of foodstuffs and then ask her husband for money to buy more, whereupon she would bring out the hidden stores and spend the money on the object of her choice. Both women and men identify in money the secret of men's stranglehold on the consumption of women. Men even buy the clothes for their women-folk; women's demands for clothes can be seen as a battle over status and dignity, for clothes are an important expression of status. Men are invariably better equipped than women from this point of view. The power dimension to spending is apparent in the following comments which convey the widely held view that women are potentially voracious spenders if given the chance. 'If women were to go to market they would want pricey clothes. They aren't reasonable. And it is the man who earns the money, so it is fair that he should spend it'. On the other hand a woman protested, 'If I went to market, I wouldn't be wearing these rags' (Belghiti, 1971, p.353). In fact, if women went to market, they could turn into money the products of their labour, learn to 'quantify' them in monetary terms. They might be tempted then to break the rules which attribute to them the right to certain conventional items of consumption – food and shelter – and not to others.

Improvements in women's income and hence consumption are often in fact a function of their relations with other women rather than those with men. In fact there is a busy exchange of goods for services which to some extent eludes the control of men, especially insofar as the parties are ostensibly 'kin'. Many women obtain clothes, food and even cash loans through the patronage of women from their region of origin. These exchanges occur within a framework of 'quasi-kin' relations in which each party recognises the right and duty of mutual help. The poorer women perform domestic chores, help cook and serve at feasts, and act as intermediaries between their various secluded patronesses (see Maher, 1976). However, it is this dependence on personal relations with other women for access to the money economy which lays women and girls open to exploitation in sweatshops and carpet factories (Anti-slavery report, 1978). The separation of women from money was nicely epitomised in the different reactions of passengers in a bus to a man and a woman beggar who came to ask for money. To the man, about 15 years older than the woman, people gave freely; they refused the woman, saying, 'She is able-bodied, she should go and work as a maid for someone'. In the town, men beggars were considered somewhat saintly, but a woman who begged regularly with her children was urged to put them in an orphanage and go back to her kin. In both these cases, we find the idea that a woman's access to money and consumption is conditional on domestic service and mediation by a man. Indeed the only 'spending money' which a woman can dispose of legitimately is that part of the bridewealth which is paid to her in cash (but which should be spent on carpets and equipment for the household), and the gifts of money which kin and friends make her on the birth of a son.

A mother often spends the money gifts on gold or silver jewellery, and a husband is supposed to express his trust and gratitude towards his wife in the same way. Thus, jewellery comes to signify the woman's satisfactory performance in her ascribed roles: those of dutiful wife and mother of sons. These roles predicate the domestic and agricultural work required to maintain the husband and raise the sons to adolescence, thus enhancing the husband's political importance in the community. In the town, the jewellery which a woman wears is not so much an indicator of her worth as of her husband's wealth. She herself, dressed and adorned, becomes an item of her husband's consumption rather than a means to improve it.

But women's desire for gold and jewellery is often a focus of conflict between husband and wife, for these things have an extra-institutional value for women. For example they flaunt their jewellery to other women at feasts and when they go to the Turkish baths. To a certain extent we must see in this flourishing of bangles a claim to personal status, since a woman's clothes and jewellery are the only items which are considered her personal property. Women attempt to accumulate gold (in poorer regions, silver) against the day of their widowhood (a not unusual event since husbands are generally at least ten years older than their wives) or divorce.

INHERITANCE, BRIDEWEALTH AND DIVORCE

The undervaluing of women's work should be considered within a context in which women are deprived systematically of any opportunity to render themselves independent of male guardianship. The fact that a woman can inherit constitutes a threat for the patrilineal group of males for they stand to lose control of her inheritance when she marries and moves away. But more important, both they and her husband would stand to lose control of her person if she were to dispose freely of means of her own. Three measures are adopted in Morocco to counter these threats. First, a woman's property is managed by her male guardian; second, she is generally disinherited by her male kin who use her land as if it were their own, sending her a token portion of the harvest; third, marriages are generally arranged with a view to the economic and political interests of the males of the contracting groups, who have therefore a collective interest in the subordination and dependence of the woman.[5]

Thus the Islamic rule, according to which a woman is entitled to inherit from her father half a share for each share inherited by his son, is without effect in the Moroccan countryside; and this is also true of the payment of bridewealth, in the form of cash, clothes and ritual gifts. Most small peasants or share-croppers have no cash or saleable property. They tend to marry girls from neighbouring villages and set up work associations with their affines. Townsmen, on the other hand, are generally able to pay bridewealth in greater or lesser quantities according to their means and the status of the girl's family. They may also marry brides from further afield since the payment of bridewealth confers the right of bride removal. Bridewealth, even though it may only be paid in full on divorce, is regarded as having been transferred to the girl by her father, to whom everything that is hers ideally belongs. It represents her inheritance and her rights to usufruct and protection in her family of origin which she invests in the new conjugal unit.

The husband becomes full guardian of his wife by paying bride-wealth (anything from 200 to 5,000 dirhams) and may control her social contacts and in particular her relations with her family of origin, whom she will see rarely, since, given the mobility of town husbands, she generally moves far from home. A small peasant who marries a bride near home without paying bridewealth does not control her movements to the same extent. Since she has not benefited economically by her marriage, she maintains a right to the protection of her male kin. Further, the bonds between women kin are particularly strong, and it is to the nostalgia of the bride for her mother and sisters, and to the continual comings and goings between them, that many Moroccans attribute the readiness of countrywomen to leave their husbands.

In my survey 52% of hamlet marriages ended in divorce compared with 28% of the town bridewealth-paying unions (Maher, 1974, p.194). On divorce a woman can claim only her personal belongings and half that year's wheat crop. In town she can claim the furnishings bought with her bridewealth only if it is not she who provoked the divorce. In fact townswomen, though isolated, enjoy a higher standard of living, and it is usually the husbands who initiate divorce. Every divorce, especially in the hamlets, is shortly succeeded by a new marriage, at least while the woman is of child-bearing age. It is only the marriage cemented by the birth of several children which is likely to endure, for women cannot take their children into a new marriage. On divorce, a woman often returns to her kin who help her to maintain and look after her children, but they are likely to favour her remarriage to relieve the strain on their resources.

It is clear that if women earned money or controlled means of production of their own, they would not be forced to enter into one unsatisfactory marriage after another, nor would they need to stay with unsatisfactory husbands for fear of losing their children. Most marriages are unsatisfactory for countrywomen, and the majority of country and hamlet divorces occur because the woman has left her hsuband. Apart from the fact that a woman's (and indeed a man's) consort is often chosen for her, her role as wife predicates hard agricultural and domestic work in rough conditions, service to her husband and his male kin, sub-ordination to female affines, separation from her home environment, and an extremely low standard of living in terms of housing, clothes and frequently, food. Given that most divorces are initiated by women the suspicion with which men view women's 'thirst for gold' is realistic; women who have acquired a minimum of financial security will be more likely to seek divorce. In fact anything which reduces woman's dependence is seen as a threat, especially within the conjugal relationship. As one man said, 'Girls don't like marriage'.

CONSUMPTION BY SEX AND AGE WITHIN THE DOMESTIC GROUP

It is not the caloric value of work which is represented in the patterns of food consumption in the hamlet family, nor is it a question of physiological needs. Rather these patterns tend to guarantee priority rights in resources to the 'important' members of society, that is, adult men. This is especially true where subsistence is precarious.

Within the community too, rights to consume are distributed differentially among the more important and less important members. The way products are distributed within the community tends to indicate not only the degree of authority inherent in certain social roles, and the relation of their incumbents to the means of production, but also the relative value of the activities attached to those roles. For example, Moroccan men eat before women and consider prized food items such as meat to be their prerogative. Women and children learn to refuse meat, and on formal occasions, to eat what the men leave.

According to the etiquette of formal occasions which is invariably followed when there are guests, and sometimes as a family routine, men and women should eat separately. Men eat with the guests and older boys, women with girls and small children. In smaller, more informal families men and women eat together. Ideally everyone eats out of one dish which is placed first before the men, and, when they have finished, the women eat what is left for themselves and the children.

The standard meal in the hamlets is composed of bread which is dipped in a vegetable relish, sometimes garnished with a small chunk of meat which is shared among all present. Great respect is shown for the food. People bless themselves before and after eating, and refrain from talking or laughing. They eat slowly and with restraint, urging their fellows, 'Eat! Eat!' Women carry this modesty to extremes. If they are guests, they will often swear that they have eaten already, and if they are not that they are not hungry. One woman used to assure her fellow-diners that she preferred bones to meat. Men, on the other hand, are supposed to be exempt from facing scarcity which is shared out among women and children. A good mother should give up her share for her children. But children, especially small girls, soon learn to offer their share to visitors, to refuse meat and deny hunger. Those between age 2 and 12 years come off worst, for by the time the evening meal comes round at about ten o'clock they are generally asleep. It is significant that there is a certain tolerance towards the children who make raids on orchards and carrot plots, for it is taken for granted that children are always hungry. The non-satisfaction of children's special needs may explain the fact that 70% of all deaths occur among children under 14 years old (Ministère du Plan, 1964, p.76). Neither are proteins for growth supplied – according to one report 50% of rural children under 12 and 36% of urban children suffer from protein-calorie malnutrition (Laure et al., 1977, p.27).

Women are the other group at risk. Pregnant and lactating mothers do not enjoy special rights to food, although they need 350 extra calories a day in pregnancy, and 550 extra during lactation, besides treble the normal intake of calcium and double that of Vitamin A (Cameron and Hofvander, 1977, p.2). In Morocco, the 'fancies' of pregnant women usually consist in an avoidance of certain foods, often meat or milk, and a change for the worse in their food intake. Lactating mothers in the hamlets are usually skeletal and clearly supply the needs of the nursing child from their own strength and not from an increased intake of food or rest. This is in conformity with the expectation that mothers will share their portion with their children, however many there are, and not expect a separate share of resources for them. The result is that women are progressively weakened by successive pregnancies. The report of one nutritionist noted that most pregnant and lactating women suffer severely from anemia because they do not receive extra food, and that this anemia is associated with a compulsion to eat earth (for minerals) (Ferro-Luzzi, 1962, p.17). It is probably that female mortality is extremely high during the years of fertility (age 15-40 years), surpassing male mortality for these years as in Algeria.[6] However the Moroccan census of 1961 gives ambiguous and unsatisfactory information on this point, suggesting that it was not a problem of which the census-takers were aware.

Just as a woman's consumption is rigidly determined, so too is her work-load, because it is inseparable from her social role. Women in the hamlets are admired for working late into their pregnancies. They are expected to rest for two weeks after childbirth, during which period they are given special nutritious food. After that, they are expected to resume normal life, with the exception of heavy field-work which is carried out by other women. However, by the time the child is a month or two old, it is common to find his mother working with the rest, sometimes with the child tied to her back, sometimes entrusting him to the care of a small girl. Men hardly ever supply the special care which women may need during pregnancy or just after child-birth. A man often falls ill or disappears at intervals during his wife's pregnancy and almost certainly at the time of the birth, so that she or a female relative has to care for him rather than the other way round. It is a woman's task to care for the sick, not a man's. Women care for their husbands, children and parents during long illnesses. But if a woman falls ill herself and can no longer work, she is more likely to be divorced than tended (see Belghiti, 1971, p.319).

The distribution of food then, is determined neither by the energy expended in work nor by the special nutritional needs of different categories of human beings, but rather by social role. This conclusion may be further demonstrated by an examination of the relation of men and women to fasting and feasting. Men observe the statutory Ramadan fast but little else, and on the whole women tend to fast more than men. Women are obliged to fast extra days during the year to compensate for the days of menstruation during Ramadan which make them impure and nullify the value of the fast. They are also impure should they bear a child or lactate. Girls tend to observe Ramadan earlier than boys, and women fast more often on a voluntary basis. During the long marriage ceremonies the bride may not eat for days but the groom does. Not eating in most circumstances has a positive moral value for women, but is neutral for men.

Feasts on the other hand, generally celebrate men and not women, although both men and women take part in them. A boy is feasted for several days at his birth and naming, a girl rarely. The circumcision of a boy is again an occasion for feasting, but there is no such occasion in the life of a girl. Women's feasts take the form of *sadaqa*, alms-giving or feast of friendship, whose focus is not so much the giver as the community. Women's feasts could more aptly be called sacrifices, for they do not celebrate their worth, but, like their fasts, are meant to redeem them from a state of inherent impurity and ransom them from misfortune. I have seen a woman make *sadaqa* at the death of a child, to favour a safe delivery or the recovery of a sick husband. There is an element of atonement for misdoing on all these occasions. Poor women and children are invited to partake, for it is presumed that they are always hungry and that to feed them is a charitable act which brings grace.

CONSUMPTION OF GOODS OTHER THAN FOOD WITHIN THE DOMESTIC GROUP

The marriage contract stipulates that a wife has a right to food and lodging and that a given sum of money should be spent on the wife's clothes during the marriage. Anything else, such as medical expenses, should be paid for by the woman's family of origin.

Money allows some members of the household to elude the canons of consumption attached to their status, and to have access to new kinds of goods without the mediation of the household head. Since married women only exceptionally have direct access to money, their consumption remains constant while that of men tends to become more evident as the cash income of the family increases.[7] Among poor families, cash is spent on cigarettes and clothes, and among better-off ones, on radios, motor-cycles and even televisions. The wage-earner who, by his access to money, evades his father's control of his consumption, acquires authority within the family, even though he often spends his wage on himself rather than in the common interest. One mother said of her wage-earning son, 'Ali is our father, our brother, our father's brother, our mother's brother'.

Especially in the town we find that the separation of the activities and the consumption of boys from the constraints of the domestic economy begins quite early. Boys are more easily released for education and peer-group activities than girls. In the hamlets, by the age of 15 they are men and begin to avoid all work connected with the domestic enterprise. They seek work as salaried farm-labourers even if this means that their own father must hire a farm-worker. Others seek paid work as apprentices to artisans or shop-keepers, but most adolescents of this age are unemployed, partly because they do not have the strength or skills needed for most jobs. However, this does not deter them from seeking the kind of consumption which they consider proper to men – clothes, cigarettes, cinema, prostitutes. Consumption is more important than work to the social role of adult male.

The case of young townswomen, usually unmarried, provides a nice contrast. Many of them work at home knitting and embroidering for the friends of kin and neighbours who are usually but not always women. In the cases which came to my notice the sewer kept her earnings and determined how they were spent. However, they tended to benefit the family as a whole, and only indirectly the sewer. For example, one 17 year old girl who earned a considerable sum by her work bought a Butagaz three-burner stove to facilitate the family cooking which was otherwise a slow, hot business over a charcoal brazier or wood-stove. Then she bought some gold-bracelets for her mother, and a sewing machine to which her father agreed to contribute a loan. The things she bought are typically female items of consumption, in the sense that they increase women's productivity and reduce their work-load, but they rarely come the way of women who do not themselves control cash. It could be said that the spending of women is not clandestine only when it is in the interest of the domestic group and not devoted to the personal needs of the worker. Women are expected to subordinate their personal interest to that of the domestic group and in particular to those of its male members, but this is not expected of men.

The fact that many more boys than girls go to school is already an indication of their dispensability to the domestic economy. Education is a form of consumption from which girls are conspicuously excluded. In the province where I worked only ten per cent of the girls of school age actually went to school, a fact which serves further to depreciate their social worth and to feed male arrogance. 'The girls here are backward. Do you think it gives us any pleasure to marry girls from our village who know nothing, are ignorant and dirty' (Pascon et Bentahar, 1971; p.184, our translation). While men attribute the high rate of divorce to the fact that women are uneducated, they still deprecate education for women, saying that it leads them to be unfaithful to their husbands.

In contrast, education has come to be an essential qualification for the effective performance of the male (representational) role, and in particular for dealing with the administration which is the most important external factor in everyone's life. Thus it is not only money which confers social value and authority. Education is the road to refinement, to a life-style which is considered urbane and prestigious. It is also seen as the road to improved material consumption but for most it leads merely to frustration. 'There are those who are ignorant and those who are educated. The former stay poor, the latter get rich. The former obey and the latter command.' (Pascon et Bentahar, 1971; p.163, our translation).

CONCLUSIONS

In a well known study of rural Morocco, the authors write:

'To spend time negotiating a contract, in trading, in talking with the villagers and taking part in the 1001 vicissitudes of the family or village, that's not "to waste one's time". One has to take as a characteristic of traditional life the importance of spending a certain amount of time on the political and social life of the city.' (Pascon 1971; p.83; our translation).

It is important, however, to recognise that the division of labour which attributes the 'entretien de la cité' to men, and with it authority and high consumption rights, and identifies women with production for and reproduction of the family, has certain grave consequences in terms of the oppression and life-chances of women. It is not as neutral as it seems.

Several conclusions may be derived from the foregoing discussion. One is that, given the ideal separation of women from money, their position tends to worsen as the part of household income which consists of money increases, because of the diffusion of wage-earning and the more frequent sale of the agricultural and craft product. Women work more, consume relatively less and are increasingly controlled by men. The situation is aggravated for those women whose children help them less because they must spend the day at school.

Women are clearly discontented with their lot, but they are trapped in their subordination to and economic dependence on men. In the light of the circumstances described above, it is difficult to exaggerate the importance of networks of relations among women, based on kinship, patronage or both, which help women to escape, to some extent, the canons of consumption which the patriarchal society would impose on them and their children. Women lend goods and services to one another, place their children with female kin when they marry again, thus ensuring that a divorce need not mean losing touch with their children, and help each other in times of crisis. Especially in the poorer sectors of the population, these exchanges tend to undermine the importance of marriage as a source of emotional and economic security and to constitute a threat to male authority and patrilineal allegiance. The vitality of these forms of solidarity among women bodes well for their future, once the series of economic and social constraints are broken. We can only hope that it is not subordinated to those constraints, bringing about new forms of exploitation.

The segregation of women, and the importance of the bonds of kinship and friendship which result in their sharing means and tasks, may explain their considerable psychological independence from men. Given this fact and the privations to which they are subjected within marriage, we may come to understand not only the high rate of divorce, but also the taboos which separate women from the market and money. Women are likely to use money in ways which would reduce their dependence on men, or would subvert the patterns of consumption which symbolize the high social value of men and low social value of women.

NOTES

1. Chayanov's estimate of the consumption of Russian peasant men (1.00), women (0.80) and children (0.50) at the beginning of the twentieth century is rashly adopted by Sahlins for Melanesian and Zambian societies. Although these estimates are based on guesswork as to physiological capacity, Sahlins dismisses out of hand Pospisil's suggestion, based on direct observation, that Kapauku women's consumption is 0.64 that of men (Sahlins, 1974; Chayanov, 1966). Such arbitrary estimates are widely used in the formulation of national policies. The French Institut National de Statistique and the Institut National d'Hygiène uses this conversion scale: a child age 0-3 consumes 0.40, age 4-9 consumes 0.70, age 10-20 consumes 1.10, a man age 21-69 consumes 1.15, a woman age 21-69 consumes 0.95, an older person 0.80 (see Sebag, 1958; p.287).

2. Urban and rural contexts have different consequences for women, and I have attempted to compare them in other publications. For this paper, a comparison was not significant, therefore I discuss 'women in general' though concentrating on the hamlets and referring only occasionally to the town.

3. According to Villeneuve, 48% of Moroccan households sow less than 2 hectares per household, and a further 24.3% sow between 2 and 8 hectares (Villeneuve, 1971, p.70). Two-thirds of the cultivating households in one hamlet I studied own less than 5 hectares.

4. Kenneth Little, writing of Xhosa Women, remarks that one of the reasons that they emigrate to the towns is that 'Town, in fact, is the only place where women can acquire real property'. Interestingly enough Xhosa women themselves say that they leave to

'dress themselves', where clothes signify dignity and independence (Little, 1973, p.21).

5. It is in this light that we should examine the strong preference for patrilateral parallel cousin marriage, which tends in practice to be marriage within a restricted group of villages, or among classificatory agnates (Maher, 1974; pp.158-9).

6. In Algeria the level of female mortality between the ages of 0 and 35 is higher than those of males, although more males die in the first six months of life, mostly from endogenous causes. The high rate of female mortality is attributed to different nutritional standards and parental care in the first fifteen years of life, and then to the risks of pregnancy and child-birth (Vallin, 1975).

7. In a series of family budgets collected in a Tunisian 'bidonville', it appears that the household head spent on his own clothes, tobacco and entertainment (little enough) more than double what he spent on those of his wife (Sebag, 1958; pp.300-302).

'I'm hungry, mum'

The Politics of Domestic Budgeting

Ann Whitehead

This article considers aspects of relations between men and women within households in economies which are very different in the way in which consumption goods are acquired – in the first case mainly through direct production (rural Ghana)[1], and in the second case mainly through the purchase of wage goods (industrial Britain). I examine both some of the processes by which household members gain unequal access to, and control over, the resources which are available to the household as a whole, and the forms of sharing that occur between husband and wife. I shall use the term *conjugal contract*[2] to refer to the terms on which husbands and wives exchange[3] goods, incomes, and services, including labour, within the household. The paper draws attention both to the necessary existence of such conjugal contracts as the basis both for marriage and the household as a collectivity concerned with the daily maintenance of its members, and to the changing terms and nature of such contracts according to the location of the household in the wider economy. The paper also draws attention to the conflicts of interest between husbands and wives which different forms of conjugal contract entail.

In demonstrating observable and institutional arrangements by which women lose access to the resources they have produced themselves, or to equal shares in the household resources, I have treated husband and wife relations at a relatively low level of abstraction. It should therefore be emphasised that the major underpinning of the discussion is an interest in power as an aspect of gender relations. These institutional arrangements are one important battleground in the establishment of male domination in the sphere of marital and family relations. At the same time, they have a relationship to the other bases of husbands' and men's power over wives and women. As the descriptions of the two empirical situations reveal, however, the relationship between the position of the genders in the sexual division of labour outside the family, and the power relationships within it, are complex and indirect.

Apart from arising out of research that I have undertaken, my interest in this general area should be seen in relation to two sets of literature. The first is feminist attempts in the last fifteen years to examine the specific nature of the family form characteristic of industrial capitalism, and to examine the analytical power of Marxist concepts to deal with gender relations in capitalist society. Within this very general theme there has been a small but growing demand for the need to distinguish between studies of the family and studies of the household (Rapp et al., 1979; Barrett, 1980). A quite unrelated set of contextual literature is that which derives from the observation that much third world production, especially in rural areas, is household based. Radical and feminist commentators have pointed out that household based production is not a single discrete type, but gets some of its basic character from the economic system in which it is embedded. Despite this, as Harris (1976 and this volume) has pointed out, many analysts of the peasant economy and household production appear to be mesmerised by the concrete existence of the household as a social form in all strata of the socioeconomic structure, in many historical and economic circumstances. This leads to both a failure to specify correctly the economic system in such a way as to apprehend its laws of motion, or the potentially different production objectives and labour relations of different forms of peasant production unit, but equally significantly to the treatment of the household as a black box. The changing nature of the production, distribution and consumption relations within the household, especially as they are affected by its position in the overall socioeconomic structure, or the changes in that structure over time, are rarely dealt with in many of the models. It is those feminists who have begun the task of 'deconstructing' the household in circumstances where the household is a productive enterprise, who have provided some basic insights on which this paper rests.

In household based production the household is the locus within which men and women cooperate as members of a single productive enterprise in which some production for own use goes on. There is a marked division of labour between men's tasks and women's tasks, including, but not confined to, the work of childbearing, and the more arduous work of childcare and domestic service and maintenance. By the sexual division of labour is meant not merely a list of men's jobs and women's jobs, nor indeed a set of cultural values about the suitability of various activities to the gender categories, but rather a system of allocating the labour of the sexes to activities, and highly importantly, a system of distributing the products of these activities. Edholm et al. (1977) stress that the sexual division of labour within household based productive enterprises renders the work that men and women do non-comparable. The allocation of different tasks to men and women has implications for the organisation of productive processes in that it involves issues of command and control. It also creates the necessity of exchanging and distributing between the sexes goods which their joint or separate labour has produced.

In these economies, the conjugal contract includes the exchange of labour in production as well as the exchanges in which personal and collective consumption needs, including the feeding and maintenance of children, are met. Here the arrangements within the conjugal contract are not separate from the way in which labour is rewarded, or from the distribution of the products of work, which in market economies by contrast take place outside the household and in the market. Edholm et al. make this comment about the problem of analysing these relations:

'. . . it is hard to analyse the relations which obtain within the unit; they are usually spoken of as relations of distribution: the product of the household is distributed according to local cultural criteria of need after outside obligations have been met. The assumption is generally made that an equal distribution is made between all active members of the household' (Edholm et al., 1977).

These comments about the sexual division of labour in household production need however to be modified in so far as the rural economies of the third world are not based entirely on self-provisioning. Production for own use occurs side by side with the production of goods and services (including labour or labour power) which are exchanged or appropriated. This production for own use may go towards provisioning a member who is in wage labour – be this rural wage labour, plantation labour or migrant wage labour; it may occur side by side with peasant production for exchange; or part of the household produce or labour may be yielded up as sharecropping rent.

But if we turn to the literature on capitalist economies to illuminate these situations we find a strong tendency for there to be relatively separate discussions of the sexual division of labour within the family, and outside it. 'Outside the household' the sexual division of labour in the wage labour and informal sector is one in which the genders enter as bearers of labour or of capital: this is the province of economic analysis whose categories are, in the infamous phrase, 'sex-blind'. 'Inside the household' the sexual division of labour concerns the behaviour of men and women in the family, including reproductive behaviour, and this is by and large the province of various forms of sociology. Efforts to link the two largely concentrate on what it is about women's position in the family which affect the terms on which they enter the labour market, and to a limited extent the way in which their positions in the occupational structure and its associated sources of sociability affect relations between men and women in the home.[4] The exception to this generalisation is the economic analysis of domestic labour, which constituted a vigorous attempt to specify the connection between the labour of women in the family with the valorised production outside it. This debate however singularly failed to provide any tools for the analysis of economic relations within the household.

The perspective taken in this paper is that, although in market economies the sexual division of labour separates men and women outside the family based household, they come together within it, and in doing so, arrangements for personal and collective consumption needs have to be met out of total household income. Thus the relations of exchange, distribution, and consumption which comprise the conjugal contract characterise household relations even where the household is not a unit of production. They thus constitute a significant area of comparison. It is for this reason that I have juxtaposed two case histories whose economic determinations take such very different forms, and indeed whose conjugal contracts are very different. One is marked by the idea of a common household subsistence fund, and the other by the family wage and the housekeeping allowance. Although in some senses the basis for making this comparison is a shaky one, my purpose is to demonstrate areas of theoretical continuity in one aspect of gender relations. It is not to deny differences in economic determination, nor to imply homologies in the sexual division of labour, in the forms of gender subordination, or in the nature of the family based household in the two cases.

Nevertheless one form of similarity does provide food for thought. What family-based households have in common is that they are small residential units, which, if not themselves biologically reproductive, are derived from biologically reproductive units. Some of their members sell their labour-power to purchase or produce by direct production the goods and services vital to the maintenance and well-being of the members of the unit. The producing and consuming collectivity is normally surrounded by ideologies of sharing and self-sufficiency. Many writers characterise the exchange and distribution of products between members of any family or kin group as governed by social definitions of need – as in Marx's description of relations within the primitive communist mode. The implication is of an absence of exploitation within such units, and this together with the folk ideologies of sharing between family kin, seems to be the source of the view that the family based household is an intrinsically democratic and cooperative unit operating in the interests of all its members. In so far as the household has an important connection with the family (see Rapp et al., 1979, and Whitehead, 1978), then the feminist literature on the family in the last fifteen years can be seen as an elaboration of precisely the opposite of this view. It is an analysis of the family as a site of subordination and domination, of sexual hierarchies of many kinds, and of conflicts of interests between its members, especially between husbands and wives.

THE HOUSEHOLD COMMON FUND IN NORTH-EAST GHANA

In this section I shall discuss the way the conjugal contract operates in a savannah farming community in North-Eastern Ghana. Exchanges between husbands and wives will be discussed both as a way in which production is organised, and a way in which members of the household are maintained and gain access to consumption goods on a household basis. The household productive enterprise, while family based, is not based on the conjugal core, nor on the nuclear family, but on a relatively large and complex extended family household. So, for the Kusasi who inhabit this area, the terms under which husband and wife exchange goods and services including labour are embedded in the set of social relations of the extended family unit. In these circumstances, the budgeting for both individuals and for the collectivity has to allow for substantial variations in household membership. The basic model is of each household having a common fund, shared by all, but I shall show that individual household members have differential access to this fund, and differing degrees of dependence on it. I shall argue that commoditisation of the economy has lessened men's dependence on the household common fund while reinforcing the dependence of women on it.

The Bawku district, in which the community under study is situated, has always been relatively inaccessible. British colonial administration had no major impact on the area until the 1920's when, like the northern territories as a whole, it was used as a labour reserve for agriculture and mining in the south (see Shepherd, 1979); this drain of labour through southwards migration of young men has continued to the present. The only colonial intervention in the area's farming system was the setting up in the 1940's of an agricultural station whose major activity was to introduce bullock plough farming and ground-nut production for sale. Agricultural policies in independent Ghana have continued to favour commercial farming and to concentrate on southern crops. The only plan to have had a substantial effect on the North-East has been the introduction in the mid-1970's of rice production on a commercial scale around Tamale, which is 70-100 miles to the South-West of Bawku. Seasonal casual male agriculture labour for these rice crops is apparently being increasingly provided by farmers from the Bawku district, thus removing even more labour from the region.

By and large the social division of labour in Bawku district is poorly developed. The district is ethnically fairly mixed, but the most numerous group are the Kusasi. Prior to colonisation the Kusasi political system was non-centralised and there were no named political leaders. Relations between groups and individuals were regulated through clan and lineage membership, where clans and lineages are patrilineally ascribed exogamous units. Today Kusasi are self-provisioning farmers who aim in a relatively short farming season to produce enough food for a whole year's consumption. They also aim to sell enough crops for cash or to get cash from other sources to obtain a range of consumption necessities (including clothes) which they cannot provide for themselves, and also a few agricultural inputs. The staple crop is millet, with ground nuts and to a lesser extent rice, grown for cash. Many households own a handful of cattle, which are used for bridewealth payments and in a number of other ceremonial and debt relationships, as well as for ploughing. Agriculture is largely non-mechanised and uses mainly locally produced inputs although about one-fifth of households own a plough which is the major non-local agricultural input.

The farming system is still sufficiently based on self-provisioning for it to be considered extremely wrong to sell millet; no-one would admit doing so. All the households in the community farm; and the majority build and repair their own houses and provide for themselves a wide range of other consumption goods. Virtually all men, women and children over 10 have some form of money income, whether this is the miniscule income of a young boy or girl from selling biscuits or oranges; the petty income of some adults from selling vegetables or hens; or the substantial incomes of adult men (or, more rarely, adult women) from hoarding and speculating in staple crops, from trading in cattle, or occasionally from wage employment.

Although this kind of society is best described as communal, in that there are no classes or strata which have different relationships to productive resources, nor is there a heirarchy of associated status, this is not to say there are no differences in income, wealth and subsistence life styles amongst the various households. A proportion of the households rarely produce all the food they need to consume in a year, while other households, regularly produce a good surplus. Individual men farm acreages which range from less than 5 acres to over 40. Land is allocated by the chief and elders; it is not in any simple sense individually owned, nor can it be bought or sold. There is however a hierarchy of competing claims on land made on the basis of inheritance, lineage membership, clan membership, 'begging' (asking for) and need. The major factor affecting a household's resource base is where its head stands in the power relations within clan and community.

At this level of technology, and without absolute land scarcity in the region, an important determinant of successful rural livelihood is command over labour. Labour is provided on a permanent basis by household members, or more intermittently by communal or exchange work parties, where a farmer 'begs' household heads who are his kinsmen, neighbours or in-laws to provide labour for a particular farming activity, on a particular farm, on a particular day. Although an ideology of reciprocity surrounds these work parties ('I beg my neighbour and then I go to help him when he calls'), surplus producing households in fact call work parties most often, and poorer households work a disproportionate number of labour days for others. Although in some cases a specific client or debt element may enter into this asymmetry, by and large it is related to resources, since the food and drink provided are of superior quality to every-day fare and thus are relatively costly.

The use of exchange labour, access to more and to better quality land, and to good income sources, mark off a handful of wealthier direct producers from their clansmen and neighbours. These farmers speculate in grain, by buying it or receiving it as payment of debt when prices are low, and selling it when prices peak before harvest. The in-hoarding and speculating are matched by the indebtedness of poorer farmers who are clan members, affine and neighbours. The wider kin and community relationships are *not* ones of mutual exchange but rather the one along which much indebtedness flows. 'Helping others' sometimes involves richer farmers providing seed for planting in return for a proportion of the harvest, leaving the 'begging' household without sufficient subsistence for the year, and having to purchase food when prices are high. The socio-economic differentiation and the cycles of post harvest selling and annual indebtedness which support it have reached the point where overall local food supply is very precarious. The capacity to withstand environmental vagaries has been considerably reduced; between 1973 and 1978, 4 out of 6 harvests were so poor that famine conditions prevailed (see Shepherd & Whitehead, 1977).

For Kusasi the cliche that the household is the basic unit of social structure is very appropriate. The Kusasi word for house – *yim* – means both the house (compound) and the people who occupy it. The household is a well defined system of statuses, authority and decision making; it is the primary locus of consumption and despite the importance of labour exchanges between other households in the community, its members form a significant production unit. Households are relatively large in size. One third of the community's households have between one and four adults in them; a further one third have between five and seven adults; while the remaining third have between eight and twenty adults within them. This large mean size of household is linked to the practice of agnatically-related married men sharing a household, to the late age of marriage for men (so that many adult single sons live with their fathers), and to comparatively high rates of polygamy.

Households in the community vary from those consisting of a man and his wife and children, through a simple polygamous household where the head has more than one wife, to complete households containing more than one married man each of whom may have more than one wife. It is probably helpful to bear in mind that the ideal Kusasi household is composed of male head, his junior brother, both of whom are married with two wives each, an unmarried adult male (brother or son) and able-bodied daughter or daughters, a woman given in pawn and one or more 'mothers'.

The Kusasi household is a complex social institution in which various forms of hierarchy coalesce to give clear lines of superordination and subordination, with the basic status markers being age, gender and marital status. Every household has a male head who is called the 'owner' of the compound or its 'landlord' and all others within it are collectively referred to as 'dependants' even when the household includes a middle-aged married brother, who may be wealthy in his own right. In terms of household composition, relations between household members, and relations between the constituent households of a community, the male head forms a pivotal point. The proper behaviour of inferiors to superiors is deference. The women always kneel when they present food and water and other things to men. All dependants crouch with their heads turned away when they have to greet or speak to a head. The 'owner' of the compound juridically mediates between household members and members of other households, and ritually represents them at, for example, the sacrifices at harvest time. The hierarchy within the household is reflected in its spatial arrangements, which are conventionally uniform with arrangements in huts, yards, and kraals reflecting the division of social space within the unit.

The way in which production is organised within the household depends on a number of factors, including the sexual division of labour. North-East Ghana, unlike many parts of Anglophone West Africa, is predominantly a male farming area. The staple crop (millet) requires a large amount of male labour input, although women's labour is important. Women in fact do not grow the staple crop. Only men have land on which millet is grown and Kusasi men argue that a woman will starve if she is not living in a household containing a male farmer, be he her husband, father or son. And despite the fact both men and women produce agricultural products, women are not really regarded as farmers at all. Although virtually all Kusasi women do some cultivation of food crops other than vegetable, the acreages they farm as their own are pitifully small (less than one acre). Women do nonetheless contribute to the agricultural cycle as the schematic outline of the gender typification of certain agricultural tasks on page 97 indicates.

While the sexual division of labour is an important factor affecting the work done by household members, the primary distinction which orders the production relations of the compound is the distinction between private farms and household farms. The household farm/farms are the most important acreages of the compound. They are distinguished linguistically from all other farms and include the manured and permanently cropped 'farm-round-the-house' as well as other outlying lands. They are always planted with millet which, once harvested, is stored in large granaries immediately outside the entrance to the house, and in the area where men sit and talk to one another and to visitors. The millet produced on these farms is supposed to feed the household for the year. It is a primary obligation of all household members to work to fill these granaries. It is also a primary obligation of the household head to see that they are filled. These farms are to be contrasted with the 'private' farms which both male and female members of the household also have. On them men grow millet, guinea corn, rice and groundnuts, while women grow rice and groundnuts. In direct contrast to the disposal of crops from household farms, the products from private farms, regardless of the labour which produced them, are owned by the individual farmer, and may be disposed of as he or she wishes.[5] Rice and groundnuts are conventionally regarded as cash crops (groundnuts having been introduced by the colonial government precisely in the drive to commoditise the indigenous economy), while the millet and guinea corn may be used to supplement the subsistence of their own wives and children. 'Surplus' grain is also required for the copious beer supplied to exchange work parties. Other cash crops include cotton, kenaf fibres and dry season vegetable gardening. These all come into the category of private farming, as does the management of small livestock (poultry, goats and sheep, pigs), but not of cattle.

Input of men and women to agricultural tasks

Crop:	Millet	Groundnuts		Rice	
Sex of Farmer:	Men	Men	Women	Men	Women
Task: Clearing	M	M	M + W	M	M + W
Planting	M + W	W	W	W	W
Weeding	M	M	M/W	M	M/W
Harvesting	M + W	M + W	M/W	M/W	M + W

Key: M + W = Men and women co-operatively.
M/W = Men and women on separate farms: either on own farms or as all male or female work parties.

The Kusasi household is a very important labour unit; one measure of the hierarchy within it is the command that individuals have over the labour of other household members. The farms which require labour are both communal and private; the private farms may belong to the household head or his dependants, and to either men or to women. The labour available includes own labour, the labour of other household members and reciprocal exchange labour. Utilising these categories the pattern of labour use is as follows: household farms are worked by all members of the household, and by exchange labour, according to gender type of activity, under the direction of the household head. Indeed, the ploughing, weeding and harvesting of the household fields, using compound labour and exchange are the mainstay of the agricultural round. The work of household members on household farms is not directly rewarded, while that of exchange labour is rewarded with food and drink. However neither the use of unremunerated household labour, nor of exchange labour is confined to work on household fields. Household heads, especially the more wealthy farmers, rely heavily on both male and female exchange labour and unremunerated household labour for the labour input to their private farms. Among dependants, however, labour provided for the private farms shows an interesting difference between men and women, the crucial point of which is that whereas men can use the unremunerated labour of their wives (and often of all the women in the household), the only way a woman can use the labour of household men is by calling small exchange working parties which are remunerated in the sense that she provides food and beer. In other words, men only work for women of the household if this work is conceptually and materially turned into another form of work ('exchange'-type).

To summarise, the Kusasi household is conceptually, and in practice, an important use-value producing enterprise in which the labour of all members contributes to the production of subsistence goods. Through the organisation of so-called reciprocal links between household heads, household members also contribute to the annual grain product of other households. 'The household' also produces goods for sale, but these crops are grown under a different form of organisation, being mainly grown on private farms, for which all men, but household heads especially, utilise the unremunerated labour of household members. The cash from products sold from these farms is owned by the private farmer, as are other forms of cash income. Some of the content of the exchanges between husband and wife are subsumed in the obligations of each male and female member in the communal production of the agricultural cycle, and in the obligations to provide labour for private farms.

Similarly, the terms under which husband and wife exchange other goods, services and income are embedded in the complex organisation of consumption and distribution within the whole household. For example, a Kusasi married woman has rights and obligations both with respect to the male household head to whom she may or may not be married, and to her own husband. It is proper to think of all of these obligations in terms of her conjugal status, in so far as she is referred to as 'wife' by the household head, and by all married men in the household.

Like the British ideology of the male breadwinner, the responsibility of the household head to provide the staple crop for all members of his household, and secondarily of a married man to ensure the staple food supply of his wives and children, are basic to Kusasi concepts of male gender identity. No other member of the household, except the head, may look inside or reach inside the granary. Each married woman in the compound receives a basket of millet from the granary every ten days or so, from which she is responsible for providing her husband and children with meals. She is also obliged to provide other food substances as soup ingredients, such as salt, fat, vegetables and dried fish powder.

Work by dependants carries with it rights other than basic subsistence which are a call on household income. For men, household labour builds up a right to the 5 cows of the marriage payment paid to the bride's male agnates. The obligation to provide the brideprice coincides with the younger men's compound labour obligations; they obtain the brideprice from the older men (compound heads) for whom they have worked, usually their father, father's brother, or their own senior brother. Work in the household also carries the rights to medical and ritual attention should this become necessary. Visits to the clinic and the diviner, or the performance of sacrifices, may be withheld if the head feels that a household member is not pulling his/her weight. Wives have a right to be clothed, as have young children who are also, in principle, entitled to be educated, although few children attend the village school. It is important to understand that these conventional claims on the common fund are subject to cultural evaluation of need and to competition made inevitable by scarcity. In both of these processes men have an undeniable, and often openly acknowledged, advantage over women.

Arguably a more significant aspect of gender differentiation than these commonly found sexual inequalities in the assessment of needs or in the power to command joint resources is the implications for men and women of the conceptual and material distinctions between the collectivity and the individual mentioned above. It is various features of this which I now wish to elaborate.

I described earlier the distinction between household farms and private farms. In part this becomes overlaid with the distinction between the staple crop and all other crops, implied in the linguistic equation of millet and food. Household farms grow the staple crop, and the staple crop is treated differently from all others in the sense that it ought not to be sold. Its production and distribution symbolise the common interests of household members, yet remain under the real and symbolic control of the household head at the same time. In contrast, the groundnuts and rice grown on private farms are potential food crops and cash crops. However, once private farm produce is sold, it becomes lost to any claims of household members, since, although attempts can be made to cajole or claim privileges, no other person has rights over an individual's cash income. In particular this applies to husbands and wives, in so far as, in common with many parts of subSaharan Africa, husband and wife do not pool resources, and do not have a common housekeeping or childrearing budget. This means both that buying and selling occur across the marital bond, and that their common responsibilities are ordered through stated conventional divisions (as in the responsibilities for different categories of food supply for meals described above), or through running accounts of who has provided what (as for example for children's education).

However, within this essential set of rules which ostensibly treats men and women equally, the potentialities for substantial gender differences arise. In the first place, despite the fact that both men and women have private farms, women's farms average less than one acre in size, so it is only men who have substantial cash incomes from private farms. There are also significant differences in the ways that men and women are supposed to dispose of their crops. Women, Kusasi say, grow groundnuts to feed to their children in the hungry season. Men farm to get cash. It is for men then, that an effectual and highly important conceptual boundary is drawn between money and subsistence. Men do not use cash income for the staple food which is part and parcel of their obligations as household head or as husband, nor normally for many other subsistence items. This boundary, while it enables individuals to retain control over their cash income, has to be seen in the light of two things: firstly the extremely poor development of the local market in such subsistence items as food, pots, baskets and building materials, all of which are rarely bought, and of the scarcity of cash in relation to compulsory expenditure (such as taxes and school fees) and desirable consumption goods (such as trousers and bottled beer), and secondly, in the light of the household's most powerful members' ability to claim that they have important duties in reconciling the competing claims of their dependants in assessing the best ways of distributing scarce resources.

The right of individuals to spend their money how they like is tempered by at least two ideologies and practices, and these also relate to men and women differently. The first is that of 'helping others'. However, there is an observable differential capacity to keep control child will go first of all to them to 'beg' when they want something. However, there is an observable differential capability to keep control over one's own income. It is much easier for a household head, married man, senior wife, unmarried son or brother and junior wives and daughter (in that descending order) to hold on to their income. There is an ideological elision between this 'helping' and 'begging', with the responsibility of the household head and/or married man to clothe wives and clothe and educate children, since they must now be provided by cash whereas before they were provided in kind. The second ideology applies particularly to mothers and is of the mother's care for her children, and especially that she will not let them starve. As I pointed out above, a woman's groundnut harvest is described often as food for her children. Kusasi say that at the beginning of the hungry season when millet hand-outs by the household head get more infrequent, mothers give their children groundnuts to prevent them from being hungry. A 'strong' woman is a wife or mother who can provide independently of her husband and/or household head during the hungry season. In households where women have other income sources throughout the year from brewing and speculating in grain, this ideology leads to *their income* being used to provide staple food during the hungry season.

In summary, in North-East Ghana, the sexes have a different relationship to different areas of the commoditised economy. Discussions of the changing sexual division of labour in commoditised rural production systems in Africa frequently find an intensification of women's work in food subsistence production, and the use of her unremunerated labour for male cash crop production (Rogers, 1980). In the situation I am describing there is a marked asymmetry in the relation of the sexes to the commoditised sector – women (except in relatively few cases) earn relatively small cash incomes from trade, from petty commodity production or from agricultural cash cropping, but the form of farming system precludes massive intensification of women's work in subsistence crops. However, commoditisation in this form has increased the comparative dependency of women on the household common fund compared to men, since women lack the cash to purchase alternatives. This throws new light on the trends in regional agricultural production. Such statistics as are available show a decline in regional millet production, which is probably the result of men's decisions to concentrate on the cash crop to the neglect of the subsistence crop.

Men and women obviously experience any decline in subsistence crop production quite differently, insofar as men have access to much more substantial alternative forms of income, but they are not, in the last analysis, responsible for the sustenance of their children. Married women, while they are wholly dependent on either a husband or a household head for staple, have little effective control over how much staple is produced, or over how it is disposed of. The introduction of cash cropping may not have altered the sexual division of labour in agriculture very substantially, but it has led to an intensification of women's work. Women are working harder to produce income from sources additional to food production, in order to purchase alternatives to make up for the shortfall in household production.

THE FAMILY WAGE AND HOUSEHOLD BUDGETING IN INDUSTRIAL BRITAIN

Let us turn now to an entirely different situation, that of intrahousehold exchanges between husband and wife within the family based household of industrial capitalism. There are several theoretical themes which underlie the material presented here, but are not discussed fully themselves. These include the nature of the characteristic working-class family under capitalism, especially features of the wage form, and of domestic labour; the sexual division of labour within the labour market and within the home; and contrasts between the normative expectations and legal obligations of husband and wife in relation to their mutual support and patterns of behaviour.

If female headed households are excluded completely from the discussion, it is most common in working class families in Britain for both husband and wife to be in wage work. As Land points out, the typical woman worker in Britain, women comprising over a third of the total formal workforce, is married and middle-aged (Land, 1977).

Proletarian women most commonly resume work when their youngest child goes to school and are more likely to work part-time than full-time. They thus participate in what is conventionally regarded as social production although they have different activity rates from their husbands and their work takes place in only certain sectors of employment. In addition these jobs are low paid. Women's employment occurs in a climate of opinion that considers that the family's income should be earned by the husband while the housework, which is unpaid, should be performed by the wife. This is not simply folk ideology: as Land (1977) has shown, while the income support part of the social security system decisively allocates bureaucratic and legal responsibilities to a husband for the economic support of his wife and children, it equally decisively allocates to a wife the care of her husband and of their home and children.

The basic model of the conjugal contract in this context derives from the exchanges made necessary by this family wage earned by the husband in the labour market, and the performance of unpaid domestic labour by the wife. In general form it consists of the idea that the husband contributes his income and some services, while the wife contributes the wide ranging services making up housework and childcare, to a mutually beneficial collectivity. It has been a common assumption that the family based household operates a single budget, enshrined in the census category of common housekeeping. As Pahl points out (1980), it is a corner stone of social policy that the income which comes into the household is available to all its members, according to their needs. Indeed historically the move to such a sharing unit, in which some members, regardless of sex, age or physical condition could be kept by others, is rightly regarded as a considerable advance from the early period of proletarianisation when families could only afford to retain those members who were independent earners. Nevertheless these assumptions about the equal availability of resources within households have been periodically questioned by feminists and others (Land, 1980), although little research has been done on family budgeting and on the respective access of husbands and wives to conjugal resources other than property.

Pahl has reviewed the data and discussions on household income allocation flows that do exist with special reference to the working-class family of a married couple and two dependent children (1980). Her findings confirm that in Britain customary ways of dividing the income that comes into the household to cover common and personal expenditure probably vary with (a) generation – most studies report that couples think there have been changes in the practices of their generation compared with that of their parents; (b) absolute level of income – poor households may well have different patterns although the comparative data is almost non-existent; (c) family structure – factors such as age of children seem to make a difference; (d) cultural factors – casual reports in the literature indicate regional differences.

Pahl distinguishes three actual household allocational forms in situations where there is a single male breadwinner or social security claimant – the whole wage system, the allowance system and the pooling system. The whole wage and allowance system appear to be most common among working class couples; the only pooling systems reported among working class couples also contained an allowance element. In the whole wage system, the entire wage is handed over to the wife for housekeeping expenses, and a sum of money is given to the husband for his personal needs. Pahl associates this system with certain geographic and occupational areas, and with poverty. These families generally have very scarce resources, and it is the mother/wife's job to manage the scarce resources to meet the household's needs. Although the husband's personal share may be a high proportion it is nevertheless absolutely small because of poverty. In the allowance system, the husband hands over a portion of his wage as housekeeping to his wife and keeps the remainder. On the whole, the housekeeping portion is fixed, and often goes together with a wife's ignorance of her husband's earnings. In both cases the woman's role as domestic manager gives her control over the disposal of a proportion of the household expenditure. It usually includes the cost of food and other weekly expenditures and she usually has more or less complete control over what is purchased with this money. It may or may not have to cover major bills such as rent, electricity and so on. Where the housekeeping is mainly for weekly expenditures only, then other money may be set aside for major bills. Whatever the arrangements and whatever these sums are called, they constitute domestic expenditure of a more or less compulsory kind.

However as Pahl's survey makes clear, in both allocational systems, the relation of the spouses to what is left after such compulsory expenditure has been accounted for is asymmetrical. Men take a sum of money, often called their pocket money, for their personal expenditure in both systems. Ideological justifications for this are that he has to have money when he goes out to work or to the pub. Working class wives' personal expenditure by contrast often comes out of what she can scrape out of 'her' housekeeping, or she may ask her husband for the money for specific items. Occasionally she may have her own allowance! Pahl reports that in those few cases where women had full 'control' of the family income, these women still expected to give the husband money for his own use. This state of affairs is sometimes justified by the fetishisation of the wage, as the authors quoted below indicate:

'The wages are paid to the wage labourer and as such they are seen as the individual property of that individual. So that whereas men can often separate two areas of expenditure (personal and family) women, for ideological reasons, tend to merge their interests with those of the family and hence we can see that the division of wages within the family very often works against women in favour of men' (Women's Studies Group, 1976, quoted in Hunt, 1977).

The non-comparability of housework and wage labour has been much discussed in the literature on the subordination of women in advanced capitalist societies. The household is a site of both use-value production and exchange of use-values. This raises the issue of the commensuration of the products of non-valorised production. Where the sexual division of labour is such that only the husband's labour power enters the market, and the wife's work is domestic labour, it is difficult for there to be any commensurability in the exchanges between husband and wife. Thus we have the familiar problem of how to measure housework, and how it should be rewarded. Similarly, in bourgeois society, the appearance that the wage is individually earned by the labour of the employed worker alone, combined with the dominant concept of private possession, create the basis for the power of the (male) employed worker to compel a sum for individual consumption. The domestic worker cannot compel such a sum, and her needs (and desires) are merged with those of other dependants, such as children.

The important case then becomes when wives enter wage work, for, under these circumstances, although it is true that the terms on which they enter the labour market are disadvantageous compared with their husbands, nevertheless they now sell their labour power in return for a cash wage, just like their husbands. They receive the wage as persons in their own right. As husband and wife are paid in money, all sums of which are equivalent and exchangeable, the only difference between them should stem from the difference in the power conferred by the different amounts of wages they receive. Potentially both husbands and wives are empowered to buy goods to the amount of their respective wages on the market outside the household, and potentially both husband and wife contribute a highly divisible object into the common budget. The form which intrahousehold economic transactions take under these circumstances is of some significance.

Hunt (1977) examined the financial arrangements between couples in a mining village in the North Midlands where both husband and wife were working. She notes the importance of the man as the breadwinner. Almost all couples thought that it demeaned men if, as in some cases, his wife was earning more than he was. She found sharing of domestic tasks when wives worked full time and brought home as much money as their husbands. She also reported that it was common for a two-income married couple to spend that income of husband and wife on different categories of consumption spending. All necessary expenditure, e.g. rent, heating, normal food bills, weekly outgoings, which cannot easily be reduced, are taken out of the husband's income, while the wife's income is used for extras, e.g. consumer durables, holidays, clothes for all family members etc. The justification for this is if the wife's income disappears then the family does not have a level of compulsory expenditure which it cannot keep up. It is not simply at the ideological level that distinctions are made between what the husband earns and what the wife earns, but also at a material level, in so far as sums of money are *concretely set aside* for different purposes.

If some of a wife's income is distinguished from her husband's by ideology and by concrete processes which set aside her wages to pay for different kinds of expenditure, what can we say about her power over its disposal as a whole, that is to say her capacity to hold on to part of her income for her own use as against her husband's? The crucial question is the extent of the benefits to women of their independent access to part of the surplus income. Women frequently report satisfaction at having a source of income of their own but their relation to its disposal is quite different from that of men in many ways.

There is little evidence of any folk category of women's pocket money similar to that of men. This despite the much vaunted category of pin money, which I think expresses the view that a woman's earnings from waged work, or from petty business, are minor, and are also her own, to be spent on items for her own use; that these are neither essential to her subsistence or normal maintenance; nor are they to be spent on routine family maintenance (despite the evidence to the contrary given above). 'Pin money' supports the model of wifely 'dependence' while implying that she has control of her own income. But in decisions about spending her own income she is subject to powerful sets of values. One of these I term 'the ideology of maternal altruism'. By this the mother and wife always put the family or the children first. In another form, no less pernicious, but more morally complex to comment upon, the altruistic mother has to deny herself resources to make scarce resources go round. As well as better and more food to the manual workers, she ensures food for the children before she eats herself. [6] An early study by Jephcott[7] suggested that the power of married women vis-à-vis their husbands could decrease when they acquired earnings of their own, because this meant that their husbands could keep more of their earnings for personal expenditure, while the women's earnings went to pay for collective family expenditure. To this must be added the evidence that, however the decisions are arrived at, husbands consume more of the household's surplus for their personal needs than do wives. Maher (this volume), Delphy (1979) and Pahl (1980) all make this general assessment although the evidence is scattered, and often has to be read off indirectly, as for example from the fact that men's leisure time pursuits outside the home tend to be more costly than women's.

It remains to be seen to what extent these findings are generally true amongst British proletarian families. The evidence certainly suggests that money wages earned by men and women, in a continuous, though possibly sectored, labour market, are rendered non-comparable when they are brought into the household by wage earners who are respectively husband and wife. Essentially I am arguing that a wife's wage enters the household and she loses control of it. This seems to me to illustrate fairly clearly hierarchies of super-subordination in operation in the household. The conjugal contract, including the ideology of maternal altruism, effectively creates barriers to women disposing of their income freely on the market, even where this income takes the money form, with the implications of personal control implied by ownership of money, and despite the free flowing character of money.

The treatment of the wife's income in this way may be a rational response to the sexual division in the labour market. As a woman she cannot command very high earnings, she is less well protected by legislation and union organisation and is liable to be forced out of wage employment at the vagaries of the market. It should not need to be pointed out that any view that the wife's income is used for holidays and non-essentials is in many families untrue. Apart from poor proletarian households, which have been specifically excluded from the discussion, and for whom the two incomes cover at most only essential expenditure, many of the items purchased by the wife's wage are simply lumpy consumption goods and items of domestic technology which have to be saved for. The particular form of joint income division that I have outlined is a powerful reinforcement of male gender stereotypes. At the point where the husband's gender identity is threatened – when his wife may be about to enter the breadwinner role – the mode of dealing with her income into the household reinstates him into this role. All such ideologies of the male wage as being different from the female wage serve to maintain the general characteristics of the sexual division of labour under capitalism.

One implication of this material is that more attention needs to be paid to the analysis of the wage form, and its relation to sexual subordination. Women's access to consumption goods, and the form of treatment of women's income, are closely linked to a sexual division of labour in capitalism in which the category of domestic labour plays a central part. It has been pointed out to me (Robin Murray – personal communication) that 'while the home is a prison it is also a zone of relative autonomy from capital', and that within it some accumulation occurs, which may be in the hands of women. This argument serves to bring out an important point of contrast. As far as women are concerned it is insufficient to characterise the nature of the autonomy at issue as autonomy from capital. Even if we were to accept the proposition that the wife in a capitalist family is autonomous from capital, it is clear that she has purchased this autonomy at the price of gender dependency within the family. To argue that the home is a zone of autonomy for women is thus misleading. A simple illustration of this is to be found in the common pattern whereby women's individual activities take place in collective areas of the house, but where space allows, there is often a designated area for husband's hobbies or activities – workshop, den, greenhouse. The set of social relations between men and women, including those in the family based household, are not totally determined by commodity relations.

CONCLUSION

This article has a deliberately narrow focus on some of the distributional aspects of intrahousehold relations. I have described as the conjugal contract the terms on which products and income, produced by the labour of both husband and wife, are divided to meet their personal and collective needs, and given details of this in two very different circumstances. In them the basis for the material maintenance of the co-residential members of the household are very different, but nevertheless I have argued in each case that inequalities of power between husband and wife become manifest in the various arrangements by which the goods, services and/or income of husband and wife are allocated and distributed. Overall a woman's effective possession of the resources she has either produced, or earned, within the family based household is determined by her relative power vis-à-vis other household members, especially her husband. This relative power is *not* simply dependent on the relative wages commanded in the labour market, or on the relative labour input into agricultural production. In both cases women are closely attached to the collective or family aspects of consumption, in one case in the form of the subsistence common fund, and in the other in the form of the housekeeping allowance, while men are much more individuated in relation to their control over resources and in their own consumption. Such a finding has close parallels with other arguments – for example, that women's role in child rearing creates an ideological mother-child dyad which is the significant social unit for women. It should be apparent, from the terms in which I have described the general features of the two situations, that these similarities are not such as to support a view that there is a 'domestic mode of production', or a non-changing category of domestic labour.

The major undiscussed perspective in this paper is what is the significance and meaning, if any, of finding such similarities between wholly different economic forms, and wholly different types of sexual division of labour. I have hardly speculated at all on the various factors which may affect the relative powers of husbands and wives over the disposal of income and produce: an important area for more substantial theoretical elaboration is the link between the differential position of the genders with respect to relations of production, and the ability to influence disposal and distribution. Similarly, although it emerges in each case that the sharing and caring which dispossess women take place in family and kinship ties, it is clear that the nature of family and kinship relations in the two circumstances are markedly different, because of their differing relationship to the production system as a whole.

Nevertheless, stress should be placed on the finding that the relative power of husbands and wives does not simply reflect relative wages commanded in the labour market. A major theme in discussions of the sexual division of labour in non wage-labour economies is that the sexual division of labour effectively renders the work that men and women do as non-comparable. And as a consequence, products are not distributed on the basis of the relative labour input into production. I have argued that both the treatment of income from waged work as being available for different categories of expenditure, and the sexual division of responsibility for specific consumption needs, are further aspects of non-comparability.

Finally both situations serve to remind us that the conjugal contract implies specific material conflicts of interest between husbands and wives. Conflicts of interest between men and women are not generic conflicts of interest, or natural antagonisms; they are, like other conflicts of interest, rooted in the nature of social relationships. In a rural area in Britain, I found that marital disputes and quarrels were often about how much time was spent outside the house by the husband, about his drinking in the pub, about his performance of domestic chores and about contraception (Whitehead, 1976). Although these could be described in terms of behavioural conflict or of differences in role expectations, many of them are, in essence, about the forms of expenditure of ostensibly 'shared' resources. I also found, as have many other studies, that financial matters are directly the subject of many other crises and disputes. Whatever the form that the material conflicts of interest between men and women in the household take, they are an expression of the extent to which, despite ideology, the household is not a collectivity of mutually reciprocal interests.

NOTES

1. The research on which this account is based was funded by the Social Science Research Council of Great Britain, to whom grateful acknowledgement is made.
2. The origin of this term is now a little uncertain to me. I think I coined it to describe the area discussed, although I was clearly influenced by the conjugal fund (Goode, 1963) and the conjugal estate (Goody, 1976), as well as by descriptions of the Hausa marriage contract (Longhurst, 1977). I hope I have not inadvertently taken it over from someone else.
3. I am using exchange in its general sociological sense, and not in the more technical sense in which it is used by economists.
4. Examples are discussions of why women are inferior bearers of labour, and whether the family makes women more suitable as a reserve army, or reduces the value of female labour power, as

well as enabling capital to pay women below that already reduced value (Elson and Pearson, this volume; Beechey, 1979; see also Humphries, 1977). Sociological literature on power relations between men and women inside the family include Bell and Newby (1976) and Whitehead (1976).

5.   This situation is not uncommon in West Africa. Roberts' (1979) description of the Niger version of *gandu* organised farming is of a similar sexual division of labour and a similar form of collective household farm. Dey (1979) describes a similar household/ private farm distinction within an agricultural system with a somewhat different sexual division of labour.

6.   Rather than a string of academic references the reader is recommended to consult the interesting collections of self written experiences of British working women (Llewellyn Davies, 1977a and 1977b).

7.   Cited in Pahl (1980).

Women, Kinship and Capitalist Development

Maila Stivens

Do kin relations in capitalist societies tend to become female-centred? The strength of kin ties among women was a striking finding of research that I carried out among middle class Australians and among rural women in Malaysia (Stivens, 1973, 1978a, 1978b).[1] This article looks briefly at evidence for female-centred kinship in capitalist societies, both in urban areas of the west and in the Third World, and suggests that the concrete conditions of capitalist development do not pare down kin relations to the isolated, male-headed nuclear family portrayed by much ideology, but rather encourage a tendency towards female-centred kin relations. My argument is that female-centredness arises because women are primarily located and subordinated within the reproductive processes embedded in kin relations. This shaping of kinship patterns is not seen as an effect of economy alone, but as the outcome of complex economic, political and cultural forces.

Social scientists have frequently labelled female-centred kinship patterns as *matrifocal* (Smith, 1973; Tanner, 1974; Yanagisako, 1977). R.T. Smith coined the term to describe an underlying pattern in which women were the focus of relationships in both male-and female-headed households. It now has wider and less exact connotations, being used to describe various situations of female-centredness in kin relations. The common features of female-centred kin patterns have been amply documented. They include women playing a central if not dominant role in kin relationships, a strong sense of female kinship solidarity, frequent interaction among female kin, strong geographical and sometimes economic concentrations of female kin and considerable material and other aid flowing through female links. A stress on women in kin relations occurs in societies with very different formal kinship systems. Use of the term matrifocal to describe these female-centred patterns however, is problematic, as it suggests a narrow concern with women as mothers and confuses domestic groups with kin structures.

MODELS OF THE FAMILY AND KINSHIP

Studies of the family have been bedevilled by ideology. Organised religion, state juridical structures, the media and much social science all present a particular model of the 'modern' family: a nuclear family that is structurally isolated from wider kin relations, reproducing itself through a sexual division of labour in which the man is the wage earner and the woman the housewife and socialiser. The distortions in this treatment of the family have been treated extensively, both in more recent history of the family, and in writings from the women's movement.[2] Some of the problems in debates about family form come from conflating the domestic grouping of the household with the structural unit of the family. For example, nuclear family households may be in the statistical majority in advanced capitalist societies, but this does not rule out important structural ties with kin outside the elementary family[3]. And many other kinds of household are supported by the wage, like single persons, single parents with children, several generations under one roof and so on. The ideology of the nuclear family is most misleading in relation to women: they are portrayed as housewives, but in fact have always acted as a reserve of labour in the advanced capitalist economy, working outside the home during wars and periods of economic demand.

These ideological confusions have especially muddied studies of family history. Much of the debate about the relationship between industrial capitalism and the elementary family has failed to distinguish clearly between household and family, getting lost in disputes about the existence of elementary families in the pre-industrial era. It is increasingly accepted that the history of the western family has been discontinuous, with multiple forms of family structure (see Poster, 1978), and that there is no simple relationship between type of economy and family and kinship forms. Kin relations in concrete social formations are shaped not only by economic forces, but also by political, juridical, ideological and cultural forces. It follows that kin relationships in capitalist societies are not specifically capitalist as such, and have their own history. Anthropologists in general have been better at seeing this than sociologists. But even quite sophisticated anthropological theorising has failed to conceptualise 'western' kinship adequately; it has tended to see kin relations outside the western elementary family as a pure, affective domain, stripped of much of the significance they have in societies where they are clearly embedded in political and economic structures (Firth et al., 1969). Such formulations obscure the structural significance of kin relations, reify kinship and the family, and fail to conceptualise the relationship between them, in both centre and peripheral societies. I am suggesting instead that we should see kin relations in such societies as a complex combination of several key structures – production, reproduction, socialisation and sexuality – which varies in historical context (cf. Mitchell, 1971). The elementary family should be seen as an aspect – not a basic unit – of kinship.

The dubious premise of the 'normal' family has been very apparent in studies of female-centred kinship both in the west and in areas of the Third World like the Caribbean. Any departure from expected male-centred patterns has been seen as anomalous or even as a deviation (Moynihan, 1965), especially where households are headed by women.

KIN RELATIONS AND REPRODUCTION IN CAPITALIST SOCIETIES

It is clear that kin relations have lost much of the direct involvement in production they had once in western societies, although they still regulate the inheritance of property and form the basis for some family enterprises, especially in farming and small businesses. But kinship is important for social reproduction, both in advanced capitalist countries and in the periphery. Capitalism relies for the reproduction of its conditions of existence upon many sectors and social forms which are not specifically incorporated into the direct capital-labour relation. Kin relations contribute to social reproduction through structuring biological reproduction, transfers of property (through inheritance) and economic reproduction in the elementary family household and wider kin circles. Kin relations (including marriage) relegate women to domestic units (as a reserve of labour) and determine the disposition of domestic labour processes – housework, childcare and other non-waged labour. A woman becomes liable to care for children, grandchildren, elderly parents or husband by virtue of being in a kin or marriage relationship. In other words, domestic labour is embedded in kin relationships. The implication of this is that kin relationships structure many of the processes of the reproduction of labour power, like childbirth, childcare, housework and the exchange of domestic labour between relatives. Similarly, property transfers and other kin redistributions contribute to the reproduction of class structures. Kin aid, especially monetary, has been shown to play an important part in helping children and others to maintain or improve their class situation (Litwak, 1965; Bell, 1968; Stivens, 1978a). Such aid also acts as a welfare system or welfare back-up, redistributing resources around kin circles. Lastly, kin relations are vitally important in psychological maintenance (Seccombe, 1974). Affection, 'moral support' and other aid between kin are integral to the reproductive aspects of kinship.

Much of the ideology surrounding kin relations is closely linked to the creation and recreation of women as ideological objects, the ideological construct of the feminine. Although women are subordinated in this construction, through socialisation women themselves also perpetuate the ideology, as feminists have pointed out. The ideological role of the 'family' has been seen by some writers in the marxist tradition as part of an ensemble of state ideological apparatuses reproducing the conditions of production (cf. Althusser, 1976). This formulation would allow us to place women's situation in the household and in kin relationships as an important apparatus of social reproduction.

The reproductive processes of kin relations contribute to women's subordination. But these relations are themselves highly contradictory, for they are also frequently the source of enormous support and solidarity among women. The ideology of conjugality in the west, for example, stresses that one's first loyalty lies within the elementary family, but there are also strong imperatives to help relatives out. Kin ties are often the main means which women use to improve their position through both economic and moral support. This female solidarity is a complex, contradictory phenomenon. It is not simply an economic and psychological defence against male dominance, nor simply a product of female domesticity. Yet while providing women with some defence, it can also act to further women's subordination. Women's solidarity with their relatives often sustains the ideological coherence of kin structures and thus increases women's submission to male control (cf. Caplan and Bujra, 1978; Whitehead, 1976).

In both centre and periphery the importance of kin relations for social reproduction is the result of a historical process we might term the *domestication* of kinship. Capitalist development in the periphery in the last few centuries has eroded the dominance of kin structures in the sense that real political power no longer derives from positions in the kinship system. Kinship has retained some of its economic importance in the transmission of property, especially land, through inheritance, although the wholesale appropriation of land by the colonial state and capitalist enterprise has greatly diminished the significance of this. These processes have often gone hand in hand with the structuring of a capitalist labour force (e.g. by 'freeing' the land and producing a proletariat). Where 'traditional' kin-based systems of land tenure do persist, they are often the result of deliberate intervention by the colonial or post-colonial state (see Clammer, 1973). In such situations, state legal structures create and/or reproduce kin relations (such as clan relations) as relations of production in dominated economic sectors.[4]

The effect of all this is that social relations of kinship in the periphery have been relegated to the domestic sphere and in the case of some dominated economic sectors, to subsistence or petty commodity production. In the domestic sphere, kin relations structure marriage and procreation, inheritance of property and the economic and ideological reproduction of the labour force. In dominated economic sectors they structure inheritance of property and frequently the organisation of labour in production. Although the kin basis of the general organisation of labour has been eroded, the subsistence producing household is frequently recruited through kinship – it usually consists of an elementary family or extended family or some other grouping of relatives.

In the centre, a similar relegation of kinship to the domestic sphere has followed the decline of the kin-based household as a productive unit. By and large, the household has become a consumption unit involved in social production rather than reproduction. But the removal of the kin based household from production – and there is considerable dispute about how far this household was in fact based on kin (Tilly and Scott, 1978; Poster, 1978) – did not automatically undermine the strength of kin ties.

MATRIFOCALITY REVISITED

The female-centredness of many diverse forms of kinship in capitalist societies has been documented in a large number of sociological and anthropological studies.[5] Many of the cases covered fall into two distinct patterns: a western, mainly urban form and a peripheral form. These two forms are not often compared in the literature, because concentration on the matrifocal domestic group has obscured similarities in the ways female-centredness is linked to social reproduction. But both forms share many common features. In particular, both forms are found in situations in which a reserve of labour is an important aspect of social reproduction. There are obviously important differences (with significant economic bases) between the two forms in that each represents forms accompanying specific patterns of capitalist accumulation. The two cases cited from my own work are concrete examples of highly specific circumstances, but they serve to illustrate a number of points common to each pattern.

THE PERIPHERY

Capitalist development in the periphery does not affect women's economic participation in any single direction. The export of first merchant and then industrial capital had differing concrete effects on peripheral economies and on women's situation within them. In some cases the interplay of capitalist development and other forces has relegated women to domestic labour and household production, as in some parts of Latin America; in others, women have been drawn into wage labour in manufacturing, especially in 'runaway' industries as in Mexico and Southeast Asia today. Yet another pattern links women's household subsistence work to plantation production (Boserup, 1970). A variant of this pattern links subsistence production to male proletarianisation (partial or complete) in parts of Africa, Latin America and Southeast Asia (Deere, 1979). This latter pattern may be combined with wage labour by younger females. All these situations share a common feature: some women are relegated to household domestic labour and/or subsistence production, to act as a reserve of labour, and to reproduce labour power.[6] This pattern is linked frequently to the labour migration, both temporary and permanent, which has been a common feature of capitalist development past and present. Men and/or younger women move from rural to urban areas and within rural areas to work in capitalist sectors. With the new international division of labour, there has for example been a fresh wave of young women migrating to work in electronics factories and other industrial capitalist enterprises.

It is in such situations in the periphery that we often find a tendency towards female-centredness in kin relations; it appears to be related to an intensification of women's reproductive work. Previous discussions of matrifocality have suggested that female-centredness arises where women are economically important (Tanner, 1974) or in conditions of marginality and poverty (Blumberg and Garcia, 1977). There is some force to these arguments, but we need to take a wider view of the economic to include reproduction. Although capitalist development often brings some labour saving in the domestic sphere, the domestic labour processes reproducing the conditions of existence of capitalism can become intensified in new directions. For example, a labour force with basic skills suited to the capitalist sector has to be produced. This involves more domestic work by women; women lose children's help as children get basic schooling; this schooling process itself requires supervision; and higher standards of care and nutrition are often required. The women also can have added tasks in processing foodstuffs for migrant members of the extended family who are provided with some subsistence by their village relatives. In many cases raised demands fall on older women who take on the sole care of grandchildren whose parents are away in the city. At the same time, many of the women face increased work in subsistence production. Even quite elderly women can be called on to replace the labour of absent migrants.

All these tasks performed by kin provide support for the migrant. Whatever the pre-capitalist kinship forms of an area, the use of bilateral ties can provide a wide range of help for the migrant. The female side of these ties is frequently stressed because this support – the domestic labour embedded in kin ties – is mainly the province of women. I now examine the link between reproduction and this female emphasis in kinship in two examples from my own research in Malaysia and in Australia.

MALAYS AND THEIR KIN

In Southeast Asia today, the arrival of massive investment by multinational companies has drawn both young men and women into wage labour in manufacturing. In Malaysia many younger male and female Malay migrants work in Kuala Lumpur and Singapore, while their parents, especially their divorced and widowed mothers, continue to work on the land in subsistence and petty commodity production.

Most Malays have a bilateral system of kinship. That is, kin on the father's side and mother's side are more or less equally important, and no one line of descent is stressed. The situation is complicated by several factors: formal family law is Islamic, which stresses the male side. On the other hand, most of the *adat* (customary laws) in the peninsular (except for the matrilineal customary law of the state of Negeri Sembilan) embody principles of equal male and female inheritance. These can come into conflict with Islamic law, which is used in land cases to assert counter claims to land. Some studies (e.g. Burridge, 1956), report a favouring of the male side in succession to positions of authority and in some residential groups. But Djamour's classic study of urban Malays in Singapore carried out in 1949-1950 (Djamour, 1965), and more recent surveys (Palmore, Klein and Ariffin bin Marzuki, 1971; Tham, 1979), show that Malays are more likely to emphasise the female side and to live with kin of the mother's side. In the case of Singapore Malays, although Djamour's informants' formal ideology (closely bound up with Islam), attributed the greater strength to the male side,

> 'in practice one finds that Malays visit their maternal relatives and go to them for advice and help more frequently than they do their paternal kin ... There is a bias towards matrilocality both in the sense of residence in the same household as that of the wife's parents and of independent residence in the native village or district of the wife' (Djamour, 1965, p.32).

Djamour reported extremely close ties between sisters and between their offspring.

The Malaysian state of Negeri Sembilan where my first hand information comes from, is characterised by a formally matrilineal system. It is thus an exception to the bilateral rule, with formal customary law (*adat perpatih*) governing a system of matrilineal clans and lineages. While the kinship system lost most of its political role with formal British rule, the upshot of a series of complex historical developments was that matrilineal law, as codified by the British, controls property in the subsistence and much of the petty commodity producing sectors.[7] But, as other writers have pointed out, there are more similarities than diffrences in the kinship systems of Malays in general (cf. Tham, 1979), and many of my findings appear to hold for other areas of Malaysia.

The Negeri Sembilan kinship system is formally centred on women. Residence is uxorilocal: that is, the husband moves to the wife's village and is therefore an outsider, with women forming the core of local groups. Matrilineal clans hold land, although women have individual titles given in the British period.

Women are also at the centre of the 'informal' kinship system in

Negeri Sembilan. Mothers are highly valued – a migrant fails to greet his mother immediately on his return to the village at his peril. Sisters share close bonds, although quarrels over property can disrupt this relationship. Like the Singapore Malays, the children of sisters are very close. In general women are the mediators in kinship, organising kin-related matters like marriages and they cooperate extensively with other female kin in a wide range of women's tasks – childcare and other domestic labour.

When Negeri Sembilan Malays move to the town and city, they often form households consisting of an elementary family. But the extended family still plays an important part in the move to the town. Kin follow each other to the city in chain migrations, live in the same household or in clusters of kin more often than not related through female ties, and provide extensive support for each other with help in housing, children, and information about jobs. The range of kin used in this way usually extends to parents, their siblings and their descendants, though it may extend to more distant relatives. Extensive outmigration in Malaysia has denuded many villages of people between the ages of 25 and 50. The migrants, however, maintain close links with their villages. Grandmothers often care for their grandchildren in the villages while the children's parents are away in the city. The latter supplement their parents' income from fruit and rubber growing with (cash) remittances, and receive rice and other produce from their village relations. Many of the present generation of migrants plan to retire to the rural areas and have kept on their homes in their home villages. Thus the advent of industrial capital in the last decade or so does not appear to have produced any great pressures towards a nuclear family form in the Malay case (see Palmore et al., 1971). Elementary families within the extended family in rural Negeri Sembilan frequently maintain separate households, although these are often in the same compound. But this was also the case during the colonial period. Significantly, during that period, many men left to become soldiers and policemen, while women were often left in the village to look after their children and to work in subsistence production.

As I noted above, the economic significance of women in such situations has been seen as a cause of matrifocality (Tanner, 1974). It is true that the financial contribution of young migrant women to the village family budget is considerable, and appears to have raised their standing in their families significantly. Older women's work in subsistence rice and petty commodity rubber production is also vital to the rural household's livelihood. With many males absent and many older women left in the village to run everyday economic affairs, women are in control of a significant proportion of the village economy. But women's importance in the economy in this narrow sense is not adequate *per se* to explain the occurrence of female-centred kin forms. We need to take account of women's economic importance in a wider sense: that is of their contribution not only to production but to reproduction. Rural women's productive and reproductive labours as I have outlined them are an important element in the relationship between the capitalist sector and other sectors not specifically incorporated into directly capitalist relations. The rural household cannot be considered in isolation from the city household of its kin as a productive and reproductive unit. The two are bound in the chain of relationships linking the village economy to the national economy. A female-centred pattern of kinship (which had cultural origins as far back as the fourteenth century) fitted the demands of capitalist development well – with some modifications. Where women's situation is 'domesticated' by capitalism, an expansion of women's control over the domestic labour processes embedded in kin relations and of the ideology sustaining these processes – kin solidarity – is logical.

It appears reasonable then to link female-centred kinship in peripheral countries with the domestication of kinship and with the creation of labour reserves in the capitalist economy. Even so, economic factors can only provide a partial explanation. A few examples illustrate the complexity involved. In Southeast Asia, women's comparative autonomy underlying matrifocality is obviously a complex cultural phenomenon (Stoler, 1977). I have noted that many of the 'traditional' legal codes governing kinship and inheritance favour women to varying degrees compared to the more 'male' principles of Islamic family law. In Malaysia, the codification of customary law in the colonial period can be seen as favouring at least bilateral and in some cases female-centred kinship and inheritance patterns. But cultural factors can also provide strong opposition to any matrifocal tendencies. For example, Malaysian Chinese retain strongly patrilineal kinship structures, although, interestingly, one study of Singaporean Chinese did in fact find a moderate tendency towards 'matricentric' kinship (Wong and Kuo, 1979).

A MIDDLE CLASS SUBURB OF SYDNEY

My second example concerns the urban bilateral kinship of a middle class suburb of Sydney.

In Australia, women are ideologically relegated to domesticity; women's primary ideological location is within kinship structures as domestic labourers. This ideology of domesticity glosses over their extensive participation in the workforce. Sociologists have tended to emphasise class differences in studies of kin relations in the west, seeing working class patterns as more female-centred than middle class patterns. I think that these differences can be exaggerated. Both middle class and working class women have structurally comparable situations as wives and mothers, located within kin relations, involved in economic and ideological reproduction.

The men in my study were mainly middle class sellers of labour, in professional, semi-professional, and routine white collar work. Less than one-fifth were skilled manual workers. They were not the status-aspiring geographically mobile spiralists of the popular stereotype of the middle class, although they had high aspirations for their children, (and more so for their sons than their daughters). Thirty percent of the women were in employment at the time of the study, seventy per cent having worked outside the home at some time in their lives, mainly in the familiar female jobs – as shop assistants, clerks, teachers and nurses. Few women gained much personal prestige from their work; most relied on vicarious satisfaction from their husbands' position, and most were in varying degrees dependent on their husbands financially.

Male and female informants agreed on the 'rules' of kinship. They felt a strong sense of obligation to kin, ranging from a minimal obligation to keep in touch, to a strong sense of moral obligation, particularly to those closely related genealogically – 'blood is thicker than water'. Many expressed the view that the ideal pattern of family and kin relationships was an important pattern for the greater good of society at large and troubles in society were often attributed to faulty family life. Informants had very developed ideas about women's focal role in kin relations; kinship was 'women's business'. It was the wife's contact with relatives they said, that determined how often they saw each other. A wife had more duties to her family, as a commercial traveller's wife put it. It was the woman, they said, who asked her husband if he had rung his mother. 'The mother-daughter tie is closer. The tie is stronger with females. I feel closer to my sister than to my brother'. Many women expressed a need to have female kin, particularly sisters, some being cited as the woman's closest friends. The most enthusiastic descriptions of kin were made by women about their sisters.

These notions were borne out by the frequency of contact between kin. Women were the main mediators of these relationships, drawing their husbands into their kin circles. Thirty-five per cent of the households interviewed had formed composite households for varying periods with parents at some point after initially leaving home, the great majority with the woman's parents. Overall, the women's contact with their parents was greater than the men's. Visits, phone calls (including long distance) and letters all maintained frequent contacts. Contacts with siblings showed the same slant towards women, although somewhat more selectively. Among siblings, the greatest contact was between sisters, although men also saw quite a lot of their brothers who were living in Sydney. Ties with kin beyond the extended family were rather limited. Again there was a decided bias towards women in contact with kin beyond the extended family. Ties with women's mothers' siblings and women's sisters' daughters were very important.

Financial and practical aid flowed in both directions between parents and adult children. The main areas of aid exchanged among these families, other than financial, were care in illness, the provision of a home for elderly parents and newly married children, babysitting, helping with D-I-Y projects, general repairs, and very importantly, emotional support. Much of this was the province of the woman, although clearly men also carried out some of this domestic labour. A great deal of help given to elderly parents was provided by daughters and their husbands, in line with most of the informants' ideas that it was the daughter's place to provide such services. Siblings also helped each other, but not as constantly.

Financial aid flowed to newly married couples from parents and from middle-aged couples to their parents. Parents helped promote their children's (sons, and daughters and their husbands) educational and professional achievements with gifts of deposits on houses, loans for cars, guarantees on mortgages and of course the payment for their daughters' weddings. Children helped elderly parents financially with rates, phone bills and other expenses, and by providing a home. There is some controversy in the sociology of the family literature as to whether financial aid flows through mainly male links (cf. Bell, 1968). But even if the husband is the financial 'manager', women often have considerable say in the giving of family aid. This is possible because 'family business' is symbolically associated with women.

In broad outline, these Australian findings were comparable to other British and North American studies which have found kin ties to be important in providing sociability, moral support and a wide range of help between kin, and in promoting the class situation of members of the extended family. The female-centredness and the female mediation of kin relations, it is suggested, are integral to the constitution of the reproductive structures of kin relations in Australia. Moreover, in the Australian case, the ideological coherence of kin structures is sustained by a complex consciousness that symbolically associates kinship with women.

CONCLUSION

These two cases have outlined very briefly and schematically the two patterns of female-centred kinship that I am proposing. I have argued that while kinship relations are determined by a complex combination of economic, political, ideological and cultural forces, capitalist development tends to domesticate kin relations. In many locations in the periphery, the social relations of kinship have been relegated to the domestic sphere and to production in dominated sectors, sectors which reproduce capitalism. In the centre, the social relations of kinship have been relegated to the domestic sphere. I argue in each case that the female focus to these relations is intrinsic to the constitution of these domesticated kin relations. In the periphery, many cases of female-centredness appear to be related to the expansion of women's domestic and subsistence production that accompanies extensive out-migration by males and younger females in conditions of capitalist development. In the centre, similarly, female-centredness appears to be related to women's domestic situation.

The two patterns clearly have much in common, but they also differ significantly in ways that I have outlined. Female solidarity is one important product of both patterns. As I have pointed out, this solidarity is a complex and contradictory phenomenon. It is not just an economic and psychological defence against male dominance, nor is it simply a product of female domesticity. Women's solidarity with female kin often sustains the ideological coherence of kin structures and so furthers the controls placed on women by their location and subordination in these structures. This solidarity can provide a very important way for women to fight male dominance, but it is often only a palliative. Without a restructuring of the reproductive relations of kinship, such struggles can only be limited by their own conditions.[8]

1. I carried out research in Sydney, Australia, from January 1968 to January 1970 (funded by a Commonwealth of Australia Scholarship held in the Department of Anthropology, University of Sydney), and in Malaysia from July 1975 to September 1976 (funded by a U.K. S.S.R.C. Studentship held in the Department of Anthropology, London School of Economics). I should like to thank members of the Subordination of Women Project, especially Olivia Harris and Ann Whitehead, for commenting on drafts of this paper.

2. See Poster (1978) and Zaretsky (1976) for accounts of the historical development of this model, Laslett (1971) and Tilly and Scott (1978) for accounts of the pre-industrial period, and Beechey (1978) and Molyneux (1979b) for references to and discussion of the domestic labour debate, which analyses the relationship between the elementary family household and the capitalist economy. See also Lenero-Otero (1977) for criticisms of the model of the nuclear family from outside feminism.

3. By *elementary family* I mean the grouping of parents and children (either dependent or independent children). 'An *extended family* is any persistent kin grouping of persons related by descent, marriage or adoption which is wider than the elementary family in that it characteristically spans three generations from grandparents to grandchildren' (Rosser and Harris, 1965, p.84). In *bilateral* kinship systems, descent is traced equally through male and female links. In *matrilineal* systems, descent is traced through the female line.

4. See footnote 7 below for a brief discussion of the history of Negeri Sembilan, Malaysia, and of the relationship between these sectors, which illustrates how those sectors can be seen as reproducing capitalism.

5. The asymmetry in bilateral kinship structures in western industrial nations has been extensively documented: see Yanagisako (1977) for a full list of references, and also Stivens (1978a) for an Australian account. For peripheral countries there is a huge literature: see again Yanagisako, and also Kandiyoti (1977) for Turkey, Vatuk (1971) for India, Geertz (1961) and Tanner (1974) for Indonesia, Potter (1977) for Thailand. The concept has been critically discussed in a large literature including Gonzalez (1970),

Sweetser (1966), Smith, (1970, 1973), Tanner (1974), Blumberg and Garcia (1977), and Yanagisako (1977).

6. See Deere (1979) for discussion of the relegation of women to subsistence production, and also my paper 'Women and their land' (1978b mimeo). Women's part in reproducing labour power is discussed extensively in the literature of the 'domestic labour debate' (see Molyneux, 1979b).

7. I have argued (1978b) that this matrilineal customary law was in some respects strengthened by colonial and post-colonial developments. The British codified the customary law, granting women what amounted to individual titles to ancestral land (riceland and fruit orchards). The historical processes which underdeveloped the Negeri Sembilan economy had a number of consequences for women's situation. After formal colonial rule was imposed, and the rubber boom of the second decade of this century collapsed, political moves by the settler class (the Stevenson scheme) acted to prevent the petty commodity producers of rubber from competing with estates and effectively limited petty commodity production. Both the latter and subsistence rice production have been relegated to backward, declining sectors, which increasingly draw on older labour as the young migrate to the towns. Older women as I suggest in the body of the article, are also responsible for a great deal of the care of the children of migrants. These developments have been accompanied by increasing control by women over property in these petty commodity and subsistence sectors. These sectors are dominated by capitalism and integrated into the reproductive mechanism of the world capitalist system. Subsistence production underwrites the cost of the reproduction of labour power for industrial capital, while surplus value is extracted from petty commodity production through the market.

8. This raises the complex issue of divorce and its relationship to female-centred kin forms. In the west, divorce can be seen as giving value to women's domestic labour, for divorce settlements often explicitly take account of the woman's contribution of unpaid labour to the household. Whether female-centred kinship encourages the dissolution of marriages, or divorce encourages these kin forms, is a moot point requiring further investigation.

Sexuality and Control of Procreation

Mirjana Morokvasić

'Most "unplanned" pregnancies are partly wanted and partly unwanted. A frequent solution to ambivalence is passivity – not using contraception, or using it haphazardly. This is a rational response when no alternative is desirable. Those family planners who speak of irrationality, of women not understanding their own interests, do not themselves understand the problem. Self-determination cannot exist if none of the options is attractive. Reproductive options cannot be separated from economic, vocational, and social choices (Gordon, 1977, p.408).

The relationship between contraception and abortion, between sexuality and procreation, is complex, and not well understood even by those who are professionally involved in family planning counselling. In this article I want to look at women's supposedly ambivalent behaviour when it comes to such important matters as their relationship to their partner and determining their fertility. It stresses the necessity of making a wide range of birth control techniques available to women so that they can freely choose the method they consider most suitable. At present, the choice is limited and the possibilities of choosing freely even more so.

The frequency of abortion in many countries including Yugoslavia despite the availability of modern contraceptive devices, leads one to believe that abortion will continue to be an important form of birth

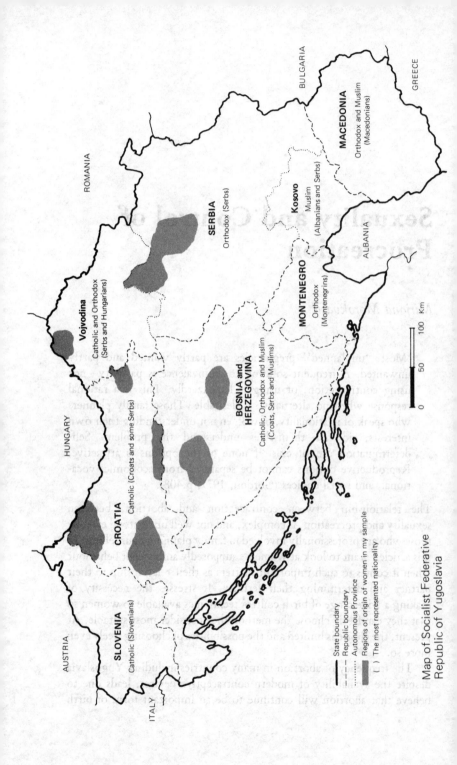

Map of Socialist Federative Republic of Yugoslavia

control, at least in the near future, whether the male legislators in some countries approve of it or not, or restrict access to it or not. For women who systematically 'choose' to have abortions, a more accessible and less costly method of pregnancy regulation should be made available. Forcing women to choose between oral or mechanical contraceptives and sterilisation 'for their own good', has all too often had objectives other than a direct benefit to women. Women will always find ways of rejecting them, even at the expense of their own health. My aim is to highlight the fact that, no matter how illogical or inconsistent their behaviour may appear, underlying it there is a rationale.

In this article I do not advocate the use of any specific form of birth control available today, although a possible alternative within abortive methods is discussed. I do argue in favour of methods that women themselves can use and control so they may enjoy to the full their right to have children only when they want to have them. These methods are not and cannot be the same for every woman.

My information comes from a survey of Yugoslav migrant women living in Western Europe (Morokvasić, 1980).[1] These migrants come from a country where abortion has been a customary and widespread practice for a long time, and where it was legalised well over a decade earlier than in many Western European countries. They also come from a society in which old values, norms and inequalities in gender relationships have been preserved. Nonetheless, the attitudes and behaviour analysed here are not specific to Yugoslavs. They are characteristic of all women who are oppressed sexually, but who, often perfectly conscious of that oppression, do not adopt the 'solutions' proposed to them in the West.

ABORTION AS FERTILITY REGULATION IN YUGOSLAVIA

Abortion is both ancient and widely practised – not only in Europe but throughout the world.[2] To say that it forms part of the traditional cultural inventory of the Yugoslavs is not an exaggeration: it has become as much a part of women's lives as having children, and often more so.

The decline in birth rates throughout almost all of Yugoslavia (despite marked regional variations) from the second half of the nineteenth century has been attributed to the adoption of various forms of birth control, particularly abortion (Breznik et al., 1972; Erlich, 1976). It has been associated with the break up of the Zadrugas[3] which reduced the demand for family labour (Erlich, 1976), as well as in the wealthy

Mirjana Morokvasić 129

agricultural regions, with the wish to preserve property by passing it on to a single heir (Breznik et al., 1972; Demeny, 1972). Abortion seems to have been widespread not only in areas where childlessness was tolerated or aimed at, but also in areas where a childless woman provoked hostility, in particular in Serbia where the incidence of abortions was the highest: 'Infertility of the women is condemned severely and it is a rare case when the woman is not forced into a divorce' (Erlich, 1976, p.303). In regions where religious influence was strong, especially Muslim or Catholic areas, abortion was less widely practised (although in the latter preventive methods were used). Such studies suggest that women in Yugoslavia, long before socialist legislation, accepted the responsibility for limiting their family size rather than seeing every pregnancy as a 'gift from God'. Where abortion was illegal and heavily penalised (Gardun, 1971) they used whatever method was at their disposal – abortifacient potions, abdominal massage. Although many of these methods were quite efficient, they frequently had an adverse effect on women's health.

Since the war, Yugoslavia like other socialist countries (Blayo, 1970) has changed its legislation on abortion a number of times; each amendment since the first law in 1952 has brought further liberalisation. In 1969 The Federal Assembly adopted a resolution on birth regulation (Zena Danas No. 269, 1969; Tomsic, 1973) and the 1974 Constitution stipulated that it is a human right to determine the size of the family and to space births. The result has been a rapid decline in the birth rate, an increase in registered abortions, and in 'completed' abortions, e.g. those which women themselves provoke either alone or with the help of a backstreet abortionist and which are completed in hospital (Breznik et al., 1972, p.318). The ratio of abortions to live births throughout Yugoslavia was in favour of abortions, although marked regional differences existed: Serbia remained the region with the highest ratio (three to one), in Vojvodina there were twice as many, in Kosovo it was equal, while only in Slovenia did births outnumber abortions (Breznik et al., 1972).[4] Despite greater attention paid to the diffusion of contraceptives since the 1969 Resolution, abortion has remained the most widely used means of birth regulation in Yugoslavia, and studies show that the use of efficient contraceptive methods is very limited, particularly in rural areas (Stampar 1971; Andolsek, 1975). Couples mainly rely upon *coitus interruptus* to prevent conception.

The message conveyed by most studies in Yugoslavia is that abortion is a necessary evil, a transitional method which involves a high risk of complications – estimated to be about 30% (Stampar, 1971; Breznik et al., 1972). They suggest that abortion will disappear once women become better informed about contraception, when their level of education improves and when they become capable of planning. Surprisingly, this message persists despite the evidence of these same studies of an impressive level of contraceptive knowledge of the population, and despite the fact that the abortion rate is higher in urban areas (for example 4 abortions per live birth in Belgrade) where educational levels are higher as are, one could assume, levels of information. Finally some studies show that additional information about and encouragement to use contraceptives have very little effect on non-users (Andolsek, 1975).

BIRTH REGULATION IN THE CONTEXT OF MIGRATION

Yugoslav women emigrate predominantly from those regions where the birth rate has been declining for some time and where abortion is most frequently practised. Through employment abroad most Yugoslav women become wage earners and members of the labour force for the first time. As wage labourers the incentive to limit their family size may augment. For, as Gordon puts it: '. . . no other variable seems to provide such a direct incentive to birth control use . . . as women's employment' (Gordon, 1977, p.412).

My interview material suggests that the majority of migrants were very clear about limiting their family size: either they had already achieved the desired number (2 on average), or they did not want any more for the moment. Their contraceptive knowledge was quite satisfactory and much better than that reported in studies in Yugoslavia. At the time of the interviews 37 percent of the women (97 out of 258) declared that they used some form of contraceptive. However, only 40 percent of 'women at risk' (those who said that they did not want any children or already had more than they originally wanted) did so. The highest percentage of contraceptive users lived in Sweden while in France and Germany the number of users was more or less equal. This is possibly due to the fact that in Sweden a very wide range of contraceptive technology is available while in France and Germany access to contraception has only been recently (since the mid '70s) facilitated.

For the women who used contraceptives the pill was the commonest method; IUDs were used by some of the migrants in Sweden, but only by 3 women in France and none in Germany. The use of a diaphragm was mentioned by women living in France. The condom or sheath was never used as a regular contraceptive by stable couples but only in cases of frequent change of partner. The majority of women used no other preventive method than *coitus interruptus*; they rely confidently on their male partner:

'My husband takes care of it'.

Men are granted the power of control and invested with anticipated responsibility in the sexual act and its outcome.

The direct consequence of this is a high rate of abortion; three-quarters of the women known to have been sexually active (i.e. they were married or living with a man) had had one or more abortions. The number of abortions per woman was the highest in France (where the majority of the migrants originate from Serbia) where most women had had as many as three and some even ten or more abortions. The lowest rate was in Sweden where women had seldom gone through more than one or two abortions each. Coming from a country in which it is relatively easy to have an abortion and where it has become a part of a woman's life and accepted as such, Yugoslav migrants probably experience difficulty in getting an abortion in the new and very different social context. In Sweden for example, abortion is not viewed as an acceptable means of fertility control. It is only 'designed as a humanitarian measure to protect women's life and health' (Luker, 1975, p.3). In France and Germany abortion was only legalised in 1975 and 1976 respectively. Yugoslav migrant women, in spite of the numerous obstacles and difficulties they have to overcome, stick to their customary practice of abortion and the majority of them are opposed or indifferent to other methods of contraception or use them erratically. However rather than having an abortion in their country of residence, most of the women travel to Yugoslavia even though this is very costly and involves the risk of losing their job. Once in Yugoslavia too they are often victims of exploitation by unscrupulous intermediaries who arrange abortions quickly. The women in the survey who reported having had abortions, had altogether an estimated minimum of 427 as against a total of 234 children. This would suggest that on average roughly two-thirds of all pregnancies are terminated. Thus it would seem clear that Yugoslav women, rather than avoiding pregnancies, seek to terminate them. Abortions remains the main means of birth regulation for them whether they are in Yugoslavia or abroad.

WHY ABORTION?

Why do women in a situation in which access to contraception is apparently easier than access to abortion still choose the latter? Or more precisely, why do Yugoslav migrants who are far from being ignorant, whose level of education is much higher than that of other migrants, and who are in the main wage earners, prefer abortion to contraception? Why do they opt for a costly, uncomfortable experience, risking not only their job but their whole migratory project, by travelling abroad to abort?

These are the questions that family planners and counsellors inevitably ask themselves, and that I originally also asked. The briefest answer to them was given me by a Yugoslav woman herself:

'Why not?'

Confronted by Yugoslav and other migrant women, social workers, doctors, interpreters and family planning practitioners, all have a common approach: they want to help these 'poor ignorant women to get rid of their backward mores and adopt modern ways'. They offer the women their medical and social expertise, tend to socialise their sexuality, and to intervene in the most intimate aspect of their lives. Full of good will and deeply concerned about eradicating ignorance, they base their whole approach on several assumptions derived from their own social and cultural background, but which are not necessarily applicable to all women. Firstly, given that abortion is physically, psychologically and financially very costly, they assume that it can easily be replaced by acceptance of contraception as a far preferable, easier method of fertility control. Secondly, they assume that women who seek abortions should have prevented their pregnancy or at least tried to do so. And thirdly, they assume that if a woman has not done so she is irrational – or even pathological – ignorant, incapable of planning and therefore in need of help from the experts.

Luker (1975) in her fine analysis based on a sample of Californian women, criticises such an approach and questions the validity of the predominant explanations of women's behaviour. She in turn puts forward a risk-taking theory in which women take rational but misinformed risks; she thus can talk about 'unwanted pregnancies'. This is a rather common expression in the literature but I would agree that it also is inadequate, because it does not distinguish between unplanned conception, unwanted pregnancy, and unwanted child. In other words most people assume that when a child is not wanted, the pregnancy is not wanted either and that the woman should have therefore prevented it. However women can be quite clear about not wanting a child, but ambivalent or even positive about wanting to get pregnant. Gordon perceptively points to the fact that 'most "unplanned" pregnancies are partly wanted and partly unwanted' (Gordon 1977, p.408). This ambivalence is deeply rooted in the significance of procreation and maternity for Yugoslav women and in their perception of women's sexuality, indeed femininity, as being closely related to procreation. Recourse to abortion may thus not be a result of lack of information or education, as the Yugoslav reports discussed earlier suggest. Abortions, and the pregnancies that precede them, may therefore be indicators of particular gender relations underlying them; so to understand the former we need to investigate the latter.

WOMEN AND MEN IN YUGOSLAV SOCIETY

Women's ability to control their generative capacities and their sexual life is an essential prerequisite to their access to a more egalitarian status in society. Fewer children and the ability to space births enable women to envisage new educational and employment perspectives outside family boundaries. However, in many cultures motherhood, (and very often the number of sons), was and still is the principal basis of women's social standing and the respect awarded them by the wider community. This is particularly true in situations where existing economic and social conditions allow women few alternatives to maternity. Double sexual standards, including deep concern about virginity and female adultery, testify to the emphasis placed on reproduction in such societies. This cultural pattern existed not so long ago and still persists in many parts of Yugoslavia although often in disguised form. Thus while the socialist revolution, in which women participated as actively as men, has opened up new possibilities for women, change in women's status has so far been confined to the public sphere where they have acquired the same legal and political rights as men, and access to all domains of economic, cultural and social life. Women are esteemed as workers and expected to take an active part in community affairs, but within the home prerevolutionary values surrounding the relationship between the genders within the family remain practically intact so that marked inequality between the genders has been preserved. A woman is expected to do all the household chores, to take the major responsibility for child care; at the same time she must accept that her husband is sexually free and irresponsible, while she must be faithful; should she allow herself any sexual freedom she must bear full responsibility for the outcome.

RELUCTANCE TO USE CONTRACEPTION: PERSISTING SUBORDINATION OF WOMEN TO MEN

Most Yugoslav migrants as we have noted above are reluctant to use contraceptives. Those who do, take the pill but are not happy about it: they complain of gaining weight, of no longer having sexual desires, of 'not being the same any more'. After a few months they stop taking it and that is generally when they get pregnant. Condoms are rejected by both women and men as reducing pleasure: 'it is no longer the same thing'. However migrants in discussing their reluctance to use contraceptives and their resentment at being harrassed by social workers to use them, reveal other more deepseated reasons for their attitude. These stem from the way in which relationships between a man and woman are structured and in particular women's position within this relationship. As an indication of this one-quarter of the women mentioned the open resistance of the male partner to using contraceptives:

> 'My husband says that a woman loses sexual desire, so if I take it he might even think that I have someone else';
> 'he always wants to be sure that any minute he "can" [impregnate me]'.

A woman's sexual drive is apparently desirable but only in order to satisfy a man's own sexual needs, while ability to impregnate at will satisfies the man's sense of control over the relationship:

> 'he always wants me with a big stomach so he can be sure of me'.

Many of the migrants I interviewed had internalised men's reasons for resisting the use of contraceptives and adopted them as their own:

> 'If I take the pill I shall become free, too';
> 'I shall become like a man. I might sleep with anybody';
> 'I shall no longer be faithful to my husband'.

These women resent one of the most important possible effects of contraception: the disruption of a deeply embedded authority structure and the double standard in which the man is dominant and sexually free while the woman is subjected and faithful. However, during their stay abroad this fatalistic attitude towards male-female relationships can be challenged by other encounters. Trenc (1973) reports cases of migrant women who for the first time in their lives experienced sexual pleasure with another man and qualified as 'wasted' the years of previous married life.

When a sexual relationship is more of a duty than a pleasure, women seek ways to refuse it. Thus another set of answers suggests that the risk of pregnancy is used as a means of refusing sexual intercourse:

'If I take the pill, he will do it every day'.

For such a woman the use of a contraceptive would remove her strongest weapon in the game of sexual politics. The fear of pregnancy is not only a weapon which gives women a reason for not having sex but it can also be an indispensable part of the sexual act:

'I can't have pleasure if I'm not afraid of becoming pregnant'.

For other women, contraception is rejected as neither natural nor healthy:

'it's not good for your health';
'one has sick children afterwards';
'one becomes sterile'.

What is 'natural' then? In the migrants' own definition of the situation, it is the absence of any intervening agent in intimate relationships between a man and woman. Since the man dominates, the most natural thing is that he should also control the possible outcome of the relationship:

'It is his duty to take care of it.'

Women refer in this way to *coitus interruptus* and associate it with an image of male virility which is deeply respected:

'he's not a man if he can't take care.'

The woman in the whole affair is dependent on what the man can do and she likes it that way; it is his job not hers:

'My husband does not drink [i.e. he is not alcoholic]. He is capable of taking care; that is the healthiest way.'

One-third of the women interviewed relied on this method and declared themselves satisfied with it. However this faith in a man's ability to control ejaculation has its limits:

'I lock myself up in the other room',

I was told by a woman who had recently had an abortion.

Although use of contraception is supposed to enable a woman to have a free sexual relationship both in terms of freedom from fear of pregnancy and freedom to decide who her partner will be, it can be argued that she is as little free as ever. A Yugoslav woman in Sweden put it this way:

'It is a myth that Swedish girls are emancipated and free. They conform to the prevailing cultural values as much as our peasant girl does. Only the values are different and the outcome is different. A Yugoslav girl might not go to bed even with someone she loves, chiefly because she fears pregnancy. A Swedish girl will go to bed with a man whether she loves him or not. She is expected to do so, everybody around her does it, and she is not supposed to have reasons for refusing – after all she is on the pill.'

For many Yugoslav men, the proposed emancipation of women has not led to any feelings of equality with their partners (Trenc, 1973) but, on the contrary, to lack of responsibility and respect for them: 'They're all whores!' For men a free woman is only an object of sexual pleasure and they profit from the relationship sexually and often financially. When they have lost interest in their partner she is left to cope with possible pregnancy or a child, with all her savings gone. Many young Yugoslav women now consider marriage as the only acceptable form under which they can have sexual relations. At least it gives them some legal protection.

Sexual relationships based on the double standard resemble a contest in which, if sexual intercourse takes place, the man is considered the winner, the woman the loser. The woman can only win if she refuses successfully: in that way she not only keeps her reputation but becomes even more desirable. One of her best weapons is fear of pregnancy – in fact it is a fear for her and a threat for him. The technology of modern contraceptives deprives women of that tool. Another weapon is pregnancy itself, though this has a somewhat different purpose.

ABORTION: SYMBOLIC PROCREATION?

Once the most likely consequence of the way in which the relationship is structured actually occurs and the woman becomes pregnant, it is entirely up to her to deal with it. Men say 'she should get cleaned up', meaning she should have an abortion. Abortion is considered a very natural, normal event. Though abortion is the opposite of procreation, it is symbolically the same – physical proof that a woman is fecund. Among older women the number of their abortions is a matter of pride and they boast to the younger women in hospital waiting rooms:

'One! That's nothing. I've had ten.'[5]

An abortion may be the result of a woman's failure to use a pregnancy as a bargaining tool to bind the man to herself. Any wavering on the man's part is met with the threat of a potential child. For example, one woman reported that she had undergone 17 abortions before having her first child at the age of 41. For twenty years she had lived with the same man whom she wanted to marry before having a child. Repeated pregnancies were her bargaining tools:

'I did not want a bastard'.

But an abortion is also proof that a woman has had sex, which for women can still be associated with having sinned. Women who travel to Yugoslavia to get an abortion avoid returning to their home village: 'When I go home alone and not for a holiday, everybody knows why I came'. For this reason some women seek to abort in secrecy and can even mutilate themselves:

'My husband was a drunkard. He beat me all the time, I didn't want a child from him. When I realised I was pregnant I tried it with needles . . . it didn't work; the child survived until I was six months pregnant. They took it out at the hospital. It was as if I gave birth to a child . . . '

Since abortion is a consequence of sin, the pain and suffering associated with it are sometimes considered purifying by some women. I was told in a Parisian hospital that many Yugoslav women sytematically refuse any anaesthetic:

'What do you think I am? I can stand it'.

Besides the need for self punishment – 'I did it; it is my fault' – this refusal also reflects their desire to ensure that the event is as natural as possible, without the use of unhealthy drugs. It may also be a way of rationalising the fact that having anaesthesia is expensive.

Though Yugoslav women are very proud of their sexual drive and their answers suggest that sex is very important to them, their sexuality and their capacity to bear children are closely related:

'When I see him I conceive'.

Preventing conception means precisely separating the two and neither men nor women are apparently ready to do this. 'For this separation to be desirable both sexes must be able to enjoy sexual activity for its own sake' (Gordon, 1977, p.408). Abortion can, of course, simply be the outcome of ignorance. But once the ignorance is overcome, as is the case with most Yugoslav migrants, behaviour does not necessarily change. I would argue this is because it is also a reflection of the established relationship of dominance within the couple in which the man dominates and takes care of the sexual act. Consequently abortion remains virtually *the* fertility control method for Yugoslavs since it leaves open the possibility of having sex and also having the occasional proof of one's virility or fecundity. When a woman has no means other than the maternal role to establish her status, then she may well turn to this even if only potentially. Abortion in this case is almost a symbolic procreation: permitting the capacity to procreate to be tested while ensuring the control of fertility.

TOWARDS AN EASIER ABORTION: A PRESENT ALTERNATIVE

Though abortion may be the result of voluntary gambling with pregnancy, it is never a pleasant experience. On the contrary it can be humiliating, painful, and often involves financial exploitation. The usual lengthy waiting period before an abortion can be arranged generates anxiety, either by increasing a woman's ambivalent feelings about it or strengthening her desire to feel free and relieved. In either case, women and abortion practitioners agree that the sooner it is done, the better.

Though women themselves decide to have abortions whether the law permits it or not, the rest of the process is out of their control. There is, however, a technique that could replace abortion and which women themselves could control. This method (called MR hereafter) is known variously as menstrual regulation, menstrual aspiration, endometrial aspiration, menses extraction or menses induction. It is a procedure 'which disrupts the intrauterine environment so that embryonic implantation either cannot occur or cannot be maintained' (Brenner & Edelman 1977, p.177). This definition suggests that both drugs and physical agents can be used but while drugs (in particular prostaglandins) may be useful in the future, the method as presently used involves 'vacuum curettage of the uterus performed either at or within a few days of the expected date of menstruation' (Davis & Potts, 1974).

MR can be performed up to the 14th day of the missed period (Savage 1979) and most clinical evidence is based on women whose pregnancies were not past that limit.

MR can be performed either on women for whom there is a positive proof of conception or those who are likely to be pregnant. The procedure lasts no more than 2-3 minutes, requires virtually no anaesthetic or cervical dilation, needs very simple equipment and can be carried out by trained para-medics. A tiny 4-5 or 6-7 mm very flexible plastic cannula is connected to a vacuum source and inserted into the uterus. Once a vacuum is created the cannula is gently rotated for about 30 seconds and the contents of the uterus evacuated.

The evidence available indicates that early termination of pregnancy by MR produces fewer side effects, and has a much lower risk of complications in hospital than abortion by suction curettage (Savage 1979). Risk of failure (i.e. not terminating the pregnancy) is less than 1%. Because it is simple, safe and cheap, MR could become a more accessible and more acceptable method of fertility control than abortion as currently performed. According to Davis and Potts (1974) the majority of women who resent contraception and prefer to terminate a pregnancy are likely to accept MR. They speculate that if a woman relied entirely upon MR she would probably have to have it done twice a year on average. There is however some evidence pointing to the negative effects of the routine use of MR.

The most important aspect of MR is that it is a technique which is potentially accessible to women and can be used by them under their own control. In a number of countries it is already being used in self-help groups.[6] However the available evidence shows that it is mainly demanded by highly educated, middle class women (for example see Gallen (1979) who reports on the experience of the Philippines). MR is not well-known among women in general, and whether its use increases may well depend on women themselves as well as on legislative measures, which are different in various countries.[7] Practitioners are themselves divided about its use and while some continue to advocate it, others have completely abandoned it. In France literature on the subject is scarce and recourse to MR is recommended only in situations like rape (Leridon, 1980). Although I have found no evidence of the use of this technique in Yugoslavia, I believe that MR could be particularly suitable for Yugoslav women who, as was shown above, are unlikely to exchange their preference from abortion. However, I am aware that a number of obstacles may come from women themselves – they would for instance have to react immediately upon a missed period, which they seldom do now – and from the medical profession.

CONCLUSION

'Birth-control use is more a measure of women's increased self-esteem and sense of opportunity than a cause of it' (Gordon 1977 p.412).

Modern contraceptive techniques may well help some women to gain control over their bodies and their sexual relationships. For other women the same techniques may have the opposite effect and strengthen male supremacy and female inferiority and subordination. The liberating potential of any form of birth control lies not in the devices themselves but in the use made of them. Yugoslav women generally manage to have only the number of children they want. This does not, however, mean that their pregnancies are planned or that they have full control over their bodies. Rather they are still in a subordinate position in their relationship to their partner and they accept that they must bear the brunt of his irresponsibility. For women who adopt the idea that they should control their fertility, but for whom at the same time pregnancy is important for asserting their womanhood to themselves, their partners and others in the community, the knowledge that they can get pregnant is important. They are thus not very likely to seek an effective means of preventing conception until changes in their status and their relationship with the partner take place, and they themselves see contraception as the most suitable way to control their fertility.

As long as women view contraception as an intrusion into the most intimate and most precious aspect of their lives, they will continue to refuse to use it or will use it erratically. When pregnant they are very likely to opt for an abortion. In this article I have argued that it is wrong to believe that they do so because they are poor planners, irresponsible, irrational, uneducated, or badly informed. Yugoslav women have first to start asking themselves questions about their roles and their relationships with men. Being able to question age-old norms that regulate their own and their men's behaviour is a first step toward change. Migration may accelerate this process of questioning and consciousness raising, not only because it entails economic independence from men but because it frees women from the grip of a binding and watchful community of origin, the strongest obstacle to change. Those women capable of grasping that independence can also be expected to want to control their own bodies, their sexuality and their reproductive capacities. Only at this point and to those women can modern contraceptive techniques become useful tools in their struggle for further change. Until such time, they may well be labelled poor choosers; the point is however that they do not have a real choice.

NOTES

I would like to express my sincere thanks to Kate Young, Michele Fellous, Ljiljana White, Penny Kane, Sharon Weremiuk and Maila Stivens for their stimulating comments and criticisms on some of the earlier drafts of this article.

1. My survey was carried out in 1975-1976 and 258 women were interviewed. Of the total sample equal numbers lived in France and Germany (37% each) and the rest in Sweden. Half the women were between 20 and 29, just under a third between 30 and 39, and the rest were between 40 and 49. More than two-thirds of the women had lived abroad for between five and ten years.

2. From his study of 250 primitive societies Devereux (1976) concludes that abortion is a universal phenomenon; see also Gordon (1977).

3. Mosely defines the Zadruga as 'an outstanding institution of peasant life in the Balkans, a communal joint family . . . a household composed of two or more biological or small families, closely related by blood or by adoption, owning the means of production communally, producing and consuming the means of livelihood jointly and regulating the control of its property, labour and livelihood communally' (1976, p.19).

4. For comparison, in the industrialised countries of the west the ratio is 1 abortion per two to three births, exactly the reverse of the Yugoslavian figures (Leridon, 1980; Luker, 1975; Blayo, 1979).

5. Pride in the number of abortions undergone is also reported by Halpern & Halpern in Yugoslavia: ' . . . it seems to be a point of pride to relate the details and numbers of abortions one has sustained . . . ' (1972, p.104).

6. A personal communication from Sharon Weremiuk (San Diego), and Mouvement pour la libération de la contraception et de l'avortement, Paris.

7. In Great Britain MR is generally assimilated to abortion since under the Offences Against the Person Act of 1861 it is the intention to terminate pregnancy which must be lawful or unlawful (Savage, 1979). This means that whether or not there is a positive knowledge that pregnancy has occurred MR falls under the 1967 Abortion Act.

    In France MR is assimilated to any endouterine action and does not fall under the Loi Veil of 1975 (Information obtained from the Conseil Supérieur de l'Information Sexuelle de l'Education et de la Planification Familiale, Ministry of Health).

The Subordination of Women and the Internationalisation of Factory Production

Diane Elson and Ruth Pearson

Since the late 1960s a new type of wage employment has become available to women in many Third World countries: work in 'world market factories' producing manufactures exclusively for export to the rich countries (Hancock, 1980b). In these factories the vast majority of employees are usually young women between the age of fourteen and twenty-four or -five. While these women are only a small proportion of all young women in the Third World, and a minute proportion of all Third World women, theirs is an important case to study, because the provision of jobs for women is often seen as an important way of 'integrating women into the development process', a demand which emerged from the United Nations Conference of International Women's Year in 1975, under the tutelage of various international development agencies.

The idea that women's subordinate position stems from a lack of job opportunities, and can be ended by the provision of sufficient job opportunities, is deeply rooted and held by a wide spectrum of opinion, from international development agencies, government bureaux, mainstream Marxists to many women's organisations. Our work in the Workshop on the Subordination of Women in the process of development has lead us to reject this perspective as a starting point. We do not accept that the problem is one of women being left out of the development process. Rather, it is precisely the relations through which women are 'integrated' into the development process which need to be problematised and investigated. For such relations may well be part of the *problem*, rather than part of the *solution*. Our starting point, therefore, is the need to evaluate world market factories from the point of view of the new possibilities *and* the new problems which they raise for Third World women who work in them.

WORLD MARKET FACTORIES: THE LATEST PHASE OF THE INTERNATIONALISATION OF CAPITAL

World market factories represent a re-location of production of certain kinds of manufactured product from the developed countries, where they continue to be consumed, to the Third World.[1] These products are often classified into two groups, those using old established (or 'traditional') technologies, such as garments, textiles, sporting equipment, toys, soft goods, furniture, etc; and those using modern technologies, such as the electrical goods and electronics industries.

The stress on the modernity (or otherwise) of the technological base can, however, be misleading. For the sophisticated, highly knowledge-intensive processes which produce the technological base for something like the electronics industry remain located in a few developed countries, in particular Japan and USA. The parts of such an industry which are relocated to the Third World share many characteristics with world market factories based on old-established technologies: their production processes are standardised, repetitious, call for very little modern knowledge, and are highly labour intensive. In many cases the reason for the high labour-intensity is that the production processes are assembly-type operations which have proved difficult and/or costly to mechanise further.

SUBCONTRACTING FROM LARGE CORPORATIONS

World market factories typically produce on subcontract to the order of a particular overseas customer, and the customer arranges the marketing of the product. The world market factory may be owned by indigenous capitalists, or may be a wholly owned subsidiary of its overseas customer, or may be a joint venture of some kind between Third World businessmen and the overseas customer (Tang, 1980). World market factories producing components for the electronics industry are typically wholly or partially owned subsidiaries of Japanese, North American, or European, multinationals (Hancock, 1980a). Large multinational trading and retailing firms based in developed countries have been very important in the development of trade in final consumer goods from world market factories. Large US and European retailing firms, like Sears Roebuck, Marks and Spencer and C & A Modes, now place very large contracts with world market factories. In South East Asia the huge Japanese trading firms (such as Mitsubishi, Mitsui, Sumitomo), are very important customers of world market factories.

Some world market factories producing final consumer goods do no more than assemble together parts supplied by their customers. Typical cases are the sewing together of products like garments, gloves, and leather luggage, the design and cutting of the parts having been carried out in the developed country by the customer. For instance, trousers are cut out in Germany, then flown in air-containers to Tunisia, where they are sewn together, packed, and flown back for sale in Germany. In such cases, the world market factory is fully integrated in to the production process of the customer firm, even though in formal terms it may be independent. Through the provision of material inputs, or design capacity, or working capital, the customer may control the production process to the extent that though the supplier has formal autonomy, in practice the customer is operating a new and more sophisticated version of the 'putting-out' system. The transfer of the goods across national boundaries, though ostensibly organised through market sales and purchases, may in substance be a transfer between two departments of an integrated production process.

In some cases there is some scope for local initiative, a certain relative autonomy. The case of Hong Kong is a good example of the form that such relative autonomy might take: faced with import controls Hong Kong businessmen in the garment industry have successfully switched to new product lines, catering for the higher quality, rather than the cheaper end of the market. But in general the degree of autonomy enjoyed by world market factories is very limited. The fundamental reason for this is that they lack the means to develop new technologies.

LABOUR FORCE REQUIREMENTS OF WORLD MARKET FACTORIES

A critical factor in the location of world market factories is the availability of a suitable labour force. It must be a labour force which provides a ratio of output to costs of employment superior to that which prevails at existing centres of capital accumulation in the developed countries. And this superior ratio must be achieved *without* superior technology. It is by now well documented that this has been achieved in world market factories by a combination of much lower costs of employment, and matching or even higher productivity than that achieved in developed countries. Wages in world market factories are often ten times lower than in comparable factories in developed countries, while working hours per year are up to 50% higher. Additional costs, such as social security payments, fringe benefits and work clothing are also much lower. The US Tariff Commission found that productivity of workers in foreign establishments assembling or processing products of US origin generally approximates that of workers with the same job classification in the USA. Several other studies have reported instances of productivity substantially higher than in the USA. This is not being achieved through superior technology: it is the result of greater intensity of work, greater continuity of production; in short, greater control over the performance of the labour force.

This greater degree of control is facilitated by the measures which have been taken by Third World governments to suspend workers' rights in world market factories. Many Third World countries which in the past had enacted progressive labour legislation, often as a result of the contribution of trade union struggles to the fight against imperialism, have by now incorporated the official trade union organisation into the state apparatus; and either suspended, or failed to enforce, major provisions of that legislation. Workers in world market factories have been left exposed by the abrogation of their rights on such matters as minimum wage payments, contributions to insurance funds, limitations on the length of the working day and week, security of employment, redundancy conditions and payments, and the right to strike. Free Trade Zones[2] have particularly stringent controls on the activity of workers' organisations. But in some countries, particularly in South East Asia, the whole country is covered by such controls, and the power of the state is vigorously used to enforce them. It is ironic that in the name of improving the lives of the poorer groups in the Third World by creating more employment opportunities for them, many Third World governments have actively reduced the ability of the poor to protect themselves against the most blatant forms of exploitation. The situation of workers in world market factories cannot, however, be analysed simply in terms of class struggle and national struggle. It has also to be analysed in terms of gender struggle.

THE EMPLOYMENT OF WOMEN IN WORLD MARKET FACTORIES

Why is it young women who overwhelmingly constitute the labour force of world market factories? This question is more conspicuous by its absence in most of the studies done by economists (Lim, 1978, is a notable exception). Perhaps this is because the type of jobs done by women in world market factories in the Third World are also done by women in the First World. It might seem to follow that the labour force of world market factories is inevitably predominantly female because the jobs to be done are 'women's work'. But to note that jobs are sex-stereotyped is not to explain why this is so.

The reproduction in world market factories of the sexual division of labour typical in labour-intensive assembly operations in developed countries rests upon some differentiation of the labour force which makes it more profitable to employ female labour than male labour in these jobs. Female labour must either be cheaper to employ than comparable male labour; or have higher productivity; or some combination of both; the net result being that unit costs of production are lower with female labour. In general, the money costs of employing female labour in world market factories do seem to be lower than would be the money costs of employing men. Kreye found that women's wages in world market factories are in general 20%-50% lower than wages paid for men in comparable jobs (Fröbel, Heinrich, Kreye, 1980). Direct productivity comparisons between male and female workers are hard to make, since so few men are employed in comparable labour intensive assembly operations. In the few documented cases where men have been employed – in Malaysian electronics factories and Malawi textile factories – their productivity was in fact lower than that of women employed in the same plants. Firms running world market factories seem firmly convinced that this would generally be the case.

What produces this differentiation? The answers that companies give when asked why they employ women, as well as the statements made by governments trying to attract world market factories, show that there is a widespread belief that it is a 'natural' differentiation, produced by innate capacities and personality traits of women and men, and by an objective differentiation of their income needs, in that men need an income to support a family, while women do not. A good example is the following passage in a Malaysian investment brochure, designed to attract foreign firms:

'The manual dexterity of the oriental female is famous the world over. Her hands are small and she works fast with extreme care. Who, therefore, could be better qualified *by nature and inheritance* to contribute to the efficiency of a bench-assembly production line than the oriental girl (emphasis added).'

Women are considered not only to have naturally nimble fingers, but also to be naturally more docile and willing to accept tough work discipline, and naturally more suited to tedious, repetitious, monotonous work. Their lower wages are attributed to their secondary status in the labour market which is seen as a natural consequence of their capacity to bear children. The fact that only young women work in world market factories is also rationalised as an effect of their capacity to bear children – this naturally means they will be either unwilling or unable to continue in employment much beyond their early twenties. Indeed the phenomenon of women leaving employment in the factory when they get married or pregnant is known as 'natural wastage', and can be highly advantageous to firms which periodically need to vary the size of their labour force so as to adjust to fluctuating demand for their output in the world market. While we agree that there is a real differentiation between the characteristics of women and men as potential workers in world market factories, in our view it is far from being natural.

WHERE DO WOMEN GET THEIR SKILLS?

The famous 'nimble fingers' of young women are not an inheritance from their mothers, in the same way that they may inherit the colour of her skin or eyes. They are the result of the *training* they have received from their mothers and other female kin since early infancy in the tasks socially appropriate to woman's role. For instance, since industrial sewing of clothing closely resembles sewing with a domestic sewing machine, girls who have learnt such sewing at home already have the manual dexterity and capacity for spatial assessment required. Training in needlework and sewing also produces skills transferable to other assembly operations:

'... manual dexterity of a high order may be required in typical subcontracted operations, but nevertheless the operation is usually one that can be learned quickly on the basis of traditional skills. Thus in Morocco, in six weeks, girls (who may not be literate) are taught the assembly under magnification of memory planes for computers – this is virtually darning with copper wire, and sewing is a traditional Moroccan skill. In the electrical field the equivalent of sewing is putting together wiring harnesses; and in metalworking, one finds parallels in some forms of soldering and welding' (Sharpston, 1976, p.334).

It is partly because this training, like so many other female activities coming under the heading of domestic labour, is socially invisible, privatised, that the skills it produces are attributable to nature, and the jobs that make use of it are classified as 'unskilled' or 'semi-skilled'. Given that 'manual dexterity of a high order' is an admitted requirement for many of the assembly jobs done by women in world market factories, and that women working in the electronics industry have to pass aptitude tests with high scores, it is clear that the categorisation of these jobs as 'unskilled' does not derive from the purely *technical* characteristics of the job. The fact that the training period required within the factory is short, and that once this period is over workers do not take long to become highly proficient, does not detract from this conclusion. Little training and 'on the job' learning is required because the women are already trained:

> 'It takes six weeks to teach industrial garment making *to girls who already know how to sew*' (Sharpston, 1975, p.105, emphasis added).

In objective terms, it is more accurate to speak of the jobs making a demand for easily trained labour, than for unskilled labour. But of course, skill categories are not determined in a purely objective way (Braverman, 1974). In particular, jobs which are identified as 'women's work' tend to be classified as 'unskilled' or 'semi-skilled', whereas technically similar jobs identified as 'men's work' tend to be classified as 'skilled' (Phillips and Taylor, 1980). To a large extent, women do not do 'unskilled' jobs because they are the bearers of inferior labour; rather, the jobs they do are 'unskilled' because women enter them already determined as inferior bearers of labour.

WOMEN'S SUBORDINATION AS A GENDER

The social invisibility of the training that produces these skills of manual dexterity and the lack of social recognition for these skills is not accidental. It is intrinsic to the process of gender construction in the world today. For this is not simply a process of gender differentiation, producing two 'separate but equal' gender roles for women and men, any more than *apartheid* produces two 'separate but equal' roles for blacks and whites in South Africa. Rather it is a process of the *subordination* of women as a gender (Whitehead, 1979). This is not only an ideological process, taking place in the realm of attitudes and values. It is not just a matter of people ascribing lesser value to women's gender roles; of simply failing to see the contribution that women make; or of believing that it is only right and proper for women to accept a second place to men. Though ideology plays a role, we would argue that the subordination of women as a gender cannot be understood simply as a matter of 'patriarchal attitudes'. Rather it is a material process which goes on not just in our heads, but in our practices.

In claiming that it is a material process we do not intend to reduce it to an economic process, to be analysed only in terms of labour, but rather to emphasise that it cannot be changed simply through propaganda for more 'enlightened' views, but requires practical changes in daily living. We would suggest that this process of subordination of women as a gender can be understood in terms of the exclusion of women as a gender from certain activities, and their confinement to others; where the activities from which women as a gender are excluded are some of those which are constituted as public, overtly social activities, and the activities to which women as a gender are confined are some of those which are constituted as private, seemingly purely individual activities.

The constitution of activities as public or private, social or individual, of course differs over time, and between different kinds of society, and is itself a matter of struggle, not a pre-determined 'given'. The importance of activities in which the social aspect is dominant, which are overtly represented as social, is that these confer social power. This is not to say that *no* power is conferred by activities in which the private aspect is dominant: but in our view it is a mistake to see private power as co-equal with social power. Social power is collective power, reproducible through social processes, relatively autonomous from the characteristics of particular individuals. But private power is purely individual power, contingent as the specific characteristics of particular individuals, reproducible only by chance.

A distinction can usefully be made between relations which are *gender ascriptive*, that is, relations which are constructed intrinsically in terms of the gender of the persons concerned; and relations which are not gender ascriptive, but which can nevertheless be *bearers of gender* (Whitehead, 1979, p.11). An example of the first is the conjugal relation: marriage is a relation necessarily involving the unions of persons of definite and opposite gender; unions between persons of the same gender are not marriage. An example of the second is the sexual division of labour in the capitalist labour process. Though the capital-labour relation is not gender ascriptive, it is nevertheless a bearer of gender (Phillips and Taylor, 1980).

Gender ascriptive relations are clearly the fundamental sites of the subordination of women as a gender, and in them women's subordination may take a literally patriarchal form, with women directly subject to the authority of the father, their own or their children's. But male hegemony in gender ascriptive relations does not always assume a patriarchal form. Rather it is a matter of the extent to which women's social being can only be satisfactorily established through the mediation of a gender ascriptive relation, whereas the same is not true for men. This kind of gender subordination is not something which an individual woman can escape by virtue of choosing to avoid certain kinds of personal relation with men. For instance, it means that the *absence* of a husband is as significant as his presence for the establishment of a woman's social identity. As Elizabeth Phillips of the Jamaica Women's Bureau has pointed out: 'the apparent independence of women from men can be misleading: while women may not be directly subordinate to a particular member of their male kin, they are nonetheless subject to an overall culture of male dominance'. For women, unlike men, the question of gender is never absent.

BEHIND THE MIRAGE OF DOCILITY

It is in the context of the subordination of women as a gender that we must analyse the supposed docility, subservience and consequent suitability for tedious, monotonous work of young women in the Third World. In the conditions of their subordination as a gender, this is the appearance that women often present to men, particularly men in some definite relation of authority to them, such as father, husband, boss. A similar appearance, presented by colonised peoples to their colonisers, was brilliantly dissected by Fanon, who showed how the public passivity and fatalism which the colonised peoples displayed towards the colonisers for long periods concealed an inner, private, rebellion and subversion. But this passivity is not a natural and original state: to achieve it requires enormous efforts of self-repression. The 'native' is in a state of permanent tension, so that when he does resist it tends to be with a spontaneity and intensity all the stronger for having been so long pent-up, and hidden. Action, not negotiation, is the characteristic response (Fanon, 1969, p.48).

That self-repression is required for women to achieve an adequate level of docility and subservience can be demonstrated on an every day level by differences in their behaviour when authority figures are present and absent. An example is the behaviour observed by Heyzer (1978) in a world market factory producing textiles in Singapore. Here the women workers were always on guard when the supervisors were around, and displayed a characteristic subservience; but in the absence of supervisors behaviour changed. Far from displaying respectful subservience, workers mocked the supervisors and ridiculed them. Another indication that the 'private' behaviour of women workers in their peer group differs from their behaviour when outsiders are present, comes from the fact that some electronics factories on the Mexican border have introduced a few men on to production lines formerly exclusively the province of women, in the belief that this will improve the discipline and productivity of the women. The stress that such self-repression can impose and the 'non-rational' forms its relief may take is exemplified in the well-documented occurrence of outbreaks of mass hysteria among young women factory workers in South East Asia.

It is interesting that governments and companies are unwilling to trust completely the personal docility of women workers and feel a need to reinforce it with that suspension of a wide variety of workers' rights which is such a selling point of Free Trade Zones. Nevertheless, in spite of being faced with extensive use of state power to control labour unions and prevent strikes, women workers in world market factories have at times publically thrown off their docility and subservience and taken direct action, though their level of participation in trade unions is reported to be very low. There are indications that these struggles tend to erupt outside the official trade union framework, taking for instance, the form of 'wild cat' sitdowns or walk-outs, rather than being organised around official negotiations (Tang, 1980).

SECONDARY STATUS IN THE LABOUR MARKET

A major aspect of the gender differentiation of the labour force available for employment in world market factories is what is generally referred to in the literature as women's 'secondary status' in the labour market (Lim, 1978, p.11). The main aspects of this secondary status are that women's rates of pay tend to be lower than those of men doing similar or comparable jobs: and that women tend to form a 'reserve army' of labour, easily fired when firms want to cut back on their labour force, easily re-hired when firms want to expand again. This tends to be explained in terms of 'women's role in the family' or 'women's reproductive role'. In a sense this is true, but it is an ambiguous explanation, in that for many people 'women's role in the family', 'women's reproductive role' is an ahistorical fact, given by biology. What has to be stressed is that women's role in the family is socially constructed as a subordinated role – even if she is a 'female head of household'. For it is the female role to do the work which nurtures children and men, work which appears to be purely private and personal, while it is the male role to represent women and children in the wider society. And it is the representative role which confers social power.

This kind of gender subordination means that when a labour market develops, women, unlike men, are unable to take on fully the classic attributes of free wage labour. A man can become a free wage labourer

'in the double sense that as a free individual he can dispose his labour-power as his own commodity and that, on the other hand, he has no other commodity for sale ... he is free of all the objects needed for the realisation of his labour-power' (Marx, 1976, p.273).

A woman is never 'free' in this way. She has obligations of domestic labour, difficulties in establishing control over her own body, and an inability to be fully a member of society in her own right. She may also obtain her subsistence from men in exchange for personal services of a sexual or nurturing kind, thus realising her labour-power outside the capitalist labour process. It is this gender difference which gives women a 'secondary status' in the labour market. Our purpose is not to deny the social reality of this secondary status. But it is to take up a critical stance towards it, rather than view it as 'natural': nature does not compel the tasks of bringing up children to be the privatised responsibility of their mother while depriving her of the social power to secure, in her own right, access to the resources required for this, thus forcing her into a dependent position.

This secondary status arising from women's subordination as a gender, means that women workers are peculiarly vulnerable to super-exploitation, in the sense that their wages may not cover the full money costs of the reproduction of their labour-power, either on a daily or a generational basis. It also means that women tend to get lower wages than men, even when those wages contribute to the support of several other people, as do the wages of many of the young women who work in world market factories (or indeed of many women workers in developed countries). Sending a daughter to work in such a factory is in some cases the only remaining strategy for acquiring an income for the rest of the family.

THE INTERPLAY OF CAPITAL AND GENDER: THE LIMITS TO LIBERATION THROUGH FACTORY WORK

Ever since large numbers of women were drawn into factory work in the industrial revolution in 19th century England there has been a strong belief that wage work can liberate women from gender subordination. The fact that the social relations of factory work are not intrinsically gender ascriptive, but are rooted in an impersonal cash nexus, gives some plausibility to such views. For instance, it seems plausible that competition between women and men for jobs would tend to undermine any material basis for gender differentiation of the labour force in world market factories. If initially capitalists prefer to employ women because they can be paid low wages, can be trained quickly, and appear to accept easily the discipline of factory life, then surely high male unemployment will tend to undermine this preference as men are induced to accept the same wages and working conditions, to acquire the same attributes that make women employable, in order to get a job. The end result of such a process would be a labour force undifferentiated by gender, with women and men doing the same jobs, in the same conditions, for the same wages, modified only by personal preferences or prejudices for this or that kind of employment or employee. There would be no objective basis for gender differentiation.

But this argument fails to consider *how it is* that women have acquired the characteristics that make them initially the preferred labour force. If men are to compete successfully, they also need to acquire the 'nimble fingers' and 'docile dispositions' for which women workers are prized. But for this, they would require to undergo the same social experience as women. In order to compete successfully, men would need to experience gender subordination. But since men and women cannot *both* simultaneously experience gender subordination, this could only happen if women were to be freed from gender subordination; i.e. a reversal, rather than an elimination of gender differentiation. Competition between women and men in the labour market can tend to produce, in certain circumstances, signs of such a reversal (Engels, 1976, pp.173-174), provoking the traditionalist critique of women's participation in wage work as an overturning of the natural order of things. But these signs of the reversal of gender roles are themselves a demonstration of the fundamental interdependence of the labour force characteristics of women and men. Though, as competitors in the labour market, women and men may at first appear as atomised individuals, they are never so completely separated. They are always linked through gender ascriptive relations, and their labour market relations become bearers of gender. The important point about the development of capitalism is that it does offer a form of interdependence – the cash nexus – which is not gender ascriptive. But though capitalist production is dominated by the cash nexus, in the sense that it must be organised to make a profit, it cannot be organised solely through cash relations (through wages and prices) but requires a specific hierarchical managerial organisation: the capitalist labour process. It has to be organised through the giving of orders, as well as the making of payments. It is because of this that capitalist production may be a bearer of gender, though it is not intrinsically gender ascriptive (Phillips and Taylor, 1980; Whitehead, 1979). Typically, the giving of orders in the capitalist labour process is defined as a male prerogative, while the role of women is defined as the carrying out of orders.

Another intrinsic limit is that the socialisation of the reproduction of labour-power cannot be accomplished completely through the cash nexus. A great deal of the labour required to provide the goods and services needed for the reproduction of labour power quite clearly can be socialised through the cash nexus. The monetisation of labour processes formerly carried out domestically, and socialised through the gender ascriptive relations of marriage, is one of the hallmarks of capital accumulation (Braverman, 1974, chp. 13). But the establishment of the social identity of children, their social integration, cannot be accomplished solely through the cash nexus. One implication of this is that the *de facto* position of women workers as major contributors to the family income does not automatically mean that they will become socially recognised as 'breadwinners', their secondary status in the labour market ended. For the position of breadwinner is not constituted purely at the economic level: it is also constituted in the process of establishing the connection of the family with the wider society. The breadwinner must be also the public representative of the family. Whitehead (1978), suggests that the wage itself, though clearly not a gender ascriptive form, tends to become a bearer of gender, in the sense that wages of male and female family members are not treated as interchangeable, but are earmarked for different things.

The recognition of this limitation does not mean that we must therefore deny capitalism *any* liberating potential: the alternative, cash-based, forms of socialisation it entails do tend to undermine and disrupt other forms of socialisation, including the gender ascriptive relations which are fundamental to the subordination of women as a gender. In this way they provide a material basis for struggle against the subordination of women as a gender. But there is no way that capitalist exploitation of women as wage workers can simply *replace* gender subordination of women. Indeed, the capitalist exploitation of women as wage workers is parasitic upon their subordination as a gender.

THE DIALECTIC OF CAPITAL AND GENDER

We would like to distinguish three tendencies in the relation between factory work and the subordination of women as a gender: a tendency to *intensify* the existing forms of gender subordination; a tendency to *decompose* existing forms of gender subordination; and a tendency to *recompose* new forms of gender subordination. We are not suggesting that these are mutually exclusive tendencies – any specific situation might well show signs of all three. They are, moreover, not categories which can be aggregated to produce a uni-dimensional conclusion that the position of women is getting worse or better. Rather, they are suggested as ways of analysing particular conjunctions of forces shaping women's lives, in the hope that this will help clarify the strategic possibilities facing women in those situations.

There is evidence of all three tendencies at work in the case of women employed in world market factories. One example of the way existing forms of gender subordination may be *intensified* is the case of a multi-national corporation operating in Malaysia which believes in deliberately trying to preserve and utilise traditional forms of patriarchal power. Instead of undermining the father's authority over the daughter by encouraging 'modern', 'Western' behaviour, it pursues a policy of reinforcement:

'the company has installed prayer rooms in the factory itself, does not have modern uniforms but lets the girls wear their traditional attire, and enforces a strict and rigid discipline in the work place' (Lim, 1978, p.37).

The enhanced economic value of daughters certainly provides a motive for fathers to exert more control, including sending them to work in the factories whether they wish to or not. On the other hand, the ability to earn a wage may be an important factor in undermining certain forms of control of fathers and brothers over young women, an advantage which has been mentioned frequently by Malaysian women working in world market factories. However, this does not mean that there is a reversal of the authority structure of the family. There is considerable empirical evidence that their wages do not confer greater status or decision-making power on the women, even though they may be the chief source of family income.

As an example of the way existing forms of gender subordination may be *decomposed*, we can cite Blake's observation (1979) of the importance of factory work as a way of escaping an early arranged marriage in some Asian countries. But the ability to resist arranged marriage and opt for 'free-choice' marriage is two-edged. In the conditions of a society dominated by the capitalist mode of production, 'free-choice' marriage tends to take on the characteristics of the dominant form of choice in such societies, a *market* choice from among competing commodities. And it is women themselves who take on many of the attributes of the competing commodities, while it is men who exercise the choice. This tendency towards the recomposition of a specifically capitalist, 'commoditised' form of making marriages is actively encouraged by the management styles of some of the large American multi-national electronics companies which provide lessons in fashion and 'beauty care' and organise beauty contests and Western-style dances and social functions for their employees. This is rationalised as the provision of fringe benefits which naturally appeal to the 'feminine interests' of the young women workers. Such interests are indeed 'feminine' in a situation where many young women are competing in a marriage market hoping to attract a husband. But they stem not from the eternal structure of the feminine psyche, but from concrete material conditions in which a young woman's face may be quite literally her fortune.

Though one form of gender subordination, the subordination of daughters to their fathers, may visibly crumble, another form of gender subordination, that of women employees to male factory bosses, just as visibly is built up. Work in world market factories is organised through a formal hierarchy with ordinary operators at the bottom controlled by varying levels of supervisors and managers. In study after study the same pattern is revealed: the young female employees are almost exclusively at the bottom of this hierarchy; the upper levels of the hierarchy are almost invariably male. Only in the lowest level of supervisors is it at all common to find women. The relationship of female employees to male bosses is qualitatively different from the relationship of male employees to male bosses. One important feature is that the sexual element in the relation between female employee and male boss is not contained and shaped by kin relations. This is one of the reasons why factory girls are often regarded as not quite 'respectable'. In some cases sexual exploitation is quite widespread – in the Masan Free Export Zone in South Korea, for example, numerous instances have occurred of sexual abuse of women employees by Japanese supervisors.

This *recomposition* of a new form of gender subordination in which young women are subject to the authority of men who are not in any family relation to them can also have the effect of intensifying more traditional forms of gender subordination of wives to husbands. The fact that if his wife works in a factory she will be subject to the authority of other men maybe a powerful reason for a husband wishing to confine his wife to the home. Husbands' dislike of their wives working in factories is mentioned by Lim (1978) as one of the reasons why so few married women are employed in world market factories in Malaysia.

INSTABILITY OF EMPLOYMENT

But the problem is not simply that young women may, through factory work, escape the domination of fathers and brothers only to become subordinate to male managers and supervisors, or escape the domination of managers and supervisors only to become subordinate to husbands or lovers. There is also the problem that the domination of managers and supervisors may be withdrawn – the woman may be sacked from her job – while the woman is without the 'protection' of subordination to father, brother, husband.[3] She may be left dependent on the cash nexus for survival, but unable to realise her labour power in cash terms through working in the factory.

This problem is particularly acute for women who work in world market factories. Some change in some distant, unknown part of the world may at any moment undercut their position, leaving their product and their labour power without a market. The recession in world demand in 1974 provoked massive cut-backs in employment in many world market factories: for instance about one-third of all electronics workers in Singapore lost their jobs (Grossman, 1979, p.10). Moreover, there is still a possibility of a resurgence of competition from firms located in developed countries. The very success of world market factories has made them vulnerable to retaliation. So far this has mainly taken the form of the growth of restrictions on imports of manufactures, particularly of consumer goods like textiles, garments and shoes. More recently there have been signs of fresh attempts to revolutionise the production process in developed countries, to eliminate the advantage which cheap labour gives to world market factories in the production of labour intensive goods. At the request of the European Clothing Manufactures Federation, the Commission of the EEC is to fund a research programme on ways of automating garment making. The fact that the mass of capital continues to be accumulated in developed countries means that market demand, and technical know-how and finance continue to be concentrated there, so that world market factories, representing relatively small dispersions of capital accumulation, are inherently vulnerable to changes in the conditions of accumulation in developed countries.

The hiring and firing practices of particular firms do, however, add to the inherent precariousness and instability of employment in world market factories. The preference of firms for young workers means that workers in their early twenties who have not yet left voluntarily are the first to be dismissed if it is necessary to retrench the labour force. Pregnancy is often grounds for dismissal. Or women are dismissed on the grounds that they can no longer meet productivity or time-keeping norms. A deterioration in performance is, in fact, often the result of some disability caused by the work itself. Women employed in the garment industry on the Mexican Border tend to suffer from kidney complaints and varicose veins. Women using microscopes every day in the electronics industry suffer eye-strain and their eyesight deteriorates. The shift work which is common in electronics and textile factories can produce continual fatigue, headaches, and general deterioration of health. The net result is that it is quite often workers who have already acquired new consumption patterns, responsibilities, and in many cases, debts, who lose their jobs, rather than those who have just entered factory life.

If a woman loses her job in a world market factory after she has re-shaped her life on the basis of a wage income, the only way she may have of surviving is by selling her body. There are reports from South Korea, for instance, that many former electronics workers have no alternative but to become prostitutes (Grossman, 1979, p.16). A growing market for such services is provided by the way in which the tourist industry has been developed, especially in South East Asia.

Our conclusions may be summarised as follows: there are inherent limits to the extent to which the provision of wage work for women through capitalist accumulation can dissolve the subordination of women as a gender. Rather than ending such subordination, entry into wage work tends to transform it. While there is a tendency for the decomposition of some existing forms of gender subordination, such as the control of fathers and brothers over the life-styles of young women, there is also a tendency to the recomposition of new forms of gender subordination, both through the recomposition of gender ascriptive relations in new forms, and through relations which are not intrinsically gendered becoming bearers of gender. Indeed, the decomposition tendency itself helps to strengthen the recomposition tendency. For the former, while it brings independence, of a sort, also brings vulnerability. This is particularly true when, as is the case with world market factory employees, this tendency affects only a small proportion of the relevant age cohort, and an even smaller proportion of the total female population of the society concerned. As an insurance against this vulnerability, individual women may often have little choice but to actively accept, indeed seek, the 'protection' of new forms of gender subordination.

WHAT CAN WOMEN DO?

Official reports about the problems of women in the Third World usually end with a list of policy recommendations which various official bodies should implement, acting 'in the interests' of women. But we orient our discussion of action around the concept of 'struggle' rather than around the concept of 'policy'. It is not that we see no role for official state agencies, whether national or international, in the process of action, but rather that our orientation towards them is to ask, not what *solutions* should they offer women, but how can women use them for purposes women have determined. For we take the most fundamental objective of action to be the development of women's capacity for self-determination.

In our view the development of world market factories does, in itself, provide a material basis for a process of struggle for self-determination. The most fundamental way in which it does this is by bringing together large numbers of women and confronting them with a common, cash-based, authority: the authority of capital. This is not the effect of most alternative forms of work for young Third World women, such as unremunerated labour in the family, or work in the 'informal sector' in petty services or 'out-work', or work as domestic servants (Blake, 1979, p.11). In these other cases women tend to be more physically isolated from one another; or are confronted with a different, more personalised form of authority; or relate to one another not as members of the same gender or class, but as members of particular households, kin groups etc.

STRUGGLE AS WORKERS

The most obvious possibility for struggle which this suggests is a struggle as *workers* around such issues as wages and conditions of work. It is therefore, at first sight, disappointing to find a low level of formal participation in trade union activities by women employed in world market factories; and evidence that in many cases they do not identify themselves as workers, or develop 'trade union consciousness' (Cardosa-Khoo & Khoo Kay Jin, 1978; Tang, 1980) – though there are exceptions (Blake and Moonstan, 1981). But we need to bear in mind both the *limitations*, as well as the possibilities, of factory-based struggle about work-related issues, and the *shortcomings* of official trade union organisations in many parts of the world.

The basic limitation in the ability of workers, no matter how well-organised, to secure improvements in pay and conditions of work, is set by the fact that control over the means of production lies ultimately with management, and not with the workforce. The limits within which workers in world market factories are confined are particularly narrow because of the ease with which the operations carried out in them might be relocated, and because the management so often enjoys the backing of particularly coercive forms of state power.

The ability to secure improvements tends to be very much conditioned by particular rates of accumulation at particular localities. It is noticeable that it is in countries like Hong Kong and Singapore where the rate of investment has been high that wage rates in world market factories have tended to rise. A higher proportion of married, and older, women tends to be found in world market factories in these countries, symptomatic of a tighter labour market.

Besides the rate of accumulation, another important consideration is the extent to which other social groups will support workers in particular factories in campaigns for better pay and conditions of work. In the case of women working in world market factories such support within their own countries is likely to come mainly from either professional and technical elite groups, or from religious organisations. There is a material basis for the support of the first group in the fact that the pay and conditions of employment in world market factories so often offend the sense of justice and fairness encouraged by other aspects of the development of capitalism, rooted in the equalising and liberalising aspect of the market economy. Unfortunately such support tends to be limited: while many members of professional and technical elite groups are willing to support the workers' right to a fair day's pay for a fair day's work, they are not so willing to face all the implications of genuine self-determination for workers, including the workers' right to control the means of production. The support offered by religious groups can often be in many ways more radical, because it tends to draw on a different set of values, rooted in a more organic vision of society. Such groups, in some countries, have become very involved in the struggle of workers in world market factories. However, from the point of view of women, such support may be particularly double-edged, because religious values tend so often to encourage the subordination of women as a gender. However, no matter how effective and far reaching the support given by religious or other groups to the workforce, the struggle for better pay and conditions of work remains contradictory. To a considerable extent, the success of the workforce in this struggle is predicated upon the success of management in making profits.

The main lesson we would draw from this is that struggle at the level of the factory cannot be judged solely in terms of its effect on pay and conditions of work. It has to be judged not simply as an instrument for making economic gains, but as a way of developing the capacities of those involved in it, particularly the capacity for self-organisation. In this context, participation in collective action in the factory itself, even of a sporadic and spontaneous character, is more important than purely formal membership of a trade union. It also helps factory workers to understand the world-wide structure of the forces which shape their lives, and helps prepare them for struggle, not just in the factory where they work, but against the economic system of which it is a part.

Struggles arising from the development of world market factories will, however, remain seriously deficient from the point of view of *women* workers if they deal only with economic questions of pay and working conditions, and fail to take up other problems which stem from the recomposition of new forms of the subordination of women as a gender. Many of these problems present themselves as a series of 'personal', 'individual' difficulties: how to attract a husband or lover; how to deal with the contradictions of female sexuality – to express one's sexuality without becoming a sex-object; how to cope with pregnancy and child care (Blake, 1979, p.12). The concern of women workers with these problems is not a sign that they are 'backward' in consciousness as compared with male workers, but that for women, it is gender subord-ination which is primary, capitalist exploitation secondary and deriva-tive. This is not to say that women spontaneously recognise that their 'personal' problems are reflections of their subordination as a gender. If social relations were so transparent there would be little need to write essays like this, or to consciously analyse women's position and plan and organise struggle.

The forms that workers' organisations have traditionally taken have been inadequate for women's point of view because they have failed to recognise and build into their structure the specificity of gender. Trade unions, for instance, have been organised to represent 'the worker', political parties to represent 'the working class'. The failure to take account of gender means that in practice they have tended to represent *male* workers. Working women have tended to be represented only through their dependence on male workers. In addition, the specific problems that concern women as a subordinated gender are often prob-lems which it is not easy for conventional forms of trade union or work-ing class political activity to tackle. New forms of organisation are required that will specifically take up these problems, offering both practical, immediate action on them, and also revealing the social roots of what at first sight appear to be a series of individual, personal prob-lems whose only common denominator lies in the supposed 'natural' propensities and capacities of women as a sex.

The employment of women in world market factories does provide a material basis for 'politicising the personal' because of the way it masses together women not simply as workers but as a gender. Women are brought together in the factory, not by virtue of being the daughter of this man, the mother of that; the sister of this, the wife of that; but simply by virtue of being women, of having the characteristics of a subordinated gender. In factory employment, women are abstracted out of particularised gender ascriptive relations.

A practical reality is given to the concept of women as a gender in the same way that a practical reality is given to the concept of labour in general (Marx, 1973, pp.103-105). This creates a basis for the struggle of women factory workers as members of a *gender*, as well as members of a *class*. This is not to say that such struggle will automatically take place – it will only happen if new forms of organisation are consciously built. To some extent this is already happening. Women workers in various parts of the Third World have formed sector based organisations which link women in different factories operating in the same industry, and 'off-site' organisations to tackle issues like housing, education and sanitation, which remain the responsibility of women.

Of course, limitations and contradictions similar to those discussed in the case of activity to improve pay and working conditions in the factory beset the struggle to ameliorate other aspects of women workers' lives especially those in the so-called 'personal' domain. Just as a limit is set to the former by capitalists' class monopoly of the means of production, so a limit is set to the latter by men's gender monopoly of the means of establishing social being, social presence. Accordingly women's struggle as a gender should not be judged in purely instrumental terms, as achieving this or that improvement in the position of women; but should be judged in terms of the way that the struggle itself develops capacities for self determination. The development of conscious co-operation and solidarity between women on the basis of recognition of their common experience of gender subordination is even more important a goal than any particular improvement in the provision of jobs or welfare services to women, than any particular reform of legal status, than any particular weakening of 'machismo' or 'patriarchal attitudes'. Improvements which come about through capital accumulation or state policy or changing male attitudes can be reversed. Lasting gains depend upon the relationships built up between women themselves.

This is the point that needs impressing upon all those policy advisers, policy makers, policy implementers, at national and international levels, who wish to 'include women in development', 'enhance the status of women' etc. The single most important requirement, the single most important way of helping, is to make resources and information available to organisations and activities which are based on an explicit recognition of gender subordination, and are trying to develop new forms of association through which women can begin to establish elements of a social identity in their own right, and not through the mediation of men. Such organisations do not require policy advisers to tell them what to do, supervise them and monitor them; they require access to resources, and protection from the almost inevitable onslaughts of those who have a vested interest in maintaining both the exploitation of women as workers, and the subordination of women as a gender. The most important task of sympathetic personnel in national and international state agencies is to work out how they can facilitate access to such resources and afford such protection – not how they can deliver a package of readymade 'improvements' wrapped up as a 'women's programme'.

NOTES

For their helpful comments in the preparation of this paper, we should like to thank: the members of the Workshop on the Subordination of Women, Institute of Development Studies, University of Sussex; the participants in the international conference on the Continuing Subordination of Women in the Development Process, IDS, September 1978; the participants in the IDS Study Seminar on Women and Social Production in the Caribbean, held in Puerto Rico, June-July 1980; and members of the Editorial Collective of *Feminist Review*.

1. The forces underlying the process of relocation are discussed in greater detail in Elson and Pearson, 1980, and Elson and Pearson, 1981.
2. Free Trade Zones are special areas which are exempt from normal import and export regulations, and also from many other kinds of regulation, such as protective labour legislation and tax laws.
3. It may seem paradoxical to talk of the protection afforded by subordination, but the paradox lies in the social relations themselves. When the social identity of women has to be established through their relation with men, the absence of father, brother, or husband, is often disadvantageous.

Women in Socialist Societies
Problems of Theory and Practice

Maxine Molyneux

It has long been the claim of socialist parties and governments that they, and they alone, can bring about the full emancipation of women. They maintain that the abolition of inequality along lines of sex can only be achieved as part of the broader socialist transformation of society through which divisions along class lines will also be abolished. Yet the persistence of sexual inequality in socialist countries is now widely acknowledged, and at the same time appears to challenge the theoretical linkage upon which the unity of socialism and women's emancipation has supposedly rested.

While it may be difficult to establish a 'necessary unity' between socialism and feminism, (especially in the absence of clear definitions of either term) and while actually existing socialist states have not eradicated sexual inequality, they have promoted substantial improvements in the position of women. Although this falls far short of full emancipation, the fact remains that these states have implemented many of the measures which feminists in both East and West have been demanding for many years.[1] In socialist states the existence of progressive legislation and egalitarian policies can be understood as the effect of both principle and necessity. There are on the one hand a range of practical considerations which arise out of the economic and social transformations that these states bring about in order to promote economic development. Many of these entail some improvement in the position of women as a necessary part of this process. On the other hand there is the influence of socialist theory and ideology with its historical commitment to, and emphasis on, the need to emancipate women as part of its general endorsement of social equality. Socialist doctrine can therefore be seen to have a certain effectivity on state policies relating to women and to the extent that these have promoted sexual equality in certain spheres it is possible to understand how socialism and feminism may claim an association, however qualified.

If it is the combination of principle and necessity which promotes sexual equality in socialist states, the unevenness of the record of achievement reflects this uneasy alliance. Despite the progress that has been made, sexual inequality persists in these countries and requires some explanation. The official view, that it is a survival of 'past' social relations may contain an element of truth as far as some of the more recently established socialist states are concerned, but it is less persuasive when applied to the long-established states of Eastern Europe. But on its own this is not, nor can it be, an adequate explanation, for it fails to recognise that specific social mechanisms and practices continue to exist through which these inequalities are reproduced. They will not therefore simply wither away in the due course of time. Moreover, certain of these inequalities are inscribed within state policies themselves and are linked into the mode of economic and political organisation of actually existing socialist states. As a result the effects of the socialist programme on women are contradictory and allow of neither wholesale approval nor impatient dismissal. It is this combination of positive and negative, emancipation and continued subordination which forms the subject of the following discussion.

In attempting to assess the record of socialist states in transforming gender relations this discussion aims to complement the debate that has already begun on the industrialised societies of Eastern Europe, by focussing on their Third World counterparts.[2] These are all too often neglected in overall assessments of the record of socialist states in improving the position of women; by incorporating their experiences into the discussion some of the fundamental issues can be posed more sharply. Moreover, a comparative overview, one which spans the advanced and Third World countries is useful not only because it facilitates contrast with capitalist states at different levels of development, but also because the policies of the less developed socialist states tend to mirror those of their more developed counterparts. Without a comparative dimension the striking degree of uniformity in matters of policy between the two types of post-revolutionary regime is easily overlooked.[3]

Before proceeding to discuss the record of these countries, a brief clarification should be made about the use of the term 'socialist' in this text. There is a large and contentious literature on how to define socialism and on how far any one definition can be applied to existing post-revolutionary societies. This is not a matter that can be clarified here and a working definition must suffice. We can begin by making the conventional distinction between socialism and communism. Whereas the former denotes a transitional form of society combining elements of different relations of production, the latter entails communal possession of the means of production, effective re-distribution of the economic surplus and popular democratic forms of control both at the general political level and at the level of the enterprise. [4] Clearly, the societies considered here fall into the former category and can be considered socialist only insofar as they have succeeded in realising part of the socialist transformation, and even this to varying degrees. Where the term 'socialist' is used in this article to describe the policies of the post-revolutionary societies, it is employed in the restricted sense to refer to those countries which are characterised by: i. an expressed commitment to constructing a socialist society; ii. an espousal of what they call 'scientific socialism' and what they understand to be the principles of Marxism and Leninism; iii. a high level of social redistribution; iv. the adoption of policies which have in the main succeeded in abolishing private appropriation and private ownership of the means of production, these latter relations being replaced by state regulation of both production and distribution according to the principle of planned economic development.

In these post-revolutionary societies a double process is taking place: there is on the one hand a destructive process, in which pre-capitalist and capitalist relations of production are progressively transformed and the power of the previous ruling classes is destroyed; on the other hand, this transformation is also characterised by a constructive process involving the introduction, extension and consolidation of new social relations and the establishment of a new form of state. How far these processes are realised depends on the nature of the formation concerned and on the level of class struggle within it. And while these post-revolutionary societies may be termed transitional, there is nothing in the nature of the transition itself which ensures that the ultimate outcome will be a communist society. Although a transition from capitalism may have occurred, the process may be arrested or reversed; alternatively, social relations may be established which cannot be assimilated into any of the existing concepts of socio-economic organisation. But even if these societies can be defined as socialist in this qualified sense, as presently constituted they are all marked by an additional, contingent limitation, namely the absence of any genuine political democracy to complement the transformations of the socio-economic sphere. There has therefore occurred a socialisation of the economy but not of political power. Despite this major limitation, these societies do exhibit some of the main features characteristic of the socialist transition, and while they retain certain features of capitalist society, they are qualitatively distinct from capitalism in their mode of social and economic organisation.

The uneven nature of the transition means that even at best, the process of social emancipation is likely to be of an incomplete and limited nature. Whilst it is necessary to avoid an apologetic explanation, attributing all forms of failure to this factor, it is evident that it plays a certain role, especially in cases where the combined effects of class resistance, conservative ideologies and the limited development of the productive forces act as a brake on all social programmes, including that of women's emancipation. Moreover, however the latter is defined it is even more problematic in post-revolutionary societies if women's oppression is to any degree attributed to the workings of the unconscious. For psychological forces not only have some independence from social factors, but they also fall under a differential temporality that may enable the social factors to have an effectivity long after the actual social conditions that helped produce them have been eroded. It will therefore be many generations after the pre-revolutionary social system has been abolished before its influence mediated via the unconscious, has ceased to take its toll. All of these considerations therefore, indicate objective and subjective limits on the process of emancipating women under socialism. They should be taken into account, not to indulge the failures of post-revolutionary societies, but rather to identify more precisely that realm of freedom within which the emancipatory process in such societies can take place.

THE THIRD WORLD

In the Third World, the realm of freedom is even more limited than in Russia and Eastern Europe. Third World revolutionary governments have come to power through combining anti-imperialist and anti-capitalist struggles in societies facing severe problems of poverty and under-development in both the economy and civil society. In most of these societies the transition to capitalism, although under way, was still at an early stage, and even today pre-capitalist relations of production and ideologies survive in the rural areas of some post-revolutionary societies. In addition to these problems many countries were devastated by war, as in the case of Vietnam, or suffered from the effects of economic blockade, as in Cuba.

When they come to power these governments face a formidable set of tasks for which they have the most meagre resources of capital, technology and skilled personnel. These tasks include developing the country's productive capacity; dismantling pre-capitalist as well as capitalist social relations; unifying an often backward and fragmented society; transforming political and juridical structures and providing the population with such welfare benefits as can be afforded. Any critique of the record of such societies in emancipating women, especially given the difficulties encountered in materially much better endowed societies, must take this background of dire scarcity into account.

This context has very direct implications for women beyond those caused by the overall shortage of resources. In the first place the prioritising of economic development, although urgent and necessary in the immediate post-revolutionary period, does make the achievement of other socialist goals, among them complete sexual equality, dependent on the success of the development strategy. In many cases this has led to the routinisation of what may be termed a productivist bias in state policies and to the indefinite postponement of the time when energies may be directed at achieving a greater fulfilment of the socialist programme. In other words, what is initially justified as short-term expediency gradually becomes an integral part of state policy.

However, whilst this productivist bias has negative effects on the position of women, it also has positive ones, especially in the immediate post-revolutionary period. For it is at this point in the transformation process that developmental goals are most closely aligned to the commitment to improving the position of women. Socialist states are committed to promoting social change as a means of accelerating and complementing the transformations in the economic sphere. These changes are of three kinds: the fulfilment of the welfarist aims of the state by providing housing, and health facilities; the mobilisation of an adequate supply of labour to meet the growing requirements generated by government policies; and the dismantling of the previous social order. All of these can directly or indirectly improve the position of women, but in the poorer, less developed countries it is the latter – dismantling the old social order – which has the most profound implications for women.

Socialist states attempt to promote the rapid transformation of what they term traditional or feudal relations on the grounds that these constitute obstacles to economic development and social reform. The previous social order and its legal, political and religious systems must be progressively replaced by a new centralised, secular and more egalitarian society. This process of erosion or transformation affects the position of women to the extent that it involves attacking some of the social relations and institutions within which their subordination is inscribed. The pre-capitalist patriarchal family is the site of many of these practices and it therefore constitutes a primary object of revolutionary reform. Institutions such as polygyny, the brideprice, child marriages and female seclusion are woven into the very fabric of pre-capitalist formations, and some of these practices may even form part of their general reproduction. Without endorsing a reductionist account of these phenomena it is clear that systems of inheritance which discriminate against women, and the strict control of marriage alliances by kin groups, may be central means by which forms of pre-capitalist property and social relations are maintained. Thus, the dismantling of structures that form an integral part of the pre-capitalist order can significantly improve the position of women; conversely, improving the position of women is seen by reforming governments as a key to dismantling the pre-capitalist social structure.[5]

These reforms generally involve a four-pronged attack on male supremacy over women, pre-capitalist property, the patriarchal family and religious orthodoxy. Not surprisingly, they have provoked considerable resistance in many countries, and if such policies are to be successfully implemented, socialist states must proceed with caution. Where they have tried to force a too rapid transformation of women's position without providing adequate support structures to help women make this radical transition, the results have been disastrous. Evidence from both Soviet Central Asia in the 1920s and China after 1949 shows that many thousands of women committed suicide or were murdered by their families for claiming their new rights; many more paid a heavy price in prolonged personal suffering for attempting to defy their families and elders (Massell, 1974; Croll, 1978).

Reform becomes even more problematic where religious doctrine and beliefs sustain sexual inequalities. In Islamic societies the extension to women of rights previously enjoyed only by men can be interpreted as an affront to Koranic principles, and this reaction, which cannot simply be seen in class terms but has a definite and irreducible religious component, may form part of a much wider counter-revolutionary response.[6]

SOCIALISM AND CAPITALISM COMPARED

These then are some of the objective constraints upon improving the position of women in the Third World. Yet even within this circumscribed realm of possibility the record of socialist states, both developed and developing, can be criticised on several important points. But before proceeding to such a critique, it is necessary to register the substantial differences that separate the record of socialist from capitalist countries in the realm of women's emancipation. These can, in a schematic way, be tabulated as follows:

1. In socialist states official ideology places considerable emphasis on the need to liberate women from the oppression they suffered under the pre-revolutionary order. This is announced in the programme of revolutionary parties, and the policies and constitutions of post-revolutionary states have always recognised women's oppression as a social and political problem requiring official intervention. By contrast, in many capitalist countries measures to improve women's position were taken only after a prolonged struggle by women and their allies to secure enfranchisement and other democratic rights. It was therefore not without some justified pride that Lenin could note in 1919 that Russia was ahead of the world in according equal rights to women and in easing the burdens that women had traditionally borne. And in the Third World today it is the socialist societies that have the greatest official commitment to bringing about sexual equality. Of course, the value of this commitment should not be overstated, but nor should it be seen as irrelevant. It influences government policy and as an official ideology it creates expectations which may induce pressure to see them fulfilled.

Socialist states therefore, move rapidly and decisively to terminate the more extreme forms of exploitation of women. Nowhere is this difference between capitalist and socialist Third World societies clearer than in the case of Muslim societies where in the contemporary capitalist versions, and in the self-designated 'Islamic socialisms' such as those of

Algeria, Libya and Somalia, traditional oppression of women continues, with polygyny, veiling, child marriage, and the seclusion of women from public life. By contrast, state policies in Soviet Central Asia, Afghanistan, and South Yemen have been consistently directed at discouraging such practices. Whilst women's employment under socialism remains subject to gender-typing, the most onerous forms of economic exploitation of women, through unpaid family labour in the fields and sweatshops, have been substantially reduced if not eradicated completely.[7] Some prostitution does survive in socialist countries, but not on the mass, flourishing scale on which it is to be found in advanced and Third World capitalist countries. The capitalist countries tolerate and even promote many of these discriminatory practices; the socialist countries try, with varying degrees of success, to hasten their disappearance.

2. Under socialism, women are encouraged to see their entry into the labour force as a *normal expectation for all active women*, and indeed as a duty to the state and to their families. The spheres of home and employment are not regarded as incompatible and in official representations, women are defined not only as domestic workers and mothers but also as wage labourers. Whilst men's wages in socialist countries are generally higher than women's, they are not considered sufficient to provide a family with an acceptable standard of living. The available evidence suggests that in order to secure this level of income both men and women are obliged to become wage earners (Heitlinger, 1979; Jancar, 1978). The 'family wage' and the full-time housewife are therefore not characteristic features of socialist societies.

3. The regulation of wage levels is linked to the commitment to maintain full employment, something that provides a further contrast with capitalist states and which has direct implications for the position of women. Whereas in the latter, women may form a large part of the reserve army of labour, socialist states have so far attempted to maintain high employment levels and this has involved actively promoting women's employment, and directing the supply of labour in accordance with the goal of economic development. The policy of moving women out of the home and into public employment is certainly influenced by such factors as capital scarcity, the restricted level of development of the productive forces, and the refusal to draw on foreign labour reserves, but these combine with a definite political commitment to mobilising women derived from the belief that this is the key to their emancipation.

Principle and practical necessity have, therefore, combined to produce a distinctive socialist policy in this regard.

4. A final difference is that socialist states accept a greater responsibility for the reproduction of labour-power and for social welfare generally than is the case under capitalism, e.g. the provision of support structures for maternity and childcare, free health care and education, housing and welfare benefits generally. However insufficient some of these may still be, especially in the rural areas, the fact remains that major advances have been made in this direction resulting in the improvement in the basic conditions of existence of the populations of socialist states – most demonstrably of those in the Third World where there is a marked contrast between the pre- and post-revolutionary periods. The implications for women of such policies are obvious enough and are most directly seen in the alleviation of responsibility for family health and childcare, and in the democratisation of the educational system.

THEORETICAL PREMISES

It is now possible to consider the record of the post-revolutionary countries, measuring it not against an abstract conception of 'liberation' nor against the practice of capitalist states, but bearing in mind the background conditions, which as we have seen, existed in these societies in the pre-revolutionary period. This section falls into two parts: first an assessment of the theoretical assumptions on the basis of which policies of women's emancipation have been formulated; and secondly, a study of the measures implemented in five key sectors of state policy.

Leaving aside the practical problems faced by post-revolutionary governments, a further set of difficulties are found not only in the implementation of government policies, but in the way in which the 'woman question' is formulated. Here, despite all the variations between states and their different socialist 'models' and international orientations, there exists a remarkable similarity of views on what core assumptions should inform socialist policies vis-à-vis women.

One important reason for the uniformity in these theories of women's emancipation is to be found in the historical formulation and subsequent reproduction of the orthodox communist position on women. This position was not a simple transposition from the Marxist classics: the writings of Marx, Engels and Lenin on women were fragmentary and, in some ways, inconsistent. What has been created is a selective canonisation of some of their observations to produce an apparently coherent theory. Just as in the aftermath of Lenin's death an orthodox corpus called 'Marxism-Leninism' was created in Moscow and disseminated through the international communist movement, so an orthodox position on women was also developed, based on an instrumental reading of the classical texts and on the official codifications of the early period of the Third International. This orthodox position on women has remained dominant and relatively unchallenged to this day; it is not only the theory officially diffused in Eastern Europe but also that with which newcomers to the 'socialist camp' and communist parties in capitalist countries continue to be supplied. Indeed even those communist parties that have cast off the official Soviet theories in other respects (e.g. the Chinese, or, in different ways, the Italian) remain relatively uncritically influenced by this codified theory on the 'Woman Question'. Even less critical distance can be expected in Third World countries that are now closely linked to, and dependent on, the Soviet Union and which lack the historical background and the cultural resources with which to evaluate and criticise this part of what they are assured is orthodox 'Marxism-Leninism'. If one adds to this the fact that the orthodox theory, with its focus on maximising women's role in production while retaining rather conventional views of motherhood, amounts to a policy which is often directly functional to the development goals of such states, then it becomes much clearer why the official code and its omissions have continued to be so uniformly reproduced.

The elements of official theory on women's subordination are derived from two main texts, Engels' *Origin of the Family, Private Property and the State*, and Lenin's *On the Emancipation of Women*. Engels' text has a pre-eminent place in that it provides the theoretical underpinning to the thesis that women's oppression results from economic determinations and is inextricably linked to the rise of class society and the formation of the state. The *Origins* is perhaps too well known to need summarising here, and more important than the argument of the text itself is the way in which it has been interpreted and appropriated. An example of this is provided by an official analysis of the position of women in Yugoslavia (Tomsic, 1978). Despite that country's degree of independence from Moscow, this text, written by an official with responsibility for women's affairs, reproduces an account of women's oppression and of what is needed to end it, which is found in every official handbook on women from Vietnam to Cuba. It can therefore be seen as representative of the orthodox analysis:

> 'Marxists have ascertained that the causes of the unequal position of women do not lie in their oppression by men, and that women do not constitute a uniform stratum; rather, their status is inextricably linked to the existence of class society based on the exploitation of man by man on the basis of private ownership. Hence the only way to achieve the emancipation of women . . . is by pursuing . . . the road to revolutionary struggle (in order to) topple the class social system.'

The text goes on to reiterate Engels' argument that 'as long as women are excluded from socially productive work they cannot be emancipated'. And in order for them to participate in social production 'housework must be only a minor burden'. In addition, the family as 'the economic unit of society' has to be abolished, and its 'educational and formative function socialised'. At the same time, Lenin's injunction to involve women in political activity is invoked on the grounds that socialism cannot be constructed without the participation of women.

This summary, which represents the core of official state policy on women's subordination has remained unaltered in its essentials since the initial codification after the Russian revolution. The policy package this gives rise to is similarly rooted in this early tradition and is set out most clearly in the resolutions of the Second Congress of the Communist International in 1920, which in many respects, was the constitutive meeting of the Communist movement. It emphasised the following policy measures: bringing women out of the home and into the economy; reorganising peasant households that keep women in subservient positions; developing communal services to alleviate domestic work and childcare; providing equal opportunities for women; mobilising women into political work and into government administration; and providing adequate working conditions to 'satisfy the particular needs of the female organism and the moral and spiritual needs of women as mothers' (Jancar, 1978).

As with the earlier analysis these policies have formed the basis of socialist countries' programmes on women throughout the world, and with the exception of the last, are ones that most feminists would endorse. Indeed were they all to be carried out, significant progress would undeniably be made. However they, and the assumptions underlying them, are open to a number of criticisms, not least on account of the economism and reductionism which prevade them. Most striking perhaps, is the fact that there is no attempt either to deal with problems in relations between the sexes or to acknowledge the differential effect of class relations on men and women; the oppression of women is held to derive from class relations and men are seen as being just as much the victims of these as women. The assumption is that if private property is abolished then the remaining residues of class society will eventually wither away through lack of support from the economic base. This argument is rather tendentious: neither Engels nor subsequent official theorists have satisfactorily established the link between women's subordination and class relations and there are many problems with the explanation of the origins of women's subordination lying in their marginalisation from productive work. This theory is nevertheless uncritically adhered to, even in Third World countries which provide empirical disproof of Engels, i.e. where women constitute important or even the main agrarian producers but are still manifestly subordinated to men. Similarly, the attempt to deal with the problem of domestic labour and childcare simply through calling for the *socialising* of a part of this work ignores the need to *equalise* responsibility within the home. But it is not a case of socialist states simply 'forgetting' to attempt to revolutionise domestic relations between men and women. On the contrary, in their official press there is a quite conscious promotion of 'motherhood' and of the idea of women as naturally suited to this role because of their supposed 'spiritual, moral and physical needs'.

At the centre of official ideology there is therefore an apparent contradiction. On the one hand, reference is made to a set of theoretical principles derived from historical materialism which attributes women's subordination to social, and ultimately economic causation. This is an explanation at least in principle, radically opposed to naturalist, essentialist or biological theories. Yet at the same time in the more popular, less theoretical material, there is continual recourse to arguments resting on one or more of these assumptions, which are then used to construct notions of the 'appropriateness' of 'women's qualities' for the domestic sphere.[8] Childcare and cooking are still regarded in many socialist countries as a woman's 'natural' sphere of activity despite official emphasis on the desirability of co-operation in the home. The result of this theoretical amalgam, however, is a set of policies which define women as primarily responsible for the domestic sphere while at the same time drawing them into relatively undemanding areas of work which are considered to be least important as far as the goal of economic growth is concerned.

THE FEMINIST CONTRAST

Not surprisingly, the orthodox socialist theory contrasts in a number of significant respects with the views held by feminists in the West. Whereas the former attempts to derive women's subordination from exploitative class relations, feminists emphasise its autonomy (or relative autonomy) from both class and economic factors. They further insist that the irreducible specificity of women's subordination is articulated through a system of stratification based on gender in which men are both privileged over women and exercise power over them. A number of implications follow from this: first, whereas the orthodox socialist position argues that women's subordination will eventually be abolished as part of the wider process of socialist transformation, feminists argue that given its independence from class and economic relations, economic transformations alone cannot guarantee the emancipation of women. For this to be achieved the complex combination of mechanisms, non-economic as well as economic, through which women's subordination is mediated, must form the object of a *specific* struggle. Secondly, whereas an economistic and reductionist bias tends to dictate the approach of socialist states to securing women's emancipation, feminist theorists have focussed on forms of oppression other than those deriving from class or economic exploitation. This has involved a recognition of the importance of such factors as ideology and psychology to the understanding of women's oppression, but it has also involved problematising relations between the sexes and exploring the ways in which men exercise domination over women both in wider societal terms and on an interpersonal level. As we saw earlier interest in these aspects of female subordination is virtually absent from socialist states' theory and practice. Thirdly, feminists have also focussed critical attention on the nuclear family and the institution of marriage, seeing these as institutions through which female subordination is mediated. These areas are regarded as relatively unproblematic under contemporary socialism in striking contrast to the more libertarian views expressed by Bolshevik radicals in the 1920s.

A further major difference between the orthodox 'Marxist-Leninist' and the feminist approaches is in the realm of sexuality. Western feminists have focussed on the sexual repression suffered by women and have called for sexual liberation as part of the general liberation of women, accompanied by demands for the rights of homosexuals and for free sexual expression outside marriage. Although the Bolsheviks were initially tolerant towards demands for sexual liberation, socialist states have subsequently given no recognition to this facet of women's (or, in the case of male homosexuals, also men's) subordination. Indeed sexual liberation is often seen as a decadent Western concern to be countered with what are, in effect, somewhat puritanical mores. Socialist states are on the whole intolerant of sexual relations outside heterosexual monogamy and they often apply severe social and legal sanctions to those considered to be 'deviants'.

The question of female sexuality is posed very directly in Third World countries where forms of female sexual mutilation persist. In both the PDRY and in Ethiopia clitoridectomy is still practised in some areas, yet in neither country has legislation been passed to ban it. Officials in the PDRY claim that with the country's economic and social development the practice would disappear. The noticeable absence of any recognition of the importance of tackling this problem directly could be attributed to the fear of provoking a hostile nationlist response of the kind encountered by the British when they tried to abolish the extreme form of female genital mutilation, known as Pharaonic Circumcision, in their African colonies. But it also forms part of a general refusal to confront directly the question of sexual relations. It is striking in this regard that while rape is a serious problem in many socialist countries, social and legislative measures to combat it and to give more protection to women have been slow to be adopted. Feminists in Yugoslavia have been lobbying for many years for improvements in this area and their efforts are only just beginning to bear fruit.

A final difference with feminism is that post-revolutionary states permit no autonomous or even 'semi-autonomous' women's movement; all women's organisations are strictly subordinated to the party, and to its social and economic priorities. This contrasts with the demand by Western feminists for autonomous and non-hierarchical women's organisations, based on a loosely federated association of grass roots groups. There is, of course, considerable debate in the West over the question of how absolute this autonomy should be and what forms of alliance women's organisations should establish with other political organisations. But however this relation is defined, and however it may vary in different historical periods, the minimum position is that women's organisations should have an irreducible area of influence over policy-formation in areas directly affecting women. This form of organisational independence is seen as an essential pre-condition for any successful women's struggle, not only by those in the Western women's movement but also by radicals in the early days of the Bolshevik Party and in the Worker's Opposition. This position is therefore one which cannot simply be dismissed as 'liberal' or 'bourgeois' but has its place firmly within the socialist tradition.

Given these divergencies, it is not surprising that Western feminists and officials of socialist states concerned with women's issues all too often regard each other with hostility. The former are aware of the limitations of the socialist states and some may even deny that anything at all has been achieved. The latter see the women's movement as it has arisen since the mid-1960s as wasting its time on 'bourgeois' or diversionary issues, and they often denigrate Western feminism in virulent tones. But whereas Western feminists base their analysis on at least some acquaintance with the writings and practice of the socialist countries, the same cannot be said of the socialist bloc, where there tends to be considerable ignorance of the Western women's movement whose writings are not available to them, any more than are those of unorthodox socialist writers in general.

POLICY MEASURES

We will now turn to the second main analytic area, socialist policy. As we shall see, this leads to a less simple conclusion than either of the above protagonists would be likely to endorse: for it neither wholly disproves nor completely validates the traditional assumptions of socialist discourse regarding women. The practical limitations of socialist policy on women leave several areas of oppression unchanged; at the same time the very real and unavoidable material constraints of Third World socialist countries compound this partial realisation of the emancipatory process. Despite the theoretical limitations of the policy, very real changes in women's position have occurred in these countries, changes that derive from both principle and practical necessity and which clearly differentiate these socialist countries from comparable capitalist ones.

The changes brought about in the position of women can be summarised by taking five distinct areas of state policy and identifying their strengths and weaknesses: legislation; family policy; education and ideology; employment; and political representation.

1 *Legislation*

The laws enacted by socialist states have occupied a place of special importance as far as women are concerned. These states have transformed the law in accordance with the view that the previous legal order served to maintain exploitative social relations and that the creation of new social relations therefore necessitated new legal instruments. In Third World societies this has often involved fulfilling what the bourgeois revolutions achieved in Europe, namely creating a unified, secular legal system, and extending the central legal authority into rural areas where customary or tribal law prevailed. Given the problems of implementing the provisions of the law, many socialist states have mounted public campaigns aimed at encouraging, within clear limits, mass participation in drawing up new codes, and explaining what the new laws mean. The popularisation of the law has been accompanied by de-professionalising legal personnel through the establishment of such institutions as people's courts and neighbourhood committees. This policy serves both to relieve the pressure of the specialised legal personnel and to publicise the aims of the state and its new codes.

The legal reforms passed in socialist states have brought about a significant improvement in women's position, particularly in the area of family law and the laws of personal status. In many Third World countries where customary, tribal and religious laws defined women's position as inferior and clearly subordinate to men, depriving them of many of the rights enjoyed by men, the very granting of formal legal equality between the sexes as between castes has represented a significant break with the past. Indeed, by establishing formal juridical equality for all citizens the new states have undoubtedly weakened, if not abolished, traditional structures of hierarchy and privilege as well as eroding the basis of the patriarchal family. The fact that this formal equality is inscribed in the constitutions of post-revolutionary states give legal support to women's demands for equality in the face of opposition from their families and the traditional social milieu.

Legal reforms which are of particular significance for women are broadly of three types. First are those aimed at removing kin control over marriages and establishing free-choice unions. Secondly, are those aimed at re-defining relations between the sexes so that they now rest on an equal footing. These include granting equal rights within marriage in matters concerning property and inheritance, and ending certain privileges previously enjoyed by men such as unilateral divorce, polygyny or sole custody of children. Thirdly, there are laws which specifically affect women as child-bearers and rearers, and which in effect constitute protective legislation. In the Third World the first two types of reform also involve liberalising the pre-capitalist family and radically changing its structure.

The juridical basis for re-defining the position of women is found in the Constitutions, in the Family Laws, and in sections of other laws such as those on land ownership and on labour. The Constitutions of socialist states proclaim women's equality with men in all spheres, and grant women the right to work, to education, and to adequate para-domestic facilities to enable women to be both mothers and wage earners. In the codes on land use and land allocation women are usually given special mention, and these measures emphasise that they are henceforth to be given the right to membership in co-operatives and state farms. In most countries only male heads of families are allowed full membership and women are -thereby excluded. The laws on employment prescribe that women are not to be discriminated against when pregnant, as they still are in many capitalist countries; instead various incentives are given to women in order to encourage them to return to work after an agreed period of absence, so that they do not see employment and child-rearing as mutually exclusive options. Maternity leave is from 16 weeks (USSR) to 26 weeks (Czechoslovakia) on full pay.[9] Even in a poor country like the PDRY paid maternity leave is between 50 and 60 days. There are also cases where 'wages' for child-care are paid directly or indirectly, such as the scheme operating in the Democratic People's Republic of Korea (DPRK) when women with three or more children under 13 are entitled to 8 hours pay for a six hour day, allowing them extra time and money for domestic duties. In Hungary where nurseries care for only 10 per cent of all children up to three years of age, this has been taken further and a 'Mother's allowance' has been introduced to pay women to stay at home for the first three years of the child's life. This 'salary' however, is only one third that of the average wage for women (Jancar, 1978; Markus, 1976). Similar 'Maternity Allowances' have also been adopted by Czechoslovakia, Bulgaria and the USSR.

Where these latter arrangements prevail however, the tendency is for women to return to work before the full period of leave, whether for economic reasons, dissatisfaction with the mothering role or in order not to damage their career prospects (Jancar, 1978). A notable inequality in these provisions is the assumption that it is the mother who is primarily responsible for the early upbringing of the child: in few countries is paternity leave even considered a reasonable request, let alone seen as a right. This is compounded by the fact that as in capitalist countries men's wages tend to be higher than women's, owing to their distribution in the occupational structure, so that the cost of withdrawal from work beyond the period of paid leave is greater for men than for women.

A similar difficulty arises in the labour codes, where measures designed to protect women also tend to confirm structures of inequality. Most of these codes specify that women should be prevented from undertaking certain kinds of work where it is thought to be detrimental to their health. Thus women tend to be excluded from heavy physical work such as lifting and construction; there are consequently no women labourers in the steel and mining industries of most socialist countries. There are also strict limits on women being allowed to do night shifts.

Protective legislation is a complex problem, but it would seem that justifiable concerns overlap with other, ideological factors. Clearly women who are pregnant cannot perform labour that is as physically demanding as they would otherwise perform, but this specific, and conjunctional, consideration slides into a more general representation of women as being 'weaker' and needing 'protection' from certain kinds of work. This is a covertly paternalistic consideration and in reality it co-exists with certain inconsistencies: women in the rural sector often perform heavy labour, yet few if any laws protect them, and in the urban sector it is often the highly-paid heavy jobs rather than more menial ones such as road-digging and garbage removal from which women are, by law, excluded. There is virtually no job which a healthy woman who is not pregnant cannot do, yet the legitimate concern to protect pregnant women is often translated, through these labour codes, into a much more diffuse ideological interpretation of women as being feeble and disqualified from playing a full economic role. While this is a difficult issue, and one by no means confined to socialist countries, it does indicate the continued effectivity of notions of women's inferiority even in the realm of the law itself.

2 The Family

As already indicated, the family is regarded as an institution of principal importance in socialist societies and is a primary target of reforming legislation. In official statements it is conventionally referred to as 'the basic cell of society', functioning as an agent of socialisation parallel to the institutions of the state and as the main focus of day-to-day responsibility for the welfare of children and the elderly. The first approved step to starting a family is marriage, a secular contract which gives its signatories equal rights within marriage and equal rights to divorce and to commonly owned property. Free unions are discouraged. But once married, it is usually not difficult to obtain a divorce, at least in the advanced socialist countries. In some Third World countries, such as China and the PDRY efforts are made by the mass organisations, state and party officials to resolve domestic conflicts and prevent the dissolution of marriages. Here the de-professionalising of the law can have its own repressive component, since it can lead to intrusive neighbourhood intervention into the family in order to suppress the demands of those (most commonly women) who want to escape from an unacceptable marriage agreement.

Legislation on the family seems designed both to promote a particular form of family, and to ensure its maximum stability and durability. The family form promoted is based on heterosexual monogamy, and in the urban centres, judging from state housing projects, the preferred form is that structured along restricted or nuclear lines. This is true even of many Third World countries where this form may not predominate. Moreover, as we saw earlier, state policy is aimed at abolishing the family as an economic unit of production, as production and distribution come progressively under state control. The only major difference with the conventional image of the family under capitalism is that both husband and wife are expected to be involved in full-time work outside the home. This latter consideration, and in particular the need to encourage the large-scale entry of women into employment, explains the fact that some aspects associated with family responsibility in the West, namely those involved in childcare, have been partially transferred to the state. Most socialist countries have made an effort to provide infant schools and nursery and daycare facilities, although the record of provision is uneven among countries and generally falls short of demand.

As far as the other aspects of socialising the domestic sphere are concerned, progress has been disappointingly slow compared with the advanced capitalist countries. Even the most advanced socialist countries lag far behind their capitalist counterparts in the mechanisation of domestic labour and in the provision of services which would alleviate the burden of housework. This failure is in part due to the productivist bias which pervades official policy, and in part to making the goal of women's emancipation dependent on the success of more universal goals. The result is that where domestic appliances, services, and items such as convenience foods are made available they are usually of poor quality, inaccessible, or too expensive for the average family to afford. Consequently domestic labour remains a considerable burden in socialist countries, even those of Eastern Europe; surveys on Hungarian households show that women still spend on average 4½ hours per day on housework and men 1½ hours, not counting childcare. And two thirds of Hungarian families do not use public services because they are too costly or are not easily accessible (Markus, 1976). If this is a problem in the more advanced countries it is compounded in the Third World by poverty and underdevelopment. Domestic labour in these conditions can be an enormous burden and can involve women in upwards of five or six hours of labour per day, on top of any other extra-domestic involvement.

Socialist states lay considerable emphasis on the importance of the family's reproductive function, an aim phrased both in patriotic terms and in terms of the need to meet the demands of the economy for labour. Women are encouraged to see themselves as having a social responsibility in this matter and are asked to limit or expand their families in accordance with the wider social goals. Where these dictate a decrease in the population growth rate, as in China, considerable pressure is placed on women to restrict the number of children they have to one or at most two. Where state policy is designed to increase the birthrate as in the Eastern European countries and most Third World countries, a greater emphasis is placed on encouraging a positive view of motherhood and larger families. A variety of incentives are offered for large families, and in most countries, as in the West, the single and childless are usually penalised through the fiscal system. The availability of abortion and contraception also tend to reflect the requirements of economic development, yet in the USSR and Eastern Europe, with the exception of Romania, abortion is legal and available either free or at a fraction of the cost in most capitalist countries. Indeed in some countries such as the USSR it has become a principal means of fertility control. In Eastern Europe demographic considerations have increasingly influenced state policy in this regard to the extent that the categories of those eligible for free abortions are being restricted to special cases. In general, government attempts to increase the birthrate in the advanced socialist countries have not proved very successful, and it is now admitted that a central factor is women's unwillingnesss and inability to cope with the combined demands of wage work and large families in the absence of a satisfactory solution to the burden of domestic responsibility. It remains to be seen whether official demographic concerns promote major policy changes in areas affecting women. It has certainly been mooted in official publications in Eastern Europe and the USSR that motherhood should take priority over employment at least for the first five years of the child's life, although opposition to this view has also been voiced (McAuley, 1981).

As far as family policy in general is concerned, the uncritical stance vis-à-vis the monogamous nuclear family might at first sight appear to be in contradiction with the call issued by Marx and Engels in the *Manifesto* to 'abolish' this family form. Yet whilst there was certainly a utopian element in their thought on this score, they seem to have focussed their criticism on the oppression and hypocrisy of the bourgeois family and the 'legalised prostitution' involved in it rather than on the 'family' in general. They believed that with the socialisation of housework, the entry of women into production and free-choice marriage, a new family free from oppressive relationships could be created. Not only did this view, as already noted, over-estimate the ease with which housework can be socialised, and underplay the non-economic elements in women's oppression, but it was distinct from the more thoroughgoing radical critique of the family developed by anarchism in the same period which stressed the *necessarily* oppressive and authoritarian nature of the orthodox family model. It is also as we have seen at variance with the more radical views expressed within the Bolshevik party during the 1920s.

The main features of the family in socialist societies today therefore derive less from a departure from the theories of Marx and Engels than from elements inherent in those theories themselves. Insofar as aspects of their theories have been over-ridden, this reflects the dominance which social and economic considerations dictating family stability have over the implicitly individualistic goals towards which Marx and Engels in their more romantic formulations hoped the family would evolve.

3 Education

Education, like the legal system, is seen as an important institutional means of building a new socialist society. The structure and curricula of schools have been radically reorganised to meet the needs of socialist development by, among other things, bringing them more into line with the specific requirements of the national and provincial economy. Beyond its contribution to the development process, education is seen as an important instrument of ideological struggle, whereby 'traditional' ideas are combatted and a 'new revolutionary personality' is created among the young. Education is also seen as a crucial step in the emancipation of women, and one which will simultaneously prepare them for taking up a place in public life and equip them to educate the children they are expected to give birth to.

States which proclaim socialist goals also commit themselves in their constitutions to provide universal education as a right for all state citizens, and even the least developed Third World socialist states have shown remarkable progress in implementing this policy. Parallel to the increase in conventional education structures, technical training courses have been provided for both women and men, and in the Third World considerable efforts have been made to eradicate illiteracy. These various initiatives have been of special benefit to women, particularly the more educationally deprived women in the rural areas.

There can be no doubting the major advances that have been made in this area both in the advanced socialist countries and in those of the Third World. However, there are a number of qualifications that must temper the record of progress. Whereas the advanced socialist countries have succeeded in virtually eliminating the discrepancy between male/female access to education, in the poorer Third World countries there often remains a marked disproportion between the sexes, and this again is particularly true of the rural areas. Female absenteeism and high drop-out rates reflect parental prejudice against the value of educating girls, and also the continuing and disproportionate pressure for them to work in the household or on the land. In higher education too there is a marked sex difference in the participation rates with female enrolment usually less than half and sometimes no more than one quarter that of the male. This problem remains despite official encouragement of women to enter education at all levels.

This differential is far less marked in the advanced socialist countries which have had the benefit of time;[10] here the main problem is not so much female non-participation as gender-typing. In all socialist countries to varying degrees, forms of gender-typing continue to operate: the majority of women continue to be assigned to, or elect to do, courses which will train them for occupations associated with the nurturing role, such as home economics, primary education, secretarial work, sewing, and health. Some Eastern European countries even practise a quota system to restrict the number of girls entering 'male' preserves (Jancar, 1978; Heitlinger, 1979). But this is not the main factor; even where courses *are* open to both sexes as for example in the physical sciences, the number of girls opting for them is still disappointingly low. Nonetheless, far more progress has been made in encouraging girls to enter areas previously restricted to boys, than in channelling men towards training in areas of 'female' employment. Whilst there are now female technicians, doctors and engineers, there are few male nurses, primary school teachers, or secretaries. Primary school teachers' training is open to both sexes, yet in most countries the recruitment is almost 100 per cent female. It is therefor clear that merely providing equal opportunities and some encouragement is not enough to eradicate sex divisions.

If men and women emerge gender-typed from the educational system, these divisions are also reflected in the conventional images of the sexes projected in socialist iconography. The burly proletarian in a heroic stance is a familiar socialist representation of masculinity reflecting the definition of men as workers, ideally located in the sphere of productive labour. Women are workers too, but they are also clearly defined in official representations as mothers, such that women are neither simply mothers *or* workers but rather working-mothers. 'Motherhood' is a central theme of official socialist propaganda about women, and the women's organisations, with special mother's brigades, mother's days, and awards for motherhood, lay considerable emphasis on this. Even in countries with a history of guerrilla struggle in which women have taken an active role in the revolutionary army, sexual divisions in this area have not been eroded, and women's special relationship with children continues unchallenged. This is exemplified by the emblem of the Women's Federation in Cuba which portrays a woman with a gun in one hand and a baby in the other. Similar images are found in the iconography of revolutionary Vietnam and in African liberation movements. In the advanced socialist countries women are not allowed to train for combat and military activity is clearly identified as a male preserve. This inevitably reinforces existing notions of gender difference.

The official representation of women is not, however, a passive one and is certainly distinct from some of the conventional stereotypes found in the West (and East). Socialist women are workers, heroines of the revolution, professionals, even astronauts; they are not 'sex objects' in the sense that they are in the West, although femininity with all its accoutrements (cosmetics, hairdos, fashion) has revived in Eastern Europe following the initial period of austerity. In China too, after decades of promoting androgenous images, unisex uniforms and the like, there has been a gradual return to the wearing of dresses and make up, which has apparently met with official as well as public approval. This is not to say that the representations of women are once again approximating those common in the West for there still remain profound differences, but the changes and their direction are nonetheless significant.

More important, perhaps, is that whilst revolutionary governments and organisations have actively sought to promote changes in the representations of women, they have done far less in respect of men. The image of women that is promoted is that of working-mothers, but there is no comparable representation of men as working-fathers or even of fatherhood, such as to complement that of motherhood. Thus in the iconography, women and not men are represented as having the principal responsibility of childcare, something which is given confirmation at other levels in the society. Few posters of men bearing gun and infant have been sighted in the socialist countries.

Beyond the problem of official support for maintaining this difference there is the question of how far men and women themselves consent to this state of affairs. This is a very difficult issue and the evidence available is both sparse and contradictory. Some surveys of Eastern European attitudes suggest that many men favour a more equal distribution of work within the home and willingly 'help out'. But even if this is true, helping out is not the issue, and there is little question of men assuming an equal responsibility for the home or of radically re-defining their self-image.

Why do women continue to perform the bulk of the domestic labour while holding down a full time job? Men's resistence to 'domestication' is obviously a powerful factor and has to do with the way in which masculinity is constructed in terms of the extra-domestic as opposed to the domestic sphere. The problem that needs tackling is not just male consciousness but women's too, for just as women acquiesced to the inequalities of the pre-revolutionary order, there are ways in which they do so still in the socialist states today. In other words ideological struggle and consciousness-raising are areas which have received too little support in socialist countries, partly because of the official view that given economic transformations, women's oppression will eventually disappear through lack of material support.

4 Employment

As note earlier, women's entry into employment is regarded as a major means of eliminating sex inequality. It is held to promote transformations in both women's consciousness and in their material circumstances. At the same time, the mobilisation of women into the labour force is regarded in these countries as a necessary component of the drive for socialist accumulation. This encouragement of women to work has had a number of significant effects. The state's backing of women's entry into employment has to some extent given women the means to attain a limited degree of leverage in dealing with their families or husbands. This is a significant consideration if one remembers that in some Muslim countries for example, women are not even legally permitted to take up employment without their husband's or guardian's permission.

The available evidence suggests that as a result of state encouragement women's participation in employment has substantially increased or has been significantly re-directed. The level of female employment in socialist countries is generally equal to or higher than that in comparable capitalist states. It is exceptionally high in the USSR where, chiefly for demographic reasons there were marginally more women than men in the labour force in the 1970s (51 per cent in 1970 and 1974). In most socialist countries, especially those of the Third World, women tended to form a hidden but sizeable percentage of the pre-revolutionary agricultural labour force, and today economically active women are still overwhelmingly to be found in the rural areas. The major change here has been the sharp increase in the number of women in paid employment as family labour becomes paid labour on state farms. However, this should not be overstated since the survival or re-instatement of a vigorous private sector in many socialist countries allows the exploitation of unpaid family labour to persist. Urban female employment has also increased substantially and this is especially noticeable in those Third World countries where participation was low in the pre-revolutionary period.

The mass entry of women into paid employment and the alteration of the prevailing conditions under which women work, have been encouraged by several state policies. In the rural areas the reorganisation of agricultural production has provided opportunities for women to work on state farms or collectives. In the urban areas the expansion of para-domestic services and new maternity leave provisions have also been incentives for women to participate in production; in both urban and rural sectors new educational and vocational training programmes have helped some women to move out of the unskilled and lowest-paid jobs. Women have also been encouraged to enter areas previously dominated by men – such as engineering, science and the medical professions. This has had some effect, particularly in the advanced socialist countries, where women now make up a sizeable percentage in those fields. However, where women succeed in attaining a majority representation in the health and education services, this advance seems to have been accompanied by a status devaluation of the occupation, as men move out and pay levels fall. Lower down the scale, a similar process seems to have been operating in the agricultural sector of some countries where women move into male occupations in the countryside as the men take up better paid employment elsewhere.

But despite some exceptions, it is at the point through which women are being introduced into the labour market that a new and discriminatory sexual division of labour is being reproduced in these countries. With the emphasis on economic development, women have been drawn into wage labour, but, as in the capitalist countries, the majority are concentrated in gender-specific occupations, which tend to be less well rewarded than those associated with the male labour force. Throughout the socialist world and with disappointing regularity, this pattern is repeated: women are drawn overwhelmingly into areas which, because of a bias towards certain areas of 'productive' labour, are not regarded as being the most important areas of the economy, i.e. principally into education, health, the service occupations and into light industry, notably textiles. According to the maxim 'to each according to his work', wages in these areas tend to be on average one third lower than the average male wage.[11] Median full-time earnings of women in Czechoslovakia were estimated to be 67 per cent of men's, 66.5 per cent in Poland and (in the state sector only) 72.5 per cent in Hungary (Michal, 1975). The pattern would seem to be similar in the Third World socialist states.

Moreover, despite having attained near equality in educational qualifications in the advanced socialist states, women's representation at higher levels of economic decision-making remains strikingly low. This seems to be as true of the more advanced socialist countries as it is of the poorer, Third World ones. In the latter it may be argued that it is as yet too early to expect significant changes in this regard, but research indicates that it is not short-term expediency so much as continuing policy to appoint male managers over female industrial workers and that this is being reproduced through overwhelmingly male recruitment to management training schemes. The overall lesson is therefore that the sexual division of labour in socialist states not only bears some similarities in *form* to that prevailing under capitalism, but also in some of its *effects*. These societies have certainly tried to reduce the degree of gender-typing in some areas of employment, and have given support to the entry of women into areas where they were previously not represented, but the problem has by no means been solved and the new structures created to deploy women have themselves reproduced new and unequal sexual relations. This asymmetry in the wage labour force is, of course, compounded by a similar determination within the home where, as noted earlier, no significant redistribution of the labour burden has occurred. The result is that women's capacity to participate equally in the workforce is seriously undermined. Herein lies a material determinant underlying women's place in secondary employment, in socialist as in capitalist countries.

POLITICAL REPRESENTATION

The question of women's political representation resolves itself into two issues: first, the degree of representation of women at different levels of the political structure – both party and state; secondly, the existence, influence and degree of independence of specific women's political organisations and the concern of the latter with identifiably feminist, as distinct from generic political, objectives.

As far as representation is concerned, there is very little of novelty to learn from the experience of socialist countries. No country in the world has achieved remotely equal representation for men and women at the highest levels of the political apparatus; the number of women in these posts is no more than a handful, in either capitalist or socialist countries. In 1976 the Eastern European bloc together with Albania and China had between them a total of 197 Politburo (or equivalent institution) posts: of these only 10 were filled by women. The USSR, Czechoslovakia, Poland and Yugoslavia had no women in their Politburos at all, and no other country had more than two. The picture is even more depressing with respect to other top government posts (ministries, state councils, chairpersons of national assemblies). For the same group of countries there werre a total of 557 such posts: only 27 of them were filled by women. The USSR, the only country to claim that women's equality had been achieved, had 75 posts in this category and not one was filled by a woman. In China, since the founding of the Republic there has been only one woman full member of the Politburo (Chiang Ching) and no women have ever been admitted to the more powerful Standing

Committee of the Politburo. There are no women with full voting rights in the Politburos of other Third World socialist states. A rung further down the ladder the position is a shade more encouraging. Women in Central Committees make up from 8.8 per cent (Cuba 1975) to 18.4 per cent (Bulgaria 1975) of the total membership. Even in Democratic Yemen, where *purdah* restrictions have militated against women taking up an active role in public life, there were six women out of about 70 in the Central Committee in 1978. The supreme Soviet of the USSR, a less powerful legislative body, has a 30 per cent female representation. But at the top levels of political power the appointment of women is still to posts which are conventionally seen as expressing, or which reflect, the occupational association of women with 'women's interests' – education, women's organisations, light industry, health and welfare. The tendency is for women to be concentrated at the lower levels of the political hierarchy and especially at local level. Here the percentage of women rises to an average of 35 per cent with some countries showing even higher figures (USSR 45 per cent; China 60 per cent). In general, the more powerful the political institution, the less women are represented within it. To some extent this pattern is reflected also in the female membership of the communist parties, since it is from these that recruits for high office are drawn. Nowhere in the bloc of socialist countries do women make up much more than a quarter of the total membership of the party. In the Third World, as would be expected, the female membership tends to be even lower; Cuba had a 15 per cent female membership (29,000 women) in 1977, six per cent of whom had been promoted to leadership positions (Jancar, 1978). This is, however, gradually increasing.

In general, despite a commitment on the part of socialist states to encourage women's political participation, two limitations prevail; women themselves are reluctant to enter the field of political activity and this is compounded by the fact that insufficient efforts have been made to secure the conditions which might make a greater involvement possible. It seems evident from available research into this area that the degree of dedication, time and effort required of politically active individuals is incompatible with the kinds of demands made on women by the combination of domestic commitments and paid work. In this way, the unresolved problem of unequal responsibilities in the home also has its effects at the political level. The problems, of course, are not all reducible to this determination and there can be no doubt that ideological and psychological factors play a part in inhibiting women's political participation.

Prejudice against women in this, as in other fields, also acts as a powerful disincentive against their entering political life.

The question of women's organisations re-introduces much broader problems about the nature of political power in socialist states. The feminist conception of a women's organisation is one that is independent of other – usually male-dominated – political groups and which, whilst quite at liberty to undertake other wider political activities, and to engage in alliances, gives special prominence to the struggle for women's emancipation. Such groups may be feminist in the contemporary sense, but as a category they would also encompass the more cautious women's reform groups that in the past focussed on such matters as legal and educational reform for women. At least some feminist groups previously existed in countries where socialist revolutions subsequently occurred – Vietnam, Cuba and China among them. But, quite apart from the denial of feminist *ideas*, the conception of political *organisation* dominant in socialist states precludes any such organisation; all political institutions are designed primarily to execute party policy and to mobilise their particular constituencies for the fulfilment of state goals. Women's organisations are technically 'mass organisations' distinct from the Party but closely affiliated to it like the trade unions and the peasant, student, youth and young pioneer organisations. Moreover, as part of a general amalgamation of different political units, even the official women's organisations in some countries have been dissolved despite the resistance of women in them. The Chinese Women's Federation, which had taken over earlier feminist organisations, was dispersed during the cultural revolution in the late 1960's, and only revived in the late 1970's. There is no separate women's organisation in the USSR and this is justified on the grounds that sexual inequalities no longer exist there. The appearance in late 1979 of an illegal feminist publication *Women and Russia* suggests that at least some women dissented from this view.[12]

The actual role of women's organisations where they do exist varies from country to country, but nowhere do they exercise any political autonomy or transgress the conventional guidelines of socialist policy on women. At most they may act as a mild form of pressure group but one without much power. In the PDRY the General Union of Yemeni Women has been engaged in providing technical training for women and running women's sewing co-operatives, carrying out hygiene and nutritional educational work among women (especially mothers), popularising the provisions of the Family Law, and practising marriage counselling. It has above all, been a social and educational organisation, of a traditional women's welfare kind, carrying out activities that were certainly important, and which could substantially improve women's position, but not mobilising women directly to confront prevailing male-female relations (Molyneux, 1979a). In this it is fairly typical.

These organisations are not merely at variance with feminist conceptions of what a women's organisation should be, but, as noted earlier they are officially quite hostile to the women's movement in the West.[13] Since the literature of the western women's movement is not made available in these countries, and discussion and study usually focus on the 'classic' texts, interpreted in a rather canonical manner, it is hardly surprising that the level of debate remains unsophisticated and confined to evaluating how successfully party directives have been implemented. Without any explicitly feminist component, these organisations do not encourage radical thinking or action; prevailing discriminatory structures are not tackled unless they are considered to be survivals from the pre-revolutionary period and obstacles to development. However, the role of the women's organisations in this regard is not merely a negative one, since these organisations are themselves agents for the implementation of offical policy. Where this dictates the mobilisation of women against the traditional structures of oppression they play a progressive role. But where this struggle is considered to have been successful, they play a more conservative role. By fostering the view that women are already emancipated or very nearly so, by diffusing a mystified ideology of 'motherhood', and by promoting gender-typed training programmes, they help to propagate forms of gender inequality. Just as the trade unions in such societies are instruments for controlling and containing workers' demands under the guise of representing their specific interests and defending an established 'workers' state, so the women's organisations, while performing many positive functions, help to divert women from demanding the further changes which are needed for their complete emancipation by supposing that the pre-conditions for this emancipation have already been secured.

CONCLUSIONS

The above discussion has enabled us to establish a provisional balance-sheet of the record of socialism as far as women are concerned. On the positive side these states have made considerable advances in some areas in comparison with the pre-revolutionary situation and in comparison with many capitalist states at comparable levels of economic development. Judged by the goals they have set themselves, they have achieved a great deal. Women have entered employment in considerable numbers; they have been involved in the political institutions of the socialist states; many inequalities in education and in the law have been, or are being, abolished, para-domestic services have been extended and the burdens of childcare and housework have in many cases been reduced. In Soviet Central Asia and in Third World socialist states traditional male privileges such as polygyny, unilateral divorce, child marriage and exclusive access to areas of public life have at least formally ended, and for the first time in these countries the issue of women's rights has been given official and sustained state support.

Of the limitations we have identified not all can be ascribed to failures of policy or theory. The relative autonomy of ideological and psychological factors dilutes the impact of the more progressive developments. At the same time there are a range of problems that can, with some justification, be traced to the continuing material constraints of the society in question and which can be expected to diminish only over time. The continuing lack of full educational facilities, particularly for older generations and rural inhabitants, means that pre-revolutionary prejudices and practices will survive, and that many women will not have the means to play a full role in public life. Limited material resources also delay the provision of child-care facilities and of appliances and utilities to lighten the domestic labour load. Such difficulties as these relate to the transitional and underdeveloped nature of some post-revolutionary societies, and with the further development of the material resources they could at least potentially be overcome.

The most significant difficulties lie as we have seen elsewhere, in the forms of inequality which are inherent in the policies of these states; they are often hidden behind the *formal* equality that women have acquired and behind the accession of women to previously unconventional occupations. These problems have been identified as: firstly, the persistence of a sexual division of labour in employment, in which the tasks allocated to women are less well rewarded and less esteemed than those of men; and secondly, the failure to alleviate the burden of housework or to equalise the burden of domestic labour and responsibility between the sexes. The result is that in effect women working outside the home have to perform a 'double shift'. Underlying this untransformed domestic situation is the failure to re-define men's roles in a manner comparable to the re-definition of women's roles – so that even the latter becomes not so much a re-definition as the addition of a new role (participation in the labour force) onto an almost completely unreconstructed older one (mother and housewife).

This problem is compounded by the prevalence in official thinking of conservative ideologies which underlie policy on the family and on women's position within it. As in most societies, the family is preceived as essential to the stability of society, and in particular to the reproduction of the labour force. But embedded in its structure are fundamental inequalities: in the typical socialist family the father is the privileged wage earner, allocated to those sections of the economy regarded as the most important in terms of official goals. Meanwhile, the mother is still allocated a special role for child-care and domestic responsibility, and this, combined with the demographic needs of some socialist countries, has resulted in the promotion of motherhood and official encouragement for the bearing of children. Women workers are therefore seen, and see themselves, in qualitatively different terms from men workers – and of course they *are* qualitatively different. As agents of production each labourer is allocated a place in the economy, not only on the basis of skill, education and physical attributes, but also on the basis of what are deemed to be the needs of certain areas of production for labourers with qualities such as 'stability', 'dedication to employment' and the like. These attributes are sought by employers not in women but in men – and with some reason since female agents are embodied in two sets of responsibilities which at crucial times in their lives set up conflicting demands on their time, energy and commitment. Male agents are free from this conflict and their prime responsibility to their family is the same as that to the state – to be regular, stable and reliable employees. In other words, despite official egalitarian ideology, the state colludes in the production of a gendered labour force by permitting fundamental inequalities to persist in both the domestic and public spheres. The evidence suggests that this is so because such a policy is functional: it corresponds to the supposed needs of production, demography, and of society at large. Thus, women *have* obtained greater equality of opportunity in employment than before, but they are unable to take full advantage of even this advance because of the unresolved material and ideological constraints to their so doing. There is even some evidence to suggest that this gender asymmetry, instead of being eroded, is in some countries being further consolidated as the desire to boost population weighs increasingly heavily on policy makers.[14]

The privileging of the relationship between men and employment and the restrictions of home and family life are therefore continuing and possibly increasing impediments to women's equal participation in all areas of public life. Yet unless the constrictive and exclusive identification of women with the domestic arena is broken, there can be little hope of achieving full equality with men. For this to be achieved changes of a major kind would be needed to abolish the sexual division of labour in both the domestic and public sphere. Most countries admit that further measures are needed to lighten the domestic labour load; but the problem is not just a technical one. Not only should more and better domestic machinery and public services be provided, but *social* transformations are required, among them the breaking down of the individualised and isolated family unit and the encouragement of greater co-operation and communal responsibility. This is especially urgent in Third World countries where scarce resources place limits on the provision of technical aids and where the extended family with its support structures for women may dissolve, leaving a vacuum which the state is unable to fill. Again, while most socialist countries have attempted to encourage the greater equalisation of the domestic labour load, this cannot be achieved without challenging both prevailing representations of masculinity and femininity with their concomitant gender-specific role-typing, and the identification of 'femininity' with inferior and 'masculinity' with superior values. If these stereotypes are eroded then men's and women's supposed superiority in the areas of respectively work and 'motherhood' would no longer disqualify the latter from demanding extra-domestic activities or the former from equal responsibility in the home. A further obstacle to the erosion of the sexual division of labour is the productivist bias which prevades official thinking and which is used to justify the continued policy of economic growth over social and political considerations. This may be acceptable for a time in the poorer underdeveloped countries but it is hardly so in the advanced socialist countries which have reaped the benefits of scientific and technological progress. The negative effects of such a bias are many, ranging from the devaluation of the work women have traditionally performed on the grounds that it is 'unproductive' to the slowness in improving services and genuinely attempting to lighten the domestic labour load. It may also be a factor in preventing the shortening of the working week, which would be a relatively simple way to facilitate the sharing of housework and childcare. And finally, women must be able to participate fully in political activity and have the right to organise with more independence around their own demands. This must form part of a more general process of democratisation and mass participation in political life. Women's full emancipation cannot be achieved 'from above' any more than can a genuine socialist transformation.

Such changes will not occur with the mere development of the productive forces: rather they require theoretical, practical and, in the last instance, a political break with the policies so far prevalent in socialist countries. Only in this way will the socialist states complete the process of women's emancipation which they have begun, and fulfil the potential promised by the policies given priority so far. For the countries of the developing world the record of the socialist bloc is therefore one which represents substantial achievements; but it contains within it permanent deficiencies that have to be identified and overcome before a genuinely comprehensive programme for women's emancipation can be realised.

NOTES

Many people have contributed to this paper in different ways and I am grateful to all of them for their time, help and encouragement. Special thanks are due to my co-members of the Subordination of Women Group at the Institute of Development Studies, Sussex, in particular to Lisa Croll and Kate Young for their comments on an earlier draft. Thanks are similarly due to Perry Anderson, Fred Halliday, Alix Holt, Martin Lockett, Alistair McAuley and Gyongy Vigh. The original version of this article was published as an IDS *Discussion Paper* (No.157); a longer version has been published in *Feminist Review* No.8 (1981) and in *World Development* Special Issue on Socialism (1981).

1. Feminism is associated historically and at the present time with a very diverse range of demands which challenge the social order at different levels and to varying degrees. It is conventional to label these demands as either reformist or revolutionary *in themselves*, yet leaving aside the problems with these labels, the limits and possibilities of determinate demands are given in part by the context in which they arise. Even such an apparently modest demand such as that for formal legal equality can have far-reaching implications in a society in which such rights are denied; moreover its achievement may be a necessary pre-condition for advancing on other fronts. Thus to argue, as some writers have done, that 'the politics

of the personal' is *necessarily* more revolutionary than demands for sexual equality is mistaken.

2. The discussion of Third World socialist countries draws on studies of China, Vietnam, Cuba, North Korea and Guinea-Bisseau as well as upon my own research in South Yemen (PDRY) and investigations in Afghanistan, Ethiopia and Cuba. This list of countries is not, of course, exhaustive. The literature on this general subject is so extensive that I have limited the bibliographical references to instances where an author has provided specific information.

3. These broad similarities in the policies should not obscure the fact that in each country state policies are both a site of, and an outcome of, struggles between contending forces producing shifts in policy over time. But these shifts have so far been within certain limits established in part by an adherence to a common set of theoretical assumptions.

4. Paul Hirst and Barry Hindess have at different times advanced this succinct formulation. See e.g. Hindess and Hirst, 1977.

5. Gregory Massell's book, *The Surrogate Proletariat,* although based almost entirely on official Russian sources, provides an interesting account of how government policy in Soviet Central Asia in the 1920's was aimed at simultaneously improving the position of women and destroying the socio-economic base of the precapitalist order.

6. As indeed, has occurred in Afghanistan, where by 1980 the Government was forced to abandon its reforming legislation designed to promote equality in the family and to give women access to education. These measures were opposed on explicitly religious grounds. Democratic Yemen has also been denounced as 'irreligious' by Saudi Arabia and other conservative Arab states after the appointment of several women judges. The Koran stipulates that only men may assume this office.

7. To Third World feminists socialist states may appear far more radical and impressive than they do to feminists in the advanced capitalist countries. The political implications of this are important to consider.

8. Engels in the *Origins* has a tendency to naturalise the division of labour especially when referring to early social forms, but he is clearly more interested in the economic and social determinants of gender inequality and in their negative effects on women. Where official ideology promotes an acceptance of the division

of labour as natural in contemporary societies this represents a departure from the aim of Engels' theorisation.

9. It is, however, rare for agricultural workers to be covered by the full-pay clause.

10. Cultural factors also play an important part here. In Soviet Central Asia, for example, which has had the benefit of time, the discrepancies between male and female enrollment are far larger than in the non-Muslim areas of the USSR.

11. See Alistair McAuley's valuable study (1981) for a full account of this problem.

12. The subsequent persecution by the authorities of the editors of these publications suggests that feminism may be regarded as a potentially subversive force. The other ideological components of some of the feminist dissidents (religion, hostility to the state etc.) must also have played an important role in attracting the attention of the authorities.

13. Some Women's Union or Party cadres who have greater contact with the outside world may revise their opinions and may, on occasion, be able to influence policy. More generally, it is possible to identify the impact of the women's liberation movement on some of the countries in the socialist bloc despite official hostility to 'bourgeois feminism'.

14. Outwork is being re-established in the USSR as a way of enabling women to combine wage labour and childcare (reported in *Soviet Weekly* 8.3.80). At the same time Leonid Brezhnev's speech at the Party Congress in February 1981 stressed the need to improve the position of women both in employment *and* at home.

Bibliography

ALTHUSSER, L. (1976), *Lenin and Philosophy and Other Essays*, New York and London, Monthly Review Press.

ALTHUSSER, L. and BALIBAR, E. (1970), *Reading Capital*, London, New Left Books.

AMSDEN, A. (1980), *The Economics of Women and Work*, Harmondsworth, Penguin.

ANDERSON, M. (1979), 'The relevance of family history', in C. HARRIS et al. (eds), *The Sociology of the Family: New Directions for Britain*, Keele, Sociological Review Monograph no. 28.

ANDERSON, M. (1980), *Approaches to the History of the Western Family 1500-1914*, London, Macmillan.

ANDOLSEK, L. (ed) (1975), *Ljubljana Abortion Study 1971-1973*, Center for Population Research, USA.

ANTI-SLAVERY SOCIETY, THE, (1978), *Child Labour in the Moroccan Carpet Industry*, London.

BACHOFEN, J.J. (1967), *Myth Religion and Mother Right – Selected Writings of J.J. Bachofen*, London, Routledge & Kegan Paul.

BAHRO, R. (1979), *La alternativa, Contribución a la crítica del socialismo realmente existente*, Barcelona, Ed. Materiales.

BANERJEE, N. (forthcoming), 'Fruits of development: prickly pears for women', in YOUNG.

BARASH, D. and van den BERGHE, P. (1977), 'Inclusive Fitness and Human Family Structure', *American Anthropologist*, Vol. 79, No.4.

BARKER, D.M.L. and ALLEN, S.A. (eds.) (1976a), *Dependency and Exploitation in Work and Marriage*, London, Tavistock.

BARKER, D.M.L. and ALLEN, S.A. (eds.) (1976b), *Sexual Divisions and Society*, London, Tavistock.

BARRETT, M. (1980), *Women's Oppression Today*, London, New Left Books.

BARRETT, M. and McINTOSH, M. (1980), 'The Family Wage', Some Problems for Socialists and Feminists', *Capital and Class*, No. 11.

BEAUVOIR, S. de (1972), *The Second Sex*, London, Penguin.

BEECHEY, V. (1977), 'Some notes on female wage labour in capitalist production', *Capital and Class*, No. 3.

BEECHEY, V. (1978), 'Women and Production: a critical analysis of some sociological theories of women's work', in KUHN AND WOLPE.

BEECHEY, V. (1979), 'On Patriarchy', *Feminist Review*, No.3.

BEECHEY, V. and PERKINS, T. (forthcoming), *Part-time Women Workers*.

BELGHITI, M. (1971), 'Les Rélations feminines et le statut de la femme dans la famille rurale dans trois villages de la Tessaout', in KHATIBI.

BELL, C.R. (1968), *Middle-Class Families*, London, Routledge and Kegan Paul.

BELL, C. and NEWBY, H. (1976), 'The Deferential Dialectic', in BARKER and ALLEN (1976a).

BENDEL, R., WILLIAMS, P. and BUTLER, J. (1976), 'Endometrial aspirations in fertility control', *American Journal of Obstetrics and Gynaecology*, June 1.

BENERIA, L. (1979), 'Reproduction, production and the sexual division of labour', *Cambridge Journal of Economics*, Vol. 3.

BENNHOLDT-THOMSEN, V. (1976), 'Los campesinos en las relaciones de producción del capitalismo periférico', *Historia y Sociedad*, No. 10.

BENNHOLDT-THOMSEN, V. (1977), 'Problemas en el análisis de clases del sector agrario en paises dependientes', *Cuadernos Agrarios*, No. 5, September.

BENNHOLDT-THOMSEN, V. (1980), 'Investment in the Poor: Analysis of World Bank Policy', *Social Scientist*, Vol. 8, No. 7 (Part 1) and No. 8 (Part 2).

BLAKE, M. (1979), 'Asian Women in Formal and Non-Formal Sectors – Review and proposals for Research-Education-Mobilisation', *Occasional Paper* No. 2, United Nations Asian and Pacific Centre for Women and Development.

BLAKE, M. and MOONSTAN, C. (1981), 'Women and Transnational Corporations (The Electronics Industry) Thailand', Honolulu, Working Paper of East-West Culture Learning Institute.

BLAYO, Ch. (1970), 'Fécondité, contraception et avortement en Europe de l'est', *Population*, No. 4.

BLAYO, Ch. (1979), 'Les interruptions volontaires de grossesse en France en 1976', *Population* No. 2.

BLUMBERG, R.L. and GARCIA, M.P. (1977), 'The political economy of the mother-child family: a cross-societal view', in LENERO-OTERO.

BOSERUP, E. (1970), *Women's Role in Economic Development*, London, George Allen and Unwin.

BOURDIEU, P. (1977), *Outline of a Theory of Practice*, Cambridge, Cambridge University Press.

BRAVERMAN, H. (1974), *Labor and Monopoly Capital*, London and New York, Monthly Review Press.

BRENNER, W. and EDELMAN, D. (1977), 'Menstrual Regulation: Risks and Abuses', *International Journal of Gynaecology and Obstetrics*, No. 15.

BREZNIK, D., MOJIĆ, A., RASEVIC, M., and RANCIĆ, M. (1972), *Fertilitet Stanovnistva u Jugosaliji*, Belgrade, Institute of Social Sciences.

BRIGHTON LABOUR PROCESS GROUP, (1977), 'The Capitalist Labour Process', *Capital and Class*, No. 1.

BRODSKY, Farnsworth B. (1978), 'Bolshevik Alternatives and the Soviet Family', in D. ATKINSON (ed.), *Women in Russia*, Brighton, Harvester.

BROWN, B. (1978), 'Natural and Social Division of Labour – Engels and the Domestic Labour Debate', *m/f* No. 1.

BROWN, B. and ADAMS, P. (1979), 'The Feminine Body and Feminist Politics', *m/f*, No. 3.

BRUEGEL, I. (1979), 'Women as a reserve army of labour: a note on recent British experience', *Feminist Review*, No. 3.

BRYCESON, D. (1980), 'Proletarianisation of Tanzanian women', *Review of African Political Economy*, No. 17.

BUKH, J. (1979), *The Village Woman in Ghana*, Scandinavian Institute for African Studies, Uppsala, Centre for Development Research Publications No. 1.

BUJRA, J. (1978), 'Female solidarity and the sexual division of labour', in CAPLAN and BUJRA.

BURMAN, S. (1979), *Fit Work for Women*, London, Croom Helm.

BURNS, S. (1975), *The Household Economy: its Shape, Origins and Future*, Boston, Beacon Press.

BURRIDGE, K.O.L. (1956), 'The Malay composition of a village in Johore', *Journal of the Royal Asiatic Society – Malayan Branch*, Vol. 29, No. 3.

CAMERON, M. and HOFVANDER, Y. (1977), *Manual on Feeding Infants and Young Children*, New York, Protein-calorie Advisory Group of the United Nations System.

CAPLAN, P. and BUJRA, J. (eds.) (1978), *Women United, Women Divided: Cross-Cultural Perspectives on Female Solidarity*, London, Tavistock.

CAPLAN, P. (forthcoming), 'Cognatic descent, Islamic law and women's property on the East African coast', in R. HIRSCHON (ed.), *Women and Property, Women as Property*, London, Croom Helm.

CARDOSA-KHOO, J. and KHOO, KAY JIN (1978 and forthcoming), 'Work and Consciousness: the case of electronics "runaways" in Malaysia', Paper presented to Conference on the Continuing Subordination of Women in the Development Process, Institute of Development Studies, University of Sussex; forthcoming in YOUNG.

CAULDWELL, M. (1978), 'North Korea – Aspects of a New Society', *Contemporary Review*, No. 1355.

CHAYANOV, A.V. (1966), *The Theory of Peasant Economy*, Homewood, Illinois, R.D. Irwin Incorporated.

CHAYTOR, M. (1980), 'Household and Kinship: Ryton in the late 16th and early 17th centuries', *History Workshop Journal*, No. 10.

CHOMSKY, N. (1978), 'Language Development, Human Intelligence and Social Organisation', in W. FEINBERG, (ed.), *Equality and Social Policy*, Urbana, University of Illinois Press.

CLAMMER, J. (1973), 'Colonialism and the perception of tradition in Fiji', in T. ASAD, (ed.), *Anthropology and the Colonial Encounter*, London, Ithaca Press.

COMER, L. (1974), *Wedlocked Women*, London, Feminist Books.

COOTE, A. and KELLNER, P. (1981), *Hear this Brother. Women Workers and Union Power*, New Statesman Report No. 1.

CÓRDOVA, A. (1977), 'Rosa Luxemburg und die Dritte Welt', in C. POZZOLI (ed.), *Rosa Luxemberg oder die Bestimmung des Sozialismus*, Frankfurt.

CREIGHTON, C. (1980), 'Family, property and relations of production', *Economy and Society*, Vol. 9, No. 2.

CROLL, E. (1978), *Feminism and Socialism in China*, London, Routledge and Kegan Paul.

DAVIES, M.L. (1977a), *Life as we have known it by Co-operative Working Women*, London, Virago.

DAVIES, M.L. (1977b), *Maternity: Letters from Working Women*, London, Virago.

DAVIS, G. and POTTS, D. (1974), 'Menstrual Regulation: A Potential Breakthrough in Fertility Control', *Journal of Reproduction and Fertility*, No. 37.

DEBRÉ, M. (1979), in *Le Nouvel Observateur*, 30 April 1979.

DEERE, C.D. (1978), 'The differentiation of the peasantry and family structure: a Peruvian case study', *Journal of Family History*, Vol. III No. 4.

DEERE, C.D. (1979), 'Rural women's subsistence production in the capitalist periphery', in R. COHEN, P.W. GUTKIND, and P. BRAZIER, (eds.), *Peasants and Proletarians: The Struggles of Third World Workers*, London, Hutchinson.

DELPHY, C. (1977), *The Main Enemy*, London, WRRC.

DELPHY, C. (1979), 'Sharing the Same Table', in C. HARRIS.

DELPHY, C. (1980), 'A materialist feminism is possible', *Feminist Review*, No. 4.

DEMENY, P. (1972), 'Early Fertility Decline in Austria-Hungary', in D.V. GLASS and R. REVELLE (eds.), *Population and Social Change*, London, Edward Arnold.

DENICH, B. (1977), 'Women's Work and Power in Modern Yugoslavia', in A. SCHLEGEL (ed.), *Sexual Stratification*, New York, Columbia University Press.

DEVEREUX, G. (1976), *A Study of Abortion in Primitive Societies*, (revised ed.), New York, International Universities Press.

DEY, J. (1979), 'Women Farmers in the Gambia, the effects of irrigated rice development programmes on their role in rice production', unpublished paper, University of Reading.

DJAMOUR, J. (1965), *Malay Kinship and Marriage in Singapore*, London, The Athlone Press.

DOBZHANSKY, T.G. (1973), *Genetic Diversity and Human Equality*, New York, Basic Books.

DONZELOT, J. (1980), *Policing the Family*, London, Routledge and Kegan Paul.

DRAPER, P. (1975), 'Kung women: contrasts in sexual egalitarianism', in REITER.

DURKHEIM, E. (1964), *The Division of Labour in Society*, New York, The Free Press.

ECKSTEIN, S., GORDON, D., HORTON, D., CARROL, T. (1978), 'Land Reform in Latin America: Bolivia, Chile, Mexico, Peru, Venezuela', *World Bank Staff Working Paper*, No. 275.

EDHOLM, F., HARRIS, O, and YOUNG, K. (1977), 'Conceptualising Women', *Critique of Anthropology*, Vol. 3, No. 9/10.

ELSON, D. and PEARSON, R. (1980), 'The Latest Phase of the Internationalisation of Capital and its Implications for Women in the Third World', *Discussion Paper* No. 150, Institute of Development Studies, University of Sussex.

ELSON, D. and PEARSON, R. (1981), 'Nimble Fingers Make Cheap Workers: An Analysis of Women's Employment in Third World Export Manufacturing', *Feminist Review*, No. 7.

ENGELS, F. (1972), *The Origin of the Family, Private Property and the State*, London, Lawrence and Wishart.

ENGELS, F. (1976), *The Condition of the Working Class in England*, St. Albans, Panther.

ENNEW, J., HIRST, P. and TRIBE, K. (1977), '"Peasantry" as an economic category', *Journal of Peasant Studies*, Vol. 4. No. 4.

ERLICH, V. (1976), *Family in Transition*, Princeton, Princeton University Press.

EVERS, H-D. (1980), 'Subsistence Production and the Jakarta "Floating Mass"', *Prisma*, No. 17, June.

FANON, F. (1969), *The Wretched of the Earth*, Harmondswoth, Penguin.

FEDERACION DE MUJERES CUBANAS, (1978), *Boletin* No. 2, Havana.

FERRO-LUZZI, G. (1962), *La Situazione Alimentare e Nutrizionale nel Marocco*, Rome, C.N.R.

FIRESTONE, S. (1979), *The Dialectic of Sex*, London, The Women's Press.

FIRTH, R., HUBERT, J. and FORGE, A. (1969), *Families and Their Relatives*, London, Routledge and Kegan Paul.

FLANDRIN, J-L. (1979), *Families in Former Times*, Cambridge, Cambridge University Press.

FRENCH, M. (1978), *The Women's Room*, London, Deutsch.

FRIEDL, E. (1975), *Women and Men. An Anthropological Perspective*, New York, Holt, Rinehart and Winston.

FRIEDMANN, H. (1980), 'Peasants and simple commodity producers: analytical distinctions', *Journal of Peasant Studies*, Vol. 7, No. 2.

FRÖBEL, F., HEINRICHS, J. and KREYE, O. (1980), *The New International Division of Labour*, Cambridge, Cambridge University Press.

GALLEN, M. (1979), 'Abortion Choices in the Philippines', *Journal of Bio-social Science*, Vol. 11, July.

GARDINER, J., HIMMELWEIT, S. and MACKINTOSH, M. (1980), 'Women's domestic labour', in E. MALOS, *The Politics of Housework*, London, Allison and Busby; first published in 1975 in *Bulletin of the Conference of Socialist Economists*, Vol. 4, No. 2.

GARDUN, J. (1971), 'Komparativna analiza pobacaja u nekim pravnim sistemima', *Zena*, No. 6.

GEERTZ, H. (1961), *The Javanese Family: A Study of Kinship and Socialisation*, New York, Free Press of Glencoe.

GOLDMAN, E. (1970), *The Traffic in Women*, New York, Times Change Press.

GOODE, W. (1963), *World Revolution and Family Patterns*, New York, The Free Press.

GOODY, J. (1972), 'The Evolution of the Family', in LASLETT.

GOODY, J. (1976), *Production and Reproduction*, Cambridge, Cambridge University Press.

GOODY, J., THIRSK, J. and THOMPSON, E.P., (eds.) (1976), *Family and Inheritance*, Cambridge, Cambridge University Press.

GORDON, L. (1977), *Women's Body, Women's Right*, Harmondsworth, Penguin.

GONZALEZ, N. de (1970), 'Towards a definition of matrifocality', in N.E. WHITTEN Jr. and J.F. SAWED (eds.), *Afro-American Anthropology: Contemporary Perspectives*, New York, The Free Press.

GREY, A. (1979), 'The working-class family as an economic unit', in C. HARRIS.

GROSSMAN, R. (1979), 'Women's Place in the Integrated Circuit', *Southeast Asia Chronicle*, No. 66 (Joint issue with *Pacific Research* Vol 9, No. 5-6).

HALL, C. (1979), 'The Early Formation of Victorian Domestic Ideology', in BURMAN.

HALPERN, I. and HALPERN, B. (1972), *A Serbian Village in Historical Perspective*, New York, Holt Rinehart and Winston.

HAMILTON, R. (1978), *The Liberation of Women*, London, George Allen and Unwin.

HANCOCK, M.A. (1980a), 'Electronics: The International Industry. An Examination of US Electronics Off-Shore Production Involving a Female Workforce in Southeast Asia', Honolulu, Working Paper of East-West Culture Learning Institute.

HANCOCK, M.A. (1980b), 'Women and Transnational Corporations: A Bibliography', Honolulu, Working Paper of East-West Culture Learning Centre.

HARRIS, C. (ed.) (1979), *The Sociology of the Family*, Keele, Sociological Review Monograph, No. 28.

HARRIS, O. (1976), 'Women's Labour and the Household', unpublished paper presented to BSA Development Study Group.

HARRIS, O. and YOUNG, K. (1981), 'Engendered Structures. Some Problems in the Analysis of Reproduction', in J. LLOBERA and J. KAHN, *Anthropological Analysis and Pre-capitalist Societies*, London, Macmillan.

HARRISON, M. (1977), 'The Peasant mode of production in the work of A.V. Chayanov', *Journal of Peasant Studies*, Vol. 4, No. 4.

HARTMANN, H. (1979), 'The unhappy marriage of Marxism and Feminism: towards a more progressive Union', *Capital and Class*, No. 8.

HAVEMANN, R. (1967), *Dialéctica sin Dogma*, Barcelona, Ariel.

HEITLINGER, A. (1979), *Women and State Socialism*, London, Macmillan.

HERZOG, M. (1980), *From Hand to Mouth: Women and Piecework*, Harmondsworth, Penguin.

HEYZER, N. (1978), 'Young Women and Migrant Workers in Singapore's Labour Intensive Industries', Paper presented to Conference on the Continuing Subordination of Women in the Development Process, Institute of Development Studies, University of Sussex.

HEYZER, N. (1981), 'International Production and Social Change in Singapore', in P. CHEN (ed.) Development Politics and Trends in Singapore, Hamburg, Oxford University Press.

HEYZER, N. (forthcoming), 'The relocation of international production and low-pay female employment: the case of Singapore', in YOUNG.

HIMMELWEIT, S. and MOHUN, S. (1977), 'Domestic Labour and Capital', *Cambridge Journal of Economics*, Vol. 1.

HINDESS, B. and HIRST, P. (1977), *Mode of Production and Social Formation*, London, Macmillan.

HOBSBAWM, E. (1969), 'La marginalidad social en la historia de la industrialización europea', in *Revista Latino-americana de Sociologia*, No. 2.

HOBSBAWM, E. (1975), *The Age of Capital*, London, Weidenfeld and Nicolson.

HUMPHRIES, J. (1977), 'Class Struggle and the Persistence of the Working Class Family', *Cambridge Journal of Economics*, Vol.1, No.3.

HUNT, P. (1977), 'The Parlour and the Pit', Unpublished MSc thesis, University of Keele.

HUNT, P. (1978), 'Cash-transactions and household tasks', Keele, Sociological Review, Vol. 26, No. 3.

HURSTFIELD, J. (1978), *The part-time trap*, London, Low Pay Unit.

JANCAR, B. (1978), *Women Under Communism*, Baltimore, Johns Hopkins.

KANDIYOTI, D. (1977), 'Sex roles and social change: A comparative appraisal of Turkey's women', in The Wellesley Editorial Committee, *Women and National Development*, Chicago and London, University of Chicago Press.

KANDIYOTI, D. (forthcoming), 'Urban Change and Women's Roles in Turkey: and overview and evaluation', in C. KAGITCI-BASI, *Sex Roles, Family and Community in Turkey*, Indiana University Press.

KHATIBI, A. (ed.) (1971), *Études Sociologiques sur le Maroc*, Rabat, Bulletin Economique et Social du Maroc.

KING, M. (1977), 'Cuba's Attack on Women's Second Shift, 1974-1976', *Latin American Perspectives*, Issues 12 and 13, Vol. IV, Nos. 1 and 2.

KOONZ, C. (1977), 'Mothers of the Fatherland: Women in Nazi Germany', in R. BRIDENTHAL, and C. KOONZ, (eds.), *Becoming Visible: Women in European History*, Boston, Houghton Mifflin.

KUHN, A. (1978), 'Structures of Patriarchy and of Capital in the Family', in KHUN and WOLPE.

KUHN, A. and WOLPE, A.M. (eds.) (1978), *Feminism and Materialism*, London, Routledge and Kegan Paul.

KUO, E.C.Y. and WONG, A.K. (eds.) (1979), *The Contemporary Family in Singapore*, Singapore, Singapore University Press.

LAND, H. (1977), 'Social Security and the Division of Unpaid Work in the Home and Paid Employment in the Labour Market', Department of Health and Social Security, (reprinted from *Social Security Research Seminar*).

LAND, H. (1980), 'The Family Wage', *Feminist Review*, No. 6.

LAPIDUS, G. (1975), 'USSR Women at Work: Changing Patterns', *Industrial Relations*, Vol. 14, No. 2.

LASLETT, P. (ed.) (1949), *Patriarcha and other Political Works of Sir Robert Filmer*, Oxford, Blackwell.

LASLETT, P. (1971), *The World we have Lost*, London, Methuen.

LASLETT, P. (ed.) (1972), *Household and Family in Past Time*, Cambridge, Cambridge University Press.

LAURE, J., ESSATARA, M.B., JAOUDI, M.T. (1977), *Besoins et Apports en Nutriments au Maroc*, (cyclostyled), Rabat, Institute Agron. et Veterin, Hassan II.

LEACH, E. (1961), 'Polyandry, Inheritance and the Definition of Marriage', in E. LEACH, (ed.), *Rethinking Anthropology*, London, The Athlone Press.

LEACH, E. (1967), 'Characterisation of caste and class system', in A. de REUCK and J. KNIGHT (eds.), *Caste and Race: Comparative Approaches*, London, J. and A. Churchill Ltd.

LEACOCK, E. (1978), 'Women's Status in Equalitarian Society: Implications for Social Evolution', *Current Anthropology*, Vol. 19.

LENIN, V.I. (1972), 'On the Emancipation of Women', Moscow, Progress Publishers.

LENERO-OTERO, L. (ed.) (1977), *Beyond the Nuclear Family Model*, Sage Studies in International Sociology 7, London, Sage.

LERIDON, H. (1980), 'La Régulation des naissances dans le monde', *Révue de Practicien*, Paris, No. 57.

LIM, L. (1978), 'Women Workers in Multinational Corporations in Developing Countries – The Case of the Electronics Industry in Malaysia and Singapore', *Women's Studies Program Occasional Paper* No. 9, University of Michigan.

LITTLE, K. (1973), *African Women in Towns*, Cambridge, Cambridge University Press.

LITWAK, E. (1965), 'Extended kin relations in an industrial democratic society', in E. SHANAS and G. STREIB (eds.), *Social Structure and the Family: Generational Relations*, Englewood Cliffs, Prentice Hall.

LEWRG, (1980), *In and Against the State*, London, Pluto.

LONGHURST, R. (1977), *The Provision of Basic Needs for Women: A Case Study of a Hausa Village in Nigeria*, Draft Report for ILO, Geneva, and MOD, UK.

LUKER, K. (1975), *Taking Chances: Abortion and the Decision not to Contracept*, University of California Press.

LUKES, S. (1973), *Emile Durkheim: His Life and Work*, London, Penguin.

LUXEMBURG, R. (1951), *The Accumulation of Capital*, London, Routledge and Kegan Paul.

McAULEY, A. (1981), *Women's Work and Wages in the USSR*, London, George Allen and Unwin.

MacCORMACK, C. and STRATHERN, M. (eds.) (1980), *Nature, Culture and Gender*, Cambridge, Cambridge University Press.

McDONOUGH, R. and HARRISON, R. (1978), 'Patriarchy and relations of production', in KUHN and WOLPE.

McINTOSH, M. (1978), 'The State and the Oppression of Women', in KUHN and WOLPE.

McINTOSH, M. (1979), 'The Welfare State and the needs of the dependent familiy', in BURMAN.

MACKINTOSH, M. (1977), 'Reproduction and patriarchy: a critique Meillassoux's Femmes Greniers et Capitaux', *Capital and Class*, No.2.

MACKINTOSH, M. (1978), 'The Sexual Division of Labour in Social Production', paper presented at Conference 133, Institute of Development Studies, University of Sussex.

MACKINTOSH, M. (1979), 'Domestic Labour and the Household', in BURMAN.

MACKINTOSH, M. (forthcoming), 'Sexual Contradiction and labour conflict on a West African estate farm'.

MACPHERSON, C.B. (1977), *The Life and Times of Liberal Democracy*, Oxford, Oxford University Press.

MAHER, V. (1974), *Women and Property in Morocco*, Cambridge, Cambridge University Press.

MAHER, V. (1976), 'Kin, clients and accomplices', in BARKER and ALLEN (1976b).

MARKUS, M. (1976), 'Women and Work: Emancipation at a dead end', in A. HEGEDUS et al., *The Humanisation of Socialism*, London, Allison and Busby.

MARTINEZ-ALIER, J. (1967), 'Un edificio capitalista con una fachada feudal?', in *Cuadernos del Ruedo Ibérico*, No. 15, Paris.

MARTINEZ-ALIER, V. (1974), *Marriage, Class and Colour in Nineteenth Century Cuba*, Cambridge, Cambridge University Press.

MARTINEZ-ALIER, V. (1975), 'As mulheres de caminhào de turma', *Debate & Crítica*, No. 5.

MARX, K. (1968), 'The 18th Brumaire of Louis Bonaparte', in Marx Engels *Selected Works*, London, Lawrence and Wishart.

MARX, K. (1973), *Grundrisse*, Harmondsworth, Penguin.

MARX, K. (1976), *Capital*, Vol. 1, Harmondsworth, Penguin.

MARX, K. (1978), *Capital*, Vol. 2, Harmondsworth, Penguin.

MARX, K. and ENGELS, F. (1958), 'Manifesto of the Communist Party', in *Selected Works*, Volume 1, Moscow, Progress Publishers.

MASON, T. (1976), 'Women in Nazi Germany, 1925-1940', *History Workshop Journal*, No. 1 (Part 1) and No. 2 (Part 2).

MASSELL, G. (1974), *The Surrogate Proletariat*, Princeton, Princeton University Press.

MEDICK, H. (1976), 'The proto-industrial family economy: the structural function of household and family during the transition from peasant society to industrial capitalism', *Social History*, Vol. 1, No. 3.

MEILLASSOUX, C. (1981), *Maidens, Meal and Money*, Cambridge, Cambridge University Press.

MICHAL, J. (1975), 'An Alternative Approach to Measuring Income Inequality in Eastern Europe', in Z. FALLENBUCHL (ed.), *Economic Development in the Soviet Union and Eastern Europe*, Vol. 1.

MIDDLETON, C. (1979), 'Sexual Divisions in Feudalism', *New Left Review*, No. 113-114.

MIES, M. (1979), 'Consequences of Capitalist Penetration for Women's Subsistence Reproduction in Rural India', in *Bulletin of Concerned Asian Scholars*, Vol. XI, No. 2.

MILL, J.S. (1977), *The Subjection of Women*, London, Everyman's Library.

MILLETT, K. (1975), *The Prostitution Papers*, London, Paladin.

MINISTÈRE DU PLAN (1964), *Résultats de l'Enquête à Objectifs Multiples 1961-1963)*, Rabat, Division Statistique.

MITCHELL, J. (1971), *Women's Estate*, Harmondsworth, Penguin.

MOLYNEUX, M. (1977), 'Androcentrism in Marxist Anthropology', *Critique of Anthropology*, No. 9/10.

MOLYNEUX, M. (1979a), 'Women and Revolution in the PDRY', *Feminist Review*, Vol. 1, No. 1.

MOLYNEUX, M. (1979b), 'Beyond the domestic labour debate', *New Left Review*, No. 116.

MOLYNEUX, M. (1981a), 'Women's Emancipation under Socialism: A Model for the Third World?, *Discussion Paper* No. 157, Institute of Development Studies, University of Sussex.

MOLYNEUX, M. (1981b), 'Socialist Societies Old and New: Progress towards Women's Emancipation', *Feminist Review*, No. 8.

MOROKVASIĆ, M. (1976), 'Les femmes immigrées yougoslaves en France et en R.F.A.', *Hommes et Migrations*, doc. 15 November.

MOROKVASIĆ, M. (1980), *Yugoslav Women in France, Germany and Sweden*, mimeo, Paris, CNRS.

MOSELY, Ph. (1976), 'The Peasant Family: The Zadruga, or Commual Joint-Family in the Balkans, and its recent Evolution', in R.F. BYRNES, (ed.) *Communal Families in the Balkans: The Zadruga*, University of Notre Dame Press.

MOYNIHAN, D.P. (1965), *The Negro Family: The Case for National Action (The Moynihan Report)*, Washington, D.C., Office of Policy Planning and Research of the Department of Labour.

MURDOCK, G.P. (1949), *Social Structure*, New York, Macmillan.

MURRAY, N. (1979), 'Socialism and Feminism: Women and the Cuban Revolution', Part I, *Feminist Review*, Vol. 1, No. 2, Part II in *Feminist Review*, Vol. 1, No. 3.

NAREDO, J.M. (1979), 'La ideología del progreso y de la producción encubre la práctica de la destrucción', *Cuadernos de Ruedo Ibérico*, Nos. 63-66.

OAKLEY, A. (1972), *Sex, Gender and Society*, London, Temple Smith.

OAKLEY, A. (1974), *The Sociology of Housework*, London, Martin Robertson.

O'LAUGHLIN, B. (1977), 'Production and reproduction: Meillassoux's Femmes, Greniers et Capitaux', *Critique of Anthropology*, No. 8.

ORTNER, S. (1974), 'Is female to male as nature is to culture?' in ROSALDO and LAMPHERE.

ORTNER, S. (1978), 'The Virgin and the State', *Feminist Studies*, Vol. IV, No. 3.

OTTO-WALTER, R. (1979), 'Unterentwicklung und Subsistenzreproduktion. Forschungsansatz der Arbeitsgruppe Bielefelder Entwicklungssoziologen', in Bielefelder Entwicklungssoziologen (ed.), *Subsistenzproduktion und Akkumulation*, Saarbrücken.

PAHL, J. (1980), 'Patterns of Money Management in Marriage', *Journal of Social Policy*, Vol. 9, Part III.

PALMER, I. (1977), 'Rural Women and Basic Needs', *International Labour Review*, Vol. 115, No. 1.

PALMER, I. (1978), *Issues and Policy Implications related to Women and Agrarian Reform*, Rome, F.A.O.

PALMORE, J.A., KLEIN, R.E. and ARIFFIN BIN MARZUKI, (1971), Class and family in a modernising society', *American Journal of Sociology*, Vol. 76.

PASCON, P. (1971), 'La main d'oeuvre et l'emploi dans le secteur traditionnel', in KHATIBI.

PASCON, P. and BENTAHAR, M. (1971), 'Ce que disent 296 ruraux' in KHATIBI.

PEARSON, R. (forthcoming), 'Women workers in Mexico's border industries', in YOUNG.

PETRIĆ, N. (1975), *The Human Right to Free Choice on Childbirth in the S.F.R. Yugoslavia*, Belgrade, The Yugoslav Committee for International Women's Year.

PHILLIPS, A. and TAYLOR, B. (1980), 'Sex and Skill. Notes Towards a Feminist Economics', *Feminist Review*, No. 6.

PHONGPAICHIT, P. (1980), *Rural Women of Thailand: From Peasant Girls to Bangkok Masseuses*, ILO, WEP10/WP14.

POSTER, M. (1978), *Critical Theory of the Family*, London, Pluto.

POTTER, S.H. (1977), *Family Life in a Northern Thai Village*, Berkely, California University Press.

RAPP, R., ROSS E. and BRIDENTHAL, R. (1979), 'Examining Family History', *Feminist Studies*, Vol. 5, No. 1.

REITER, R. (ed.) (1975), *Toward an Anthropology of Women*, New York, Monthly Review Press.

REITER, R. (1977), 'The search for origins', *Critique of Anthropology*, No. 9/10.

RESEARCH GROUP ON HOUSEHOLDS AND PRODUCTION (1978), 'Group Formation in the Historical Development of the Modern World-System', *Working Paper*, Fernand Braudel Center, State University of New York.

ROBERTS, M. (1978), 'Sickles and Scythes', *History Workshop Journal*, No. 7.

ROBERTS, P. (1978), 'The Intervention of Capital in Rural Production Systems and its effect on Women', Paper presented at Conference 133 on the Continuing Subordination of Women in the Development Process, Institute of Development Studies, University of Sussex.

ROBERTS, P. (1979), 'The Integration of Women into the Development Process: Some Conceptual Problems', *IDS Bulletin*, Vol. 10, No. 3.

ROBERTS, P. (forthcoming), 'Rural women in Western Nigeria and Hausa Niger: a comparative study', in YOUNG.

ROGERS, B. (1980), *The Domestication of Women: Discrimination in Developing Societies*, London, Tavistock.

ROSSER, C. and HARRIS, C.C. (1965), *The Family and Social Change*, London, Routledge and Kegan Paul.

ROSALDO, M. (1974), 'Women, culture and society: a theoretical overview', in ROSALDO AND LAMPHERE.

ROSALDO, M. and LAMPHERE, L. (eds.) (1974), *Women, Culture and Society*, Stanford, Stanford University Press.

ROWBOTHAM, S. (1974), *Women, Resistance and Revolution*, New York, Vintage Books.

RUBIN, G. (1975), 'The Traffic in Women', in REITER.

RUPP, L.J. (1977), 'Mother of the Volk: The Image of Women in Nazi Ideology', *Signs*, Vol. 3, No. 2.

SACKS, K. (1974), 'Engels revisited: Women, the Organisation of Production and Private Property', in ROSALDO and LAMPHERE.

SACKS, K. (1979), *Sisters and Wives: The Path and Future of Sexual Equality*, Westport, Connecticut, Greenwood Press.

SAHLINS, M. (1974), *Stone Age Economics*, London, Tavistock.

SAHLINS, M. (1976), *The Use and Abuse of Biology: An Anthropological Critique of Sociology*, Ann Arbor, The University of Michigan Press.

SANDAY, P. (1974), 'Female Status in the public domain', in ROSALDO and LAMPHERE.

SAVAGE, W. (1979), 'Menstrual Aspiration', *Fertility and Contraception*, Vol. 3, No. 1.

SCHMIDT, A. (1970), 'Der strukturalistische Angriff auf die Geschichte', in A. SCHMIDT (ed.) *Beiträge zur Marxistischen Erkenntnistheorie*, Frankfurt.

SEARLE, G.R. (1978), 'Eugenics and Class', Paper presented at the Conference of the Past and Present Society, London.

SEBAG, P. (1958), 'Le Bidonville de Borgel', *Cahiers de Tunisie No. 23-24, 3-4 Trimestre*.

SECCOMBE, W. (1974), 'The housewife and her labour under capitalism', *New Left Review*, No. 83.

SHARPSTON, M. (1975), 'International Subcontracting', *Oxford Economic Papers*, March.

SHARPSTON, M. (1976), 'International Subcontracting', *World Development*, Vol. 4, No. 4.

SHEPHERD, A. (1979), 'The Introduction of Capitalist Rice Farming in Northern Ghana', unpublished Ph.D. thesis, University of Cambridge.

SHEPHERD, A. and WHITEHEAD, A. (1977), 'The Socio-Economic Background to the Famine in North East Ghana', Draft Notes to Rural Development Conference at St. Peter's College, Oxford.

SHORTER, E. (1977), *The Making of the Modern Family*, London, Fontana.

SINGLEMANN, P. (1978), 'The peasantry and peripheral capitalist development', Paper presented at the IX World Congress of Sociology in Uppsala, Sweden.

SMITH, R.T. (1970), 'The nuclear family in Afro-American kinship', *Journal of Comparative Family Studies*, Vol. 1.

SMITH, R.T. (1973), 'The matrifocal family', in J. GOODY (ed.), *The Character of Kinship*, Cambridge, Cambridge University Press.

STACEY, M. and PRICE, M. (1980), 'Women and power', *Feminist Review*, No. 5.

STAMPAR, D. (1971), 'Neki aspekti planiranja obitelji: demografska politika u S.R. Hrvatskoj', *Zena*, No. 5.

STIVENS, M. (1973), 'Kinship and Class: A Study in a Sydney Suburb', M.A. (Hons.) thesis, University of Sydney.

STIVENS, M. (1978a), 'Women and their kin: kin, class and solidarity in a middle-class suburb of Sydney, Australia', in CAPLAN and BUJRA.

STIVENS, M. (1978b), 'Women and their land', Paper presented at Conference 133 on the Continuing Subordination of Women in the Development Process, Institute of Development Studies, University of Sussex.

STOLCKE, V. (1980), 'Mulheras e trabalho', *Estudos Cebrap*, No. 26, San Paulo.

STOLER, A. (1977), 'Class structure and female autonomy in rural Java', in The Wellesley Editorial Committee, *Women and National Development*, Chicago and London, University of Chicago Press.

STOLER, A. (forthcoming), 'The company's women: a history of plantation women and labour policy in North Sumatra', in YOUNG.

STRUVE, W. (1973), *Elites against Democracy: Leadership Ideals in Bourgeois Political Thought in Germany*, 1890-1933, New Jersey, Princeton University Press.

SWEETSER, D. (1966), 'The effect of industrialisation on intergenerational solidarity', *Rural Sociology*, Vo. 31.

SYMONS, D. (1980), *The Evolution of Human Sexuality*, London, Oxford University Press.

TANG, S.L. (1980), 'Global Reach and its Limits: Women Workers and their Responses to Work in a Multi-national Electronics Plant', mimeo, Department of Sociology, Chinese University of Hong Kong.

TANNER, N. (1974), 'Matrifocality in Indonesia and Africa and among black Americans', in ROSALDO and LAMPHERE.

THAM, S.C. (1979), 'Social Change and the Malay Family', in KUO and WONG.

TILLY, L.A. and SCOTT J.W. (1978) *Women, Work and Family*, New York, Holt, Rinehart and Winston.

TOMSIC, V. (1973), 'The status of women and family planning in Yugoslavia, *Faits et Tendances*, No. 10.

TOMSIC, V. (1978), 'The Communist Party of Yugoslavia in the Struggle for the Emancipation of Women', unpublished mimeo.

TRENC, P. (1973), 'Utjecaj ekonomske emigracije na odnose medju spolovima, brak i planiranje porodice (Impact of economic emigration on gender relations, marriage and family planning)', Paper presented at Conference on Yugoslav migrant women, Zagreb, 6.11.1973.

TRIBE, K. (1978), *Land, Labour and Economic Discourse*, London Routledge and Kegan Paul.

TROTSKY, L. (1970), *Women and the Family*, London, Pathfinder Press.

VALLIN, J. (1975), 'La Mortalité en Algerie', *Population*, Vol. 30, No. 6.

VATUK, S. (1971), 'Trends in north Indian urban kinship: the matrilateral asymmetry hypothesis', *Southwestern Journal of Anthropology*, Vol. 27.

VILLENEUVE, M. (1971), *La Situation de l'Agriculture et son Avenir dans l'Economie Marocaine*, Paris, CNRS.

WALLERSTEIN, M. (1974), *The Modern World-System: A Capitalist Agriculture and the Origins of the European World-Economy in the Sixteenth Century*, New York, Academic Press.

WERLHOF, C. von (1980a), 'Notes on the relation between sexuality and economy', *Review*, Vol. IV, No. 1.

WERLHOF, C. von (1980b), 'Women's Work: The Blind Spot in the Critique of Political Economy', *Jornades d'Estudi sobre el Patriarcat*, Universitat Autónoma de Barcelona.

WHITE, B. (1976), 'Production and reproduction in a Javanese village', unpublished Ph.D. thesis, Columbia University.

WHITEHEAD, A. (1976), 'Sexual antagonism in Herefordshire', in BARKER and ALLEN (1976b).

WHITEHEAD, A. (1978), 'The intervention of capital in rural production systems: some aspects of the household', Paper presented at Conference 133 on the Continuing Subordination of Women in the Development Process, Institute of Development Studies, University of Sussex.

WHITEHEAD, A. (1979), 'Some Preliminary Notes on the Subordination of Women', *IDS Bulletin*, Vol. 10, No. 3.

WHITEHEAD, A. (forthcoming), 'A Conceptual Framework for the analysis of the effects of technological change on women', Geneva, ILO.

WILSON, E.O. (1975), *Sociobiology: The New Synthesis*, Cambridge, Mass., Harvard University Press.

WOLF, M. (1974), 'Chinese Women: Old Skills in a New Context', in ROSALDO and LAMPHERE.

WOMEN'S STUDIES GROUP, CENTRE FOR CONTEMPORARY CULTURAL STUDIES (1976), *Women Take Issue*, London Hutchinson.

WONG, A.K. and KUO, E.C.Y. (1979), 'The urban kinship network in Singapore', in KUO and WONG.

YANAGISAKO, S.J. (1977), 'Women-centred kin networks in urban bilateral kinship', *American Ethnologist*, Vol. 4, No. 2.

YOUNG, K. (1978), 'Modes of Appropriation and the Sexual Division of Labour: a case study from Oaxaca, Mexico', in KUHN and WOLPE.

YOUNG, K. (ed.) (forthcoming), *Just one big happy family*.

ZARETSKY, E. (1976), *Capitalism, The Family and Personal Life*, London, Pluto.

Notes on Contributors

VERONIKA BENNHOLDT-THOMSEN studied social anthropology at the University of Bielefeld, West Germany, and now teaches sociology there. She is also a leader of the women's studies course at the Institute of Social Studies at The Hague. She has done fieldwork in different rural areas in Mexico on the political economy of population growth and peasant production and movements. She has a small child.

DIANE ELSON read Philosophy, Politics and Economics at St Hilda's College, Oxford. She has researched and taught in the field of development economics in the universities of Oxford, York and Sussex. Her particular interests have been the economics of employment, including a project on shift work, labour legislation and employment opportunities in Indonesia, and international trade and imperialism. She is now living in Manchester where she teaches courses in the university on Women and Development, and Women, Science and Technology. She was a member of SOW and is now active in a local women's group, and in the Conference of Socialist Economists. She has a young son.

OLIVIA HARRIS lectures in anthropology at Goldsmiths' College, London. She has been involved in the women's movement since 1970. 1972-4 was spent doing research in a rural Andean community in Bolivia with a particular focus on gender relations. She is on the editorial collective of *Critique of Anthropology* and was a member of the SOW Workshop.

ROSLYN McCULLAGH studied politics at the University of Queensland and Sussex University. She has done research on Papua New Guinea, Uganda and Ghana, and taught in Australia, England and Ghana. She has been involved in feminist groups in Australia and England, and is an active member of the Conference of Socialist Economists.

MAUREEN MACKINTOSH teaches economics at North London Polytechnic, though is currently working at the Centre for African Studies at Maputo, Mozambique. She has done research on agriculture, international firms and industry in Senegal, and formerly worked at the Institute of Development Studies, Sussex. She has been active in the women's movement in Britain, and was a member of SOW.

VANESSA MAHER was born in Kenya and educated in Tanzania and England. She studied social anthropology at Cambridge University. She has taught in Nigeria and has conducted research in Morocco and Italy. She worked with a group of women on the history and anthropology of childbirth and maternity. At present she is engaged in research with seamstresses in Turin.

MAXINE MOLYNEUX was born in Pakistan and brought up in India and Latin America. She now teaches sociology at Essex University. She was a member of the SOW Workshop and is on the editorial collective of *Feminist Review*. She has written about Ethiopia, and on the position of women in the People's Democratic Republic of Yemen, Cuba and Afghanistan.

MIRJANA MOROKVASIĆ was born in Yugoslavia and studied psychology at the Sorbonne, Paris. She taught social psychology and sociology of education at the University of Lille, and is now a research fellow at the Centre National de la Recherche Scientifique, Paris. Her research focuses on the migratory movements of labour within Europe with emphasis on female migration. She is married with children.

RUTH PEARSON studied economics at Sussex University and has worked in Argentina, Mexico and at the UN Economic Commission for Latin America. She was a member of the SOW Workshop. She now lives in Norwich with her husband and two small children and teaches economics.

MAILA STIVENS was born in Australia and studied anthropology at Sydney University and the London School of Economics. She has done research in Sydney on middle class kinship and in Negri Sembilan, Malaysia, on women and underdevelopment. She was a member of the SOW Workshop. She now lives in London with her husband and child and teaches anthropology at University College.

VERENA STOLCKE was born in Germany and studied social anthropology at Oxford. She has lived and worked also in Argentina, Cuba and Brazil. At the moment she is engaged in writing a book on women agricultural workers in Sao Paulo and teaches anthropology at the Universidad Autonoma de Barcelona. She has two daughters and a part-time husband, and is active in women's groups in Barcelona.

ANN WHITEHEAD studied anthropology at Cambridge and Swansea Universities. Since 1971 she has been a lecturer in the School of Social Sciences at the University of Sussex, where she teaches anthropology and women's courses. Before teaching she worked as a research officer in social policy for the Labour Party. She lives in London with a small son, and belongs to a number of feminist study groups and organisations, and was a member of SOW.

CAROL WOLKOWITZ was born in the USA and was educated at Smith College and Sussex University. She is a sociologist who has spent a number of years in India; her major research interest is women's involvement in politics in India. She is active in feminist groups and the Conference of Socialist Economists.

KATE YOUNG was born in Malawi and educated in Scotland, Germany and the United States. She studied anthropology at the London School of Economics. Her main fieldwork experience has been in Mexico. As a research fellow at the Institute of Development Studies, Sussex she organises short study seminars on various development issues and their importance to women in a number of third world countries – Peru, Puerto Rico, Sri Lanka. She has been a member of a number of feminist groups, and was a member of SOW. She lives in London with her son and long-suffering helpmate.

CSE Books

CSE Books was founded by members of the Conference of Socialist Economists to promote the practical criticism of capitalism which the CSE as a whole is committed to and to facilitate wider participation in the debate and analysis going on in the CSE. By coordinating with CSE activities in general, by publishing *Head & Hand: A Socialist Review of Books*, and by organising dayschools on issues thrown up by our own publications, we hope to narrow the gap which exists in bourgeois society between the producers and consumers of books.

For further information on CSE Books titles and the CSE Bookclub, write to 25 Horsell Road, London N5.

The Conference of Socialist Economists

The Conference of Socialist Economists was formed in 1970. Since that time there have been many changes. CSE is committed to development of a materialist critique of capitalism in the Marxist tradition. The membership of CSE now covers a broad spectrum of political and research activities which generates a wide-ranging debate, for CSE is as far as possible, unconstrained by the traditional academic divisions of intellectual labour into, say, 'economists', 'politics', 'sociology' or 'history'.

Instead the groupings are around the CSE working groups. Currently, groups actively working on material are the Ideology Group, Housing, Capital and the State, State Economic Policy, Capitalist Labour Process, Political Economy of Women, European Integration, Health and Social Policy. There is a Labour Process Historians' Group and there may at different times be other groups in operation. Groups are in various parts of the country.

For further information on membership, write to CSE, 25 Horsell Road, London N5.

HEAD & HAND: A SOCIALIST REVIEW OF BOOKS

Head & Hand is the only English-language periodical devoted to reviewing a wide range of publications from a socialist perspective. It provides an alternative to its liberal counterparts and to the scattering of socialist reviews in more specialist journals. It carries highly readable, well-informed and often provocative reviews: novels, politics, history, trade unions, children's literature, feminism, health, community publishing, socialist theory and practice, international affairs, nuclear power, Ireland etc. As well as essay reviews, it also contains short reviews and notices, reading lists and news from CSE Books and other publishers. 24 A3 pages.

Subscription £3.00 (overseas £4.00) for 3 issues per year.

Microelectronics: Capitalist Technology and the Working Class,

CSE Microelectronics Group.
Now that the post-war boom has ended, microelectronic technology will be the key element in restructuring the factory and the office as capital attempts to lay the basis for a new period of accumulation. Cheap mass-produced processors etched onto tiny chips will enable management to re-organise jobs in ways that undermine or exclude workers' collective power. This book examines capital's strategy for reasserting its control over the labour process in different sectors of the economy as well as the complementary role of the state in promoting the development and application of microelectronics. 152 pages illust.

Hb 0 906336 16 3 £8/Pb 0 906336 17 1 £2.95.

Living Thinkwork: Where Do Labour Processes Come from?

Mike Hales.
Mike Hales describes his experience doing operations research at ICI, where even mental workers learn that ultimately 'You're not paid to think'. Through an account of 'scientific' work in a capitalist firm, his book shows the place of knowledge-production in the politics of management. A concrete intervention in Marxist theory of the labour process, this book is also a document in the history of the 'class of '68', exploring the contradictory social relations between theory and personal experience, theory and practice, and academic and industrial work. 192 pages illust.

Hb 0 906336 14 7 £10/Pb 0 906336 15 5 £3.50.

Northern Ireland: Between Civil Rights and Civil War,

Liam O'Dowd, Bill Rolston & Mike Tomlinson.
This book is the first major study to document the origins and nature of Direct Rule in Northern Ireland, particularly the social-democratic model which Britain has attempted to superimpose upon the Orange State. The authors argue that Direct Rule has not been overcoming the notorious sectarianism of Stormont but has instead reconstituted class sectarian relations more subtly within the new state institutions. Their argument is illustrated through detailed studies of the economy, trade unions, local government, housing, community politics and repression. 224 pages illust.

Hb 0 906336 18 X £12/Pb 0 906336 19 8 £3.95.

The Alternative Economic Strategy: A Labour Movement Response to the Economic Crisis, CSE London Working Group.

This book argues that there is an alternative to Tory monetarism: a socialist transformation of the economy.

Hb 0 906336 22 8 £7/Pb 0 906336 23 6 £2.95.

Science, Technology and the Labour Process: Marxist Studies, Volume I, ed. Les Levidow and Bob Young.

The current restructuring of capitalism is centred on science and technology, yet very little has been written which analyses this development from a Marxist perspective. The forces of production are being transformed: greater subordination of the labour force is being achieved in traditional and new areas; a new generation of products based on sophisticated technologies is being produced.

   This book is the first of a series of collections which attempts to integrate the analysis of science and technology with marxist critiques of the capitalist mode of production. It looks at general features of the role of science and provides detailed case studies in the areas of microelectronics, biotechnology and photographic processing. The book moves from the scientific revolution of the 17th century to Marx on science and technology to recent and future areas of class struggle around new technologies. 216 pages illust.

Hb 0 906336 20 1 £12.00/Pb 0 906336 21 X £4.95.

Value: The Representation of Labour in Capitalism, ed. Diane Elson.

Marx's theory of value has been a controversial and constant matter of debate since the time it was first published. This collection of essays focuses on some of the more difficult and neglected concepts at the very beginning of *Capital*: abstract labour as the substance of value; the relative and equivalent forms of value; the commodity as a symbol. The book also contains a useful annotated bibliography of all Marx's references to value. 192 pages.

Hb 0 906336 07 4 £12.00/Pb 0 906336 08 2 £4.95.

A Workers' Enquiry into the Motor Industry, IWC Motors Group.

Examines redundancies, speed-ups, payments systems, automation, health and safety and the international reorganisation of capital investment – all from the point of view of labour. A4 size, 102 pages illust.

0 906336 05 8 £2.25.